Amskapi Pikuni

Amskapi Pikuni

THE BLACKFEET PEOPLE

Clark Wissler
and
Alice Beck Kehoe
with the collaboration of Stewart E. Miller

FRONT COVER PHOTO: "Scouts," sculpture by Jay Labre, at northern highway entrance to Blackfeet Reservation. Credit: Alice Kehoe.
BACK COVER PHOTO: Tribal bison herd on Blackfeet Reservation. Credit: Alice Kehoe.

Published by State University of New York Press, Albany

For information, contact State University of New York Press, Albany, NY
www.sunypress.edu

Production by Ryan Morris
Marketing by Kate McDonnell

Library of Congress Cataloging-in-Publication Data

Wissler, Clark, 1870-1947.
  Amskapi Pikuni : the Blackfeet people / Clark Wissler and Alice Beck Kehoe ; with the collaboration of Stewart E. Miller.
     p. cm.
  Includes bibliographical references and index.
  ISBN 978-1-4384-4334-8 (pb : alk. paper)
  ISBN 978-1-4384-4335-5 (hardcover : alk. paper) 1. Siksika Indians—History. 2. Siksika Indians—Government relations. 3. Siksika Indians—Cultural assimilation. I. Kehoe, Alice Beck, 1934– II. Miller, Stewart E., 1950–2008. III. Title.
  E99.S54W488 2012
  978.004'97352—dc23

                                                                    2011048815

10 9 8 7 6 5 4 3 2 1

In memory of Stewart Miller (1950–2008),
(center, with Walter Lamar, left),
whose intelligence and knowledge, and deep kindness,
greatly benefited his nation, and his friends

Contents

Plates follow page 176

Illustrations

Figures

Tables

Preface

Amskapi Pikuni, like other American First Nations, have emerged from the shadow of imperial domination that darkened their land when the bison herds disappeared. Now that bison once more live among us, the people of this nation want to retell their history as it was experienced.

Just a century ago, a young man who had grown up in Indiana farm country came out to Browning to purchase Blackfoot manufactures for exhibit and study in New York's American Museum of Natural History. Clark Wissler hired as his interpreter David Duvall, son of Yellow Bird (Louise Big Plume) and her French Canadian husband from Fort Benton trading post. Duvall's father died when he was a young boy, so Yellow Bird returned to her reservation and settled in Heart Butte, where she married Jappy Takes Gun On Top. David was sent to Fort Hall Indian School, in Idaho, where he learned to speak and write English as well as the trade of blacksmithing. Wissler's project of preserving Piegan elders' knowledge by means of writing excited Duvall, and Wissler, in turn, was impressed by Duvall's talent for interviewing and his intellectual ability. Soon Duvall became a full collaborator in the project, working throughout the year while Wissler was in New York. Tom Kyaiyo (Sanderville) and other men of Heart Butte seem to have willingly dictated to Yellow Bird's son: we must remember that then, 1905–11, the first generation to have grown up on the reservation had come to adulthood, everyone had settled into the new way of life, and more and more children were taken from their families to be drilled into Anglo speech and habits. No one was coercing the men to cooperate with Dave Duvall; his employer, Wissler, took pains to avoid antagonizing the agency superintendent but was much more comfortable with Indian people. Wissler and Duvall openly respected the people, in an age when it was conventional to call them degraded savages.

Wissler gave up coming to the reservation in 1909, weakened by a chronic condition that persisted until 1928. Memories of the beauty of the mountains and High Plains, and the impressive people native to the land, remained strong. As he applied himself to supervising the American Museum's wide range of research with First Nations, Wissler never stopped thinking about how Blackfoot had survived and prospered for thousands of years in country so different from the farmlands Europeans knew. His framework for analyzing Blackfoot success would be "human ecology," a term Wissler seems to have been the first anthropologist to use in our contemporary sense. Twenty years after completing writing up the material collected by Duvall (who committed suicide in 1911), Clark Wissler began a "history of the Blackfoot Indians in contact with white culture." In simple words, it would be a history of Piegan standards of living, how they interacted with their natural world and, when that was disastrously disrupted in the 1870s, how they coped with Anglo invasion. The book was well sketched out in 1933, then left unfinished as Wissler addressed more immediate obligations.

In 2003, I stopped in Muncie, Indiana, to look at an archive of Wissler's papers held in the anthropology department of Ball State University. Most of the boxes held routine correspondence from his years at the American Museum. One box contained a surprise: his unsuspected manuscript on Blackfoot history. The more I read of the manuscript, discussed the human ecology approach with colleagues, and talked with Piegan friends, the more I was convinced it would be worthwhile to complete what Wissler had shelved.

What follows is Wissler's manuscript, filled in with references he notated but left uncopied, presented as chapter 1. Chapter 2, written by Earl Old Person, chairman of the Blackfeet Tribal Council for most of a half-century, carries on Amskapi Pikuni history from the 1950s to 2010. Chapters on "Bungling" (Wissler's term for Indian Agents' mismanagement), "Schooling," and "The Ranchers" amplify major aspects of reservation life. I've added an introduction, chapter 6, to Clark Wissler's life and work.

The book took its shape from discussions with several Piegan colleagues, particularly Stewart Miller, Linda Matt Juneau, Carol Tatsey Murray and John Murray, Darrell Robes Kipp, Dorothy Still Smoking, Shirlee Crow Shoe, Rosalind La Pier, Kathy New Breast McDaniel, Fred and Ramona DesRosier, Lea Whitford, Marvin Weatherwax, Wilbert Fish Sr., and Stan Juneau. I am deeply grateful to them and to those many others at the Blackfeet Community College, Browning Public Schools,

Nizipuhwahsin School, and elsewhere on the reservation who have extended such warm hospitality and friendship. My gratitude goes also to Alberta Blackfoot scholars, especially Narcisse Blood, and my Calgary colleagues, particularly Sarah Carter, Donald B. Smith, Brian and Susan Kooyman, Gerald and Joy Oetelaar, Gerald Conaty, Barbara Belyea, and Mary Eggermont-Molenaar. Piegans Darrell Norman, David Dragonfly, and Jim Kennedy contributed from their specialties. I acknowledge Earl Old Person, now and forever Chief of the Blackfeet Tribe, the late Bob Scriver who knew more about most people than they wanted, and his surviving partner Mary Scriver. I thank Mike Wikstrom for special friendship, and in Milwaukee, archivist par excellence Mark Thiel. Eric and Beth Lassiter got me to Muncie, and made visiting it a treat. Let me close with memorializing Mollie and George Kicking Woman, Mae Williamson, Katie Croff, and Stewart Miller. They shine brightly now in the night sky.

NOTE ON NAMES: Aamsskaapi-piikani, usually spelled Amskapi Pikuni, are the Southern Pikuni, spelled Piegan in English. The United States government officially terms them Blackfeet, the Blackfeet Tribe on the Blackfeet Indian Reservation. Anthropologists use Blackfoot, as do the Canadian government and the Canadian First Nations descended from Blackfoot alliance groups who remained north of the 49th parallel. Amskapi Pikuni using English generally refer to their nation as Blackfeet or Piegan.

In Memoriam

Stewart E. Miller
Nixokow
1950–2008

First and foremost among Amskapi Pikuni who assisted me in developing this book was Stewart E. Miller (1950–2008). Employed in the Blackfeet Tribe Planning Office, Stewart worked ceaselessly to build a database of information and photographs for Amskapi Pikuni history. He shared these with me, and more significantly, steered me toward a fuller and more balanced view of his people's lives over the past century and a half. The chapter on "Ranchers" in particular derives from Stewart's efforts to help me go beyond the stereotypes. Cut down by an illness that cascaded into fatal cardiac arrest, Stewart Miller was well described in the local *Glacier Reporter* obituary: "Stew was extremely intelligent and patient which was only equaled by his modesty." This book is a small portion of his legacy. His full, rounded life, virtually a model of Amskapi Pikuni men of the later 20th century, is described by his kinsman Walter Lamar in the Eulogy that follows.

(Editor's Note: Stewart Miller was an exemplary Amskapi Pikuni in all respects. This eulogy describes a man whose life experiences typify those of his contemporaries among the Blackfeet people. The author, Walter Lamar, is cousin to Stewart by English reckoning but his brother in Blackfoot kin terms.)

Eulogy Presented at Little Flower Catholic Church, Browning, Montana, Services For Stewart Miller, December 2008
By WALTER LAMAR

Stewart Edward Miller, born May 20, 1950, in Everett, Washington, to Dolores "Dorrie" and Ted Miller.

He was a proud member of the Blackfeet Nation, attended his school years in Browning where he graduated high school in 1968. He attended Carroll College in Helena where he proved to be a true scholar.

His school years in Browning formed lifelong friendships.

His summers were spent on his grandfather Percy De Wolf's ranch where he honed his skills as a cowboy rancher.

Stewart has one sister, Renee Miller Blaney of Browning.

In 1971 Stewart married Lillian Henderson and together they had two fine sons, Robert and Michael Miller.

Stewart's professional career included vice-president of 1st National Bank, owner of the Corner Grocery Conoco/Sporting Goods Store, insurance agent, a founding contributor of the first TERO program, and director for the Blackfeet Tribe's housing and planning departments. Stewart embodied the value of community service, serving twenty-six years for the volunteer fire department where he retired as the fire chief. He was also a fire marshal for the state of Montana.

Stewart passed from our lives on December 5, here in the community he loved and served.

As we join here, not to mourn Stewart's passing, but to celebrate his life and legacy, I am honored to represent our family along with Stewart's sons Bobbie and Mike. I am Stu's cousin—Walter Lamar.

I prayed about my words today and the first thing I realized is that I wanted to ask Stu what to say? As we think about Stu today I think we all now wonder—*who do we ask now?*

Considering Stu's deep commitment to the history of our Blackfeet people and specifically our family—I think it appropriate to first explain our family history. Mountain Chief had a daughter Margrite who married Rock Gobert in Ft. Benton around 1880. Among their children they had a son Edward Rock Gobert. I should note that all of our Gobert relatives are descended from this one man—Rock Gobert who came from Switzerland. Edward Gobert married Mary Johnson and they had two daughters Charlotte, Edna. When Mary died Edward married Abigail Devereaux and they had three daughters Anna Mae Gobert Kipp, June Gobert Douglas, and Catherine "Cassine" Gobert Lamar. So—Charlotte had Dorrie, Stu's mother—Edna had Mary Jean Billideaux and Curly Bear Wagner; Anna Mae had Patsy Kipp; June had Dale, Rocky, Cathy, Linda, and Anna Douglas; and Catherine had me and my sisters—Marsha, Regina, and Judith. In fact, my mother, Stu's Auntie is here today. As Mom was reminiscing and sharing her thoughts over these past few days she told of Grandpa Ed's apartment building, where it seemed during various points the whole family lived. She said during all the coming and goings a little voice would be heard—here comes Tooo Miller.

This little bit of history and family connection is the type of information Stu researched, not only about our family but many of your families as well. It is also interesting to note that Mountain Chief had six wives, so Stu knew how we are all related and was always willing to share the information freely, because he knew it important to our future that we know our past.

I talked to our cousin Curly Bear (Clarence) Wagner this morning who is in the hospital—please pray for him. Curly Bear told me he researched everything about Glacier Park and thought he knew quite a bit about the subject. So one day he went to visit Stu—he always called him "Spider Lake Stu"—he mentioned his research and asked Stu about the Park—Stu proceeded in his quiet way to explain about many mountains, lakes, streams—the names of each and what their meaning was to the Blackfeet people. He told Curly Bear where the streams emptied—Hudson Bay, Gulf of Mexico, and the Pacific Ocean. He talked about the way the Park was taken and that it actually still belonged to the Blackfeet. Curly Bear said he felt like a "Piker" after the hour and a half lesson. He said, as we all do, that Stu knew about all subjects in detail. He wondered, *who do we ask now?*

Our Grandfather Edward Gobert was a musician, semipro baseball player, basketball player, rancher, owned the first telephone company in Browning, built Gobert Hall—the first community building in Browning, was a master carpenter, a long time Deputy Sheriff of Glacier County and community leader. He was a hunter and fisherman.

Stu's Dad, Ted—was Navy sailor, lineman, fireman, and community leader. He too was a hunter and fisherman.

Both were men's men and had skills in many areas—both devoted their lives to serving their communities.

Is this sounding familiar? Over the past few days I have heard folks say about Stu, "He was a jack-of-all-trades; could do anything and knew about everything; devoted himself to serving the community; was a true hunter and fisherman. In fact he transcended being "good at"—and was an expert at everything he did. I think many of us experienced his unintentional way of making one feel somewhat inadequate—or as Curly Bear said a "Piker"—when he would politely step in and take over what you were doing to do it the right way with such ease—or after explaining a plan or idea to him, he would, in a polite way, talk about the plan until it was realized that the grand idea or plan was purely idiotic. It was interesting that he never criticized, but he could make you try so much harder. *Who do we ask now?*

Steve Juneau, Stu's son-in-law, and I work together. I know Steve saw Stu like many others—a true mentor. I have heard that word over and over describing Stu. Steve wonders—*who do I ask now?*

Stu's colleagues from his days at Blackfeet Housing gave me a paper last night and asked me to relate the words to you. They want to note that during his tenure there he brought in over 26 million dollars in funding. He implemented NAHASDA housing program over a five-year period. He contributed significantly to the College Homes Project, Community Center, rental and mutual homes project, the elderly housing project, and the elderly care center. He initiated and implemented the first tax credit project which consisted of twenty homes. He started and implemented the GAP/Down payment Assistance Program which brought 100-plus homes to first-time homeowners. He wrote HIP grants in the early days of the program. He was instrumental in getting fire halls built in the communities of Babb and Heart Butte. Recently he was instrumental in securing a grant for over one hundred thousand dollars for homes damaged by high winds. In fact Stu brought millions of dollars to the reservation just in the form of emergency assistance to fix or replace homes damaged by natural disaster. They said it would be difficult to point out all the structures and projects he had a hand in or managed individually, simply because there are just too many. They concluded with these words: "Stu was a brilliant, but humble man as he went about his endeavors in life. He didn't have to raise his voice if angry to emphasize a point—his "Paul Harvey" like vocabulary would take care of it. Stu's very presence was enough to make any gathering important with his stately appearance and almost arrogant, if you will, attitude that any situation was a piece of cake. Pillar of the community isn't adequate in describing Stu's contributions to this reservation, his friends, and his family. They said he contributed at one point or another to virtually every tribe program and department—They wonder, *who we ask now?* Sincere words from Stu's friends and colleagues at Blackfeet Housing.

Everybody talks of Stu's service to the community—he was counted on to direct operations during fires, floods, high winds, and blizzards. People sought him out for advice on proposal writing, letter writing, federal rules and regulations, land issues (he knew about every detail of our family land), natural resources, and even personal issues. Like the song played at the Rosary said—he was our Rock, our anchor in the storm. He provided technical expertise and creative assistance to tribal leaders, community members, friends, and family. His tremendous intelligence and patience were only equaled by his modesty. Always in the background, never seeking accolades or headlines—many have said the impact of his loss will greatly affect the whole community—the whole reservation. *Who do we ask now?*

Stu was not an emotionally expressive person, his deep love for family and community was demonstrated not by words but deeds.

Like you I have many stories I wish I could relate today—but let's just each take a moment today to think of our own stories. Renee said she and Stu still had so much yet to do together—and we all feel the same way, but we should concentrate on what **did** we do together. Relish the stories, bask in the memory of a real man.

Ted, Dorrie, Renee, and Stu always welcomed everyone to their spot on the lake for good fun and laughter—Stu carried on the tradition so kids, grandkids, friends, and relatives had the same opportunity to create new memories.

Thank you for allowing me to honor my cousin, my brother.

ONE

Manuscript on the History of the Blackfoot Indians in Contact with White Culture, 1933

by Clark Wissler, edited and completed by Alice B. Kehoe

The usual published study of a tribal culture is projected on the assumption that the culture as described is a highly standardized form of social behavior, which existed with little change over an indefinite period of time preceding white contact. It is doubtful if this assumption is warranted, since the form of culture as stated is based upon observed occurrences and the recollections of tribesmen living at the time the data were recorded. This is especially true of current studies in the culture of North American Indian tribes, most of these studies having been made during the interval 1890–1920. Assuming that the oldest native informants used in such studies were on the average seventy years of age, the culture as described could be established only for a period falling between 1860 and 1910. On the other hand, for some of the best-known Indian tribes, there are available historical publications giving fragmentary descriptions of culture at various intervals during the entire period of white contact. It may thus be possible to select an Indian tribe studied in detail during the period 1890–1920 and for which there are historical accounts ranging from 1600–1890. It is obvious that should this historical information be found reasonably complete, a comparison of these data with the standardized culture for the later period would indicate to some extent the stability of tribal culture during the whole period. Further, it is possible to accumulate data on such culture changes as may have occurred in the tribe in question, since the observations of ethnologists were published. Again, it is possible to examine the records of the Department of Indian Affairs for information as to cultural changes in progress at the time the ethnological studies mentioned above were in progress, thus giving us a more or less complete account of the cultural activities of the tribe selected throughout the whole period of white contact. It is possible that the presentation of a tribal culture in such time perspective will give a truer picture of living culture than can be observed in ethnological studies of the usual type. Everyone now agrees that even so-called primitive cultures change in response to contacts with each other, as well as with white cultures, but as yet we have no body of data from which the forms and rates of change can be evaluated.

The group of tribes in the northern Plains generally known under the name Blackfoot offer a promising opportunity to try out the above suggestion. The published standardized culture is based upon observations and individual narratives recorded during the period 1890–1915. For the earlier period we have a fair amount of culture data scattered over the entire period from 1754–1890. The chief sources for these data are to be found in the writings of Umfreville, under the date of 1784; Henry in 1809; and Maximilian in 1833. These accounts give not only good descriptions of manners and customs, but, since they are in part in the form of diaries, they give daily pictures of Blackfoot culture as it was lived. Naturally, additional details of culture for this group are found in other writers of the period, a full list of which is given in the bibliography. [Editor's note: no bibliography was included with the 1933 manuscript; I endeavored to find and include Wissler's sources in the bibliography for this book.]

The first step in this investigation is to prepare a digest of the standardized culture, which in this case can be considered as functioning around 1880. The data used for the compilation of this statement can be taken from the published studies of Grinnell, McClintock, and Wissler.

The historical data available suggest that certain changes in this contact have occurred, according to which at least four periods of Blackfoot culture history may be assumed. These are: (1) 1670–1750: Period of indirect fur trade; (2) 1750–1850: Direct fur trade; (3) 1850–85: Treaty period; (4) 1885 to the present: The reservation period.

Period of Indirect Fur Trade

To fully understand the culture influences surrounding the Blackfoot during this period, an exhaustive review must be made of the ethnography of the time and the history of the fur trade. The Hudson's Bay Company began operations around 1670. French traders pressed in from the Great Lakes a few years later. Both had easy water routes to Lake Winnipeg and thus to the Saskatchewan River and the Plains. The northern end of the Plains area ends with the northern branch of the Saskatchewan, bounded on the west by the Rocky Mountains and on the east by Lake Winnipeg.

The Assiniboine tribes occupied the territory east of the lake and seemed to have formed the habit of visiting the Hudson's Bay posts via Nelson River early in 1680. This may have been due to a long standing acquaintance with the Cree, who were in direct contact with the Hudson's Bay Company. Further, the Assiniboine, from their own initiative and by direct encouragement, became traders carrying trade goods to the tribes west of them and in return transporting furs, etc., to Hudson's Bay. The history of this interesting procedure is probably lost, yet there may be additional interesting information in the archives of the Hudson's Bay Company. [Editor's note: See A. J. Ray, *Indians in the Fur Trade* (1974), drawn from these archives.]

At that time all of the territory between the Saskatchewan and the United States boundary was held by the Assiniboine and the Blackfoot groups. Therefore, it is certain that the Assiniboine traded with the Blackfoot during this period and thus were the carriers of some phases of white culture. To evaluate this influence is a fascinating problem, but can be best approached after the other periods in Blackfoot culture history have been investigated.

However, some white influence may have reached the Blackfoot from another direction. We have reason to believe that before 1670 the Blackfoot had absorbed the horse culture out of the Plains. In contrast to the Assiniboine of the time, who went mostly on foot and by canoe, the Blackfoot made no use of canoes and were provided with horses in sufficient number to transport their entire tribe personnel and belongings. We infer this because such was the status when first observed by French and English explorers in 1751 and again in 1754. Obviously, to have reached this state of saturation for horse culture, they must have begun to acquire it some decade or two before.[1]

When observed in 1751 they possessed horse trappings and other arts of trade recognized by the French as Spanish in origin. Further, the Indians stated that these objects came by trade from the Southwest, in which direction were to be found trading posts kept by "white men with beards." There is no evidence to indicate that the Blackfoot came in direct contact with these Spanish or French traders, but that their contact was indirect by tribal trade through an intermediary.[2] According to traditions of the Blackfoot recorded later, this intermediary seems to have been Shoshone or, as stated later, the Snakes.[3]

The most important influence to bear upon the Blackfoot was the horse culture pattern already developed by the Snakes and other Plains tribes. As stated, this was fully assimilated before 1750 and may be considered one of the first major results of white contact (Fig. 1), though in this case the contact was indirect.

FIG. 1. Pikuni on horseback, 1855, by Gustavus Sohon.

No doubt, personal contact between white men and natives sets in motion culture change. It is possible that white men, or at least mixed-blood Indians, visited the Blackfoot before the historically recorded visit of 1751. There are mentions of such visits following that date, but there is no good reason for assuming that these were the initial instances. We know, for example, that Henry Kelsey from Hudson's Bay visited the Assiniboine of the Plains as early as 1690–91, spending more than a year in their camps. We know this because he was sufficiently educated to leave a journal. It is not impossible that he was preceded or immediately followed by adventurous white traders who left no written records.[4] In 1751, the French seemed to have been on the north Saskatchewan in Blackfoot territory; in 1754, Henday mentions a French "leader" with Indians at Buffalo Lake, south of what is now Edmonton; Cocking, in 1772, mentions "a forlorn Frenchman who had been living with these Indians (Assiniboine) for seven years." However, we can take the date 1750 as definitely making the beginning of the period in which there was more or less constant direct contact between the Blackfoot and white traders.

When the Blackfoot first began to visit trading posts instead of dealing with the Assiniboine and other middlemen is uncertain. The early accounts of the traders stress the fact that the Blackfoot would not leave the Plains, being unwilling to travel by foot or canoes. There is reason to believe that French trading houses were set up among the Assiniboine before 1740, some of which would be accessible to the Blackfoot. The first definite statement is by Henday in 1754, who, while on the South Saskatchewan states that the Piegan had come to the northeast to visit a trading post, presumably a French post in the vicinity of Fort La Corne [at the Forks of the Saskatchewan River in central Saskatchewan]. However, such visits would not have been frequent before 1750.

We may summarize the probable contact influence by stating that indirectly the Blackfoot had acquired horse culture and, in addition, knowledge of the existence of white men and familiarity with certain trade goods, especially metal tools, guns, kettles, trade tobacco, mirrors, beads, and a few other trinkets. There is no reason to believe that many of these objects were possessed by the Blackfoot before 1750, but that they were quite familiar with them and understood their value is reasonably certain. Horse culture must have raised the standard of living and increased the ease of supplying the camps with the furniture needed. Also, the use of the horse for transportation greatly lessened the drudgery of traveling, gathering wood, etc.[5] Again, this superior means of transportation made possible a great increase in the size of tents, their furniture, and personal equipment. It may be assumed that the horse introduced a new type of property, since the early accounts of these people stress the fact that certain individuals possessed herds of horses. The possible effect of this increase in well-being and luxury upon other phases of culture, particularly social and ceremonial organization, is one of the interesting problems developed by this investigation.

Direct Fur Trade

This period is approximately a century long, dating from 1750 to 1850, and may be characterized as a period during which the Blackfoot group of tribes were not in contact with any governmental or commercial activities except those directly concerned with the fur trade. No settlements were set up near their traditional hunting ranges, nor do we find the respective governments of Canada and the United States sufficiently concerned with these tribes to make treaties with them until the end of the period. No missionaries were resident among them, nor had they made serious attempts to extend their activities to the Blackfoot country. In Montana some settlements for mining and grazing were set up late in the period, but these fell well without the territory claimed by these tribes. In short, they were free to live their own life so long as they remained within their habitat, and no white control was in evidence except such indirect influence as the fur traders could exercise by threatening to withhold trade goods. On the other hand, it seems to have been the policy of the fur trade companies to discourage the intrusion of settlers, missionaries, etc., and further, to maintain the political independence of the tribes concerned. They rightly assumed that the preservation of such independence and the prevention of other types of white intrusion would be to the advantage of the fur trade. Our problem is then to discover in what way, if any, the new conditions of the fur trade changed the older Blackfoot culture. Also, in how far the fur traders were able to direct the social behavior of these tribes.

As preliminary to the consideration of this period, a general statement of the territorial range and relationships of the tribes is advisable. Referring to a map (Fig. 2) will make clear that the Blackfoot group resided in the northern Plains, around the headwaters of the Saskatchewan rivers, between the north branch and what is now the boundary line between the United States and Canada. It will be noted further that the Saskatchewan enters the Lake Winnipeg drainage and that in the main all the country between the Rocky Mountains and these lakes is grassland, whereas all the land immediately north of the north branch of the Saskatchewan is forest. This area was occupied by the Blackfoot group, the Assiniboine and the Plains Cree. Whether the Plains Cree were here before 1700 cannot be determined, but it seems likely that their movements westward of Winnipeg were stimulated by the fur trade. The early accounts indicate that while these tribes were more or less at war with each other, they were more often in friendly contact, since we note that the first white observers were able to find interpreters who could speak two or three of the languages belonging to these tribes. Further, as previously stated, the Cree and the Assiniboine carried on trade with the Blackfoot group.

Fig. 2a. Original Blackfoot Territory, 1800.

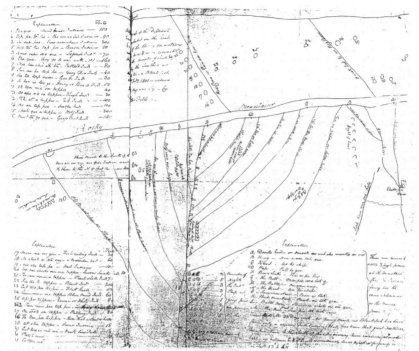

FIG. 2b (above). Map drawn by the Akai Mokti, principal chief of the Blackfoot alliance, for Hudson's Bay trader Peter Fidler in 1801. Annotated by Fidler as directed by the Akai Mokti, to show all the First Nations he knew, their territories, and the principal rivers and Rocky Mountains. The map shows the Snake-Columbia River route to the Pacific. North is to the right. See also map of Blackfoot territory, Fig. 2a shaded section. FIG. 2c (below). Blackfeet Reservation, Montana. Figs. 2a and 2c drawn by Marjan Eggermont.

Another important point is to consider the objective of the fur trader in this area. During this period the furs most desired for export to Europe were beaver, otter, and other fine furs, but of these beaver was the staple. Certainly it was the fur sought by the first traders in this region. The beaver is a forest animal[6] but was fairly abundant in this part of the Plains, because even the small streams were skirted by thick growths of aspen, willow, mountain ash, etc., all excellent food material for beaver. Further, the north branch of the Saskatchewan afforded a continuous waterway either to Hudson's Bay or to Montreal. It also furnished easy access to the northern forests of Canada, a region rich in furs. It so happens that the tribes of the Blackfoot group were not disposed to trap beaver; in fact they seem to have had an aversion to killing this animal which in some cases amounted to a tabu. The Assiniboine, on the other hand, especially those bands living to the eastward in the timbered districts around the Winnipeg lakes, would trap beaver. These Assiniboine were encouraged by the traders to enter the Blackfoot country to trap beaver and so far as known the Blackfoot made no serious objection to the procedure.[7] If, as assumed, the Plains Cree came to the area after the opening of the fur trade, they also were stimulated to enter the region to take beaver and trade with the other Indians. This may account for the tendency of the Plains Cree and Assiniboine to spread westward during the fur trade period and to some extent to filter into the range of the Blackfoot group. However, during all this time the Blackfoot group seems to have been the stronger, both in numbers and morale, which might account for the observed fact that the penetration of the Assiniboine and Cree was chiefly along the north branch.

We have noted that the Blackfoot were not disposed to trap beaver and the Assiniboine and Cree were willing to do so. However, we note in the reports of Henry and other traders that whenever the Cree and Assiniboine took to the open Plains they were disinclined to produce beaver especially if they were equipped with horses. In general this was the experience of traders in the United States, who found it necessary to introduce hunters into the Plains to trap beaver, since the typical Plains Indians were disinclined to engage in this work. We suspect that there is something incompatible between Plains horse culture and trapping beaver. Beaver trapping seems to call for a more or less fixed winter residence of scattered families. The pattern for Indian trapping in all the forest land east and north of the Plains was to scatter out in family groups over a wide range of territory. These groups were outfitted by the traders and soon came to be economically dependent on them. Furthermore, their trapping efficiency was increased by breaking down their old tribal solidarity rather than otherwise. We suspect, then, that the rapid breaking down of the old Cree culture was largely due to this new form of living, which was in the main antagonistic to the old tribal organization. In other words, it tended to introduce family individualism as opposed to village and tribal communism.

In contrast, life upon the open Plains, following the horse culture type, was favorable to the maintenance of large well-organized tribal groups. Such a large body would be readily fed upon buffalo meat, provided it was sufficiently mobile to follow the herds. The earliest accounts state that these Plains Indians usually operated in camps of approximately two hundred tents. When the Cree and Assiniboine took to the Plains they seem to have adopted this mode of life, though less habituated to it than the Blackfoot. As we shall see later, the Blackfoot suffered less damage by white contact during this period than did their neighbors, which may be largely due to their resistance to the production of beaver.

If these Indians did not produce beaver, why did they offer an important field of activity for fur trade? They were industrious trappers of wolves and wolf skins were in some demand for export. The reason why the Blackfoot group produced wolf skins is not wholly clear, but it seems that before white contact the skin of the wolf was a necessary part of a warrior's equipment. Further, according to Umfreville, great numbers of wolves followed the Plains camps, living upon the rejected carcasses of the buffalo, and that they were easily taken by traps and by pursuit on horseback.[8] However, one important part of Blackfoot trade was pemmican. The boat crews transporting furs and goods through the Saskatchewan country and westward depended largely upon pemmican for a traveling ration. Also, pemmican was sought as a reserve food for all trading posts. We note in reports of traders that this food formed a large part of the goods received from the Indians. Naturally, there was some demand for buffalo robes, deer skins, etc., all of which were occasionally turned in by the Plains Indians. In addition, horses were frequently sold to the traders. Thus, it is clear that even though these Indians did not produce beaver, they were able to offer goods sufficient for the trading posts within their country.

What the Indians desired in return for these goods was, first of all, firearms and ammunition. In addition, knives, hatchets, and kettles. Cloth did not appeal to them.

Since the traders entered this country by water, the important posts were to be found on the two branches of the Saskatchewan and their tributaries. The traders seldom went far inland. Trading posts in the United States were not opened on the Upper Missouri before 1820 and trade with the Blackfoot did not become active until the last decade of this fur trade period.

The Human Ecology of the Area

Ethnologists are usually content to describe the cultures of a tribe in an area, but rarely concern themselves with questions of population, environment, and health; but if one is concerning himself with the changes of culture over a given period, he can scarcely avoid giving serious consideration to such questions as the following: (1) the magnitude and stability of the tribal populations; (2) how the people are clothed and housed; (3) the state of health.

There are some difficulties in arriving at a satisfactory notion of the density of population in this area during the fur trade period. However, the traders found it advantageous to make careful estimates of the population in each tribe and subdivision in order to satisfactorily forecast the amount of trade goods to be provided. Further, with this information in hand each trader could know to what extent he was serving the whole tribe and what inroads his rivals had made upon his trade. As a rule, these early estimates are not based upon counts by individuals but on the number of tents. Assuming that the tribal organization was fairly constant during the period, it was safe to assume that each tent represented a reasonably stable social unit. Further, tents were objective and so could be readily counted, both by Indian and white. There is reason to believe that each chief or band leader knew the approximate number of tents in his party at any given time. However this may be, several writers of the period give the number of tents for each division of the Blackfoot and neighboring tribes.

The first, and perhaps the most reliable, statement is by Henry in 1809. This writer is remarkably accurate in all his observations subject to modern check, and so it may be taken for granted that his population counts are equally accurate. Since 1809 is approximately the middle point in the fur trade period, the estimate of Henry may be taken as typical for the period as a whole, provided it checks satisfactorily with the later estimates of other writers. To this end we have prepared a table showing the successive population counts for all the tribal divisions of the area.

It will be noted that Henry used two methods of counting, one, the number of tents, as just stated, the other, a count of warriors. According to his own statement, the term *warrior* means any able-bodied male capable of bearing arms. An examination of the table suggests that these two counts were made independently, since there is no definite mathematical relation between the number of tents and the number of warriors. Dr. Richardson, a member of the Franklin Expedition, states that according to his observations among the Gros Ventre the average number of persons per tent is ten. This may be somewhat too high an average, but if accepted would give the three Blackfoot tribes a total population of 6,500 according to Henry's count, and approximately 10,500 according to Richardson. As we shall see later, these two estimates fairly well represent the population estimates between 1809 and 1850.

Under another head we shall note that the number of women among these tribes is greatly in excess of the men, the estimates suggesting a ratio of four to three. On the assumption that this is a conservative average, Richardson's estimate of ten persons to a tent may not be much too large, though, if Henry is correct in his count for warriors, we estimate at the ratio of four females to three males a total Blackfoot population of 7,000. However this may be, a study of the table leads to the conclusion that during the last half of the fur trade period, there was no significant change in the population of the Blackfoot and the neighboring tribes. This is an important matter since the opinion prevails that every contact between primitive and white peoples results in a marked decline in population for the former. Consequently, we have given careful and detailed consideration to all the available estimates. The best known general study for population of aboriginal America is by Mooney [Mooney 1928:13], who, it may be noted, credits the Blackfoot tribes with 15,000 about the year 1780. In areas where it has been possible to check Mooney's estimates they appear liberal, suggesting that a reduction of one-fifth might be nearer the truth. In any case, we feel that the data presented here do not warrant the assumption of such numbers as given by Mooney, but that the actual population for the period ranged between seven and ten thousand, with the chances favoring the smaller figure.[9] It is true the literature contains some estimates higher than the figures of Mooney, but in no case does the person making the estimate indicate that it is any more than a guess, and the experience with the literature indicates that guesses as to tribal populations in the Plains are usually far in excess of the actual figures. However, it would be unwise to accept our estimate for the Blackfoot tribes without attempting additional checks.

Such a check may be found in the area occupied by these tribes. In 1809, Henry defined the territory occupied and claimed by the Blackfoot group, including the Sarsi and Gros Ventre, which boundary was consequently reasserted by these tribes in all subsequent treaties with Canada and the United States. The area enclosed by these boundaries is approximately 70,000 square miles. The population estimates for the Gros Ventre vary greatly, but a liberal interpretation would be 1,500, and for the Sarsi 1,000. Thus, the total population for the Blackfoot group would range from ten to thirteen thousand. This would give a population density of approximately 5.5 to 7 square miles per capita. This compares favorably with the population density for the whole Plains area which, according to Mooney's relatively high estimate, is about 7 square miles per capita. Recalling that these tribes depended almost entirely upon buffalo flesh, the above seem to approach the saturation point. In 1833, Maximilian reports that traders on the Missouri established a necessary ration of one buffalo a day to twenty-five persons. Upon this basis the annual food supply per capita would require [fourteen] buffalo. Assuming the minimum population of 10,000 for the Blackfoot area, the total annual requirement would be [146,000, or 189,000 for a population of 13,000].[10] It is difficult to estimate the number of buffalo the region could maintain, but in later years, when cattle raising became an important industry in the same region, two to four head a square mile was considered proper.[11] We note that to feed this population for one year each square mile in their habitat must produce a surplus of [two] buffalo. Denig [1930:462] estimates that one buffalo cow will produce seventeen head in eight years.[12] If this is correct, to maintain itself a herd of buffalo in this area must have exceeded the number killed annually by approximately [100,000?]; this would give a density in buffalo population of [3.5] per square mile. Too much weight should not be given these calculations, but they do show within wide range the limits the available food supply would place upon the Blackfoot population. While it is true that the Blackfoot hunted beyond the borders of their Plains territory, on the other hand, as we have seen, the neighboring tribes poached upon theirs, hence there is no reason to assume the above estimate to be invalidated by the failure of a tribe to observe its boundaries. Also, they were surrounded by other equally numerous tribes dependent upon the buffalo. Consequently, we offer the hypothesis that the suggested stability of tribal population in this area was chiefly due to environmental limitations.

Denig [1930:460–462] makes certain statements about the buffalo that bear upon this discussion. Because of his long experience and reliable observation on other subjects, his remarks should be given considerable weight. Thus, he states in 1854 that for the last 21 years the number of buffalo seems to have remained constant for the whole upper Missouri country. In fact, he believes that during his residence in that country the number increased rather than diminished.[13] However, this opinion seems to be based upon his assumption that smallpox and other diseases had greatly reduced the native population. For example, he states that since 1780, fifteen to twenty thousand Indians died of this and other white man's diseases.

Denig [1930:462] estimates the total number of buffalo in the Plains area as approximately three million. We have previously referred to his calculations to show that if there were no losses to offspring the total would soon rise to 51 million. This may be somewhat imaginative, but is offered here as the opinion of a competent observer.

Denig does not give actual estimates of the amount of buffalo meat consumed by the Indians, but comments at length as to the extraordinary capacity of an Indian, indicating that the amount of meat he may consume in a day exceeds belief. According to his observation, an Indian may eat continuously for ten hours. On the other hand, Denig states that these Indians resist starvation readily, being able to go many days without food [1930:509].

These statements are similar to those of other observers and might also apply to the Eskimo.

Catlin (1844:262–263) estimated the total Indian population of the Plains area at 300,000. The number of buffalo killed by the Indians annually for food is not stated, but he does say that in excess of 200,000 are killed for their skins, most of which are traded for liquor. Curiously enough, Catlin estimates that 1,500,000 wolves are also dependent upon the buffalo and take their toll from the herd. No doubt these estimates from Catlin are based upon statements of those engaged in the fur trade. [Editor: later in the manuscript, after his narrative text, Wissler copied this passage from the Report of the U. S. Commissioner for Indian Affairs for 1853, page 354, written from Ft. Pierre:]

> I have taken no little pains to ascertain the supposed number of buffalo annually destroyed in this agency, and, from the best information, the number does not fall very far short of 400,000. Not less than 100,000 robes have been shipped by the two companies who are licensed to trade amongst the Indians under my charge. 150,000 are destroyed, of which a small portion of their flesh is consumed; they are killed for their hides, to make lodges, which they are compelled to make very secure to protect them from the extreme severity of the weather during the winter. Numbers of these lodges are disposed of to the traders for securing their peltries and robes, when traded, from exposure to inclement weather; numbers [of bison] freeze and starve to death in snowbanks, which for months are found in drifts from five to ten feet in depth, and numbers are drowned in crossing and re-crossing the Missouri river, owing to the large numbers in crossing crowding on each other. [RCIA for 1853:354]

We may now give some consideration to conditions and practices of the Blackfoot which may of themselves have tended to limit the population.

Table 1.1. The estimate per capita consumption of meat by Maximilian can be checked by data supplied by Henry (p. 444), who gives an itemized statement of the provisions consumed at his post during nine months 1807–1808. The consumers he states as comprising 17 men, 10 women, 14 children and 45 dogs. His statement of food consumed has been condensed as follows:

147 buffalo	63,600 lbs.
3 red deer	905 lbs.
5 bears	460 lbs.
Grease	410 lbs.
Pemmican,	140 lbs.
Total	65,515 lbs.

In addition his list includes:

    4 beaver
    52 game birds
    1,925 fish
    325 bushes of potatoes
    Kitchen vegetables—a large quantity

If dogs were not included in this list, a fairly accurate per capita consumption could be calculated. Further, Henry states that a large part of the fish were given to visiting Indians. Further, unless he kept a separate account of other food given to visiting Indians, some allowance must be made for this item. However, since he does not indicate that any of the meat was given away, and if we assume that a dog will consume as much as a person, the daily per capita consumption would be 2 4/5 lbs. of meat.

Thompson (1797) says his Canadian companions consumed eight (8) pounds of fresh meat a day (p. 209). Again he says the daily allowance of fish is eight pounds, equal to five (5) pounds of meat (p. 112). Palliser [describes] Fort Edmonton [with a] "population of about 40 men, 30 women, and 80 children, almost entirely supported on buffalo meat, the hauling of which, for sometimes upwards of 250 miles across the plains, is the source of great and most fruitless expense. Indeed, the labour and the difficulty of providing for a consumption of 700 lbs. of buffalo meat daily, would frequently become very precarious, were it not for an abundant supply of fish from Lake St. Anne, about 50 miles to the west of the fort, whence they are capable of hauling 30,000 or 40,000 in a season; these are a fine wholesome white fish, averaging four pounds weight each" (Palliser:1859:41).

Henry speaks of this as starving. Maximilian estimated for Fort Mackenzie a daily ration of about 16 lb. per capita, no available supply of fish and vegetables indicated. If we assume that the dogs received none of the meat at Henry's home post, the ration would have been about 5.9 lb. Doubtless, somewhere between these extremes would fall the average ration of the true plains Indian, suggesting that our estimate of the food consumption in the Blackfoot country is high enough to offer a safe margin.

According to Henry's tables, the average weight of edible meat for buffalo cows is approximately 400 lbs. Upon this basis the meat allowance at Henry's post was much less than the allowance at Fort Mackenzie, as recorded by Maximilian. This suggests that in our estimate of the normal food consumption of the Blackfoot we have understated the rate necessary to a desirable standard of living.

While it is true that the Blackfoot tribes and others in the area were in frequent contact with each other and every now and then camped in close proximity, nevertheless there was more or less friction between individuals, resulting in frequent murders and retaliations. Further, war parties organized privately were out constantly raiding the surviving tribes. Consequently, the loss of able-bodied men was considerable. Every now and then the entire party would be annihilated. Even among themselves, these tribes were far from peaceable, since the journals of traders reveal frequent cases of quarrelling, resulting in the death of one of the parties, usually followed by other deaths in revenge. One's impression is that these Indians were wild and but lightly disciplined, and that the prevailing pattern of behavior was to resort to violence at the least provocation. Murders were more common among men than among women which, in addition to the losses from war, made a heavy drain upon the male population.

Early observers agreed that drunkenness was responsible for many deaths and, while no accurate statistics are given, the impression of the reader is that in fatalities due to this cause, the sexes were about equal. Drinking was not confined to one sex, all participating freely in this celebration; intoxication resulting in quarrels and assaults on the part of both sexes. It may be that the traders have emphasized the evils of drinking because of the danger and trouble of such affairs. It must be remembered that it was only when the Indians visited a post for trade that liquor was distributed. Hence, it is not likely that a given group of Indians would have more than three or four drinks a year. Nevertheless, among a people where the death rate is high, even a slight increased mortality due to drinking would be an important factor in limiting the population.

It is also pertinent to consider the mode of life and the degree of exposure resulting therefrom. In the first place it is observable that the costume used by these tribes seems, from our point of view, wholly inadequate. The winters in this area are long and often severe, yet during the whole of the fur trade period the regular costume for the men was rarely more than moccasins, leggings, and buffalo robe. For example, Henry states:

> The ordinary dress of these people is plain and simple, like that
> of all other Meadow [prairie] Indians; plain leather shoes, leather
> leggings reaching up to the hip, and a robe over all, constitutes
> their usual summer dress, though occasionally they wear an
> open leather shirt, which reaches down to the thigh. Their winter
> dress differs little from that of the summer; their shoes are then
> made of buffalo hide dressed in the hair, and sometimes a leather
> shirt and a strip of buffalo or wolf skin is tied around the head.

They never wear mittens. The young men have a more elegant dress which they put on occasionally, the shirt and leggings being trimmed with human hair always obtained from the head of an enemy. . . . The gun which they carry in their arms, and the powder-horn and shot-pouch slung on their backs, are necessary appendages to the full dress. The bow and quiver of arrows are also slung across the back at all times and seasons, except that, when the Indian is sleeping or setting his tent, these weapons are hung on a pole within reach. [Henry 1897:725–726]

Other observers make similar statements and ethnological studies for the latter period record traditional statements from Blackfoot informants wholly consistent with the above. The costume for women was equally simple, though possibly more adequate in that they wore a dress of skin reaching below the knees. It seems curious that a people in so cold a climate, within relatively short distance of northern forest tribes who used more adequate skin clothing, that the Blackfoot should not have adopted some of the conveniences such as caps, mittens, etc. It is true that some of the men of the period were said to have worn skin shirts and occasionally a fur cap, but it is curious to note that such caps and shirts seem for the most part to have been objects of regalia rather than belonging to everyday costume. The shirt, for example, was distinctly an article of dress for distinguished persons and more often something to be worn in battle, the decorations on which were expected to have magical and protective values. In other words, these shirts were worn not as clothing but as protective charms. More than once in the literature of the times we are told that young men, even in winter, would carry their shirts and other finery in a bundle, themselves wearing only robes, leggings, and moccasins.

It seems likely that such costumes, while undoubtedly ensuring a hardy race, would greatly increase mortality and thus be at least one of the factors in limiting this population. Another consideration in the well-being of a people is that of housing. In this respect there is little to consider because the skin tent of the Plains Indians was a satisfactory shelter at all times of the year. In fact, from a standpoint of health, it was superior to the present type of housing on many Indian reservations (see Plate 4). It is doubtful, therefore, if this can be set down as a limiting factor. Another important consideration is the food supply. This we have considered above, insofar as quantity was concerned. However, it is necessary to give attention to the food itself. For the most part, meat formed the entire diet, but since practically all parts of the animal were eaten, such as liver, brain, fat, etc., there is no reason why this diet should not have been adequate. On the other hand, some vegetable food was used, especially berries,[14] eaten fresh, dried, and mixed with meat. Again, if hunting should fail for a few days, various edible wild plants might be utilized. So, granting that there was an adequate supply of food, there seems no reason why this population should not have been healthful and virile.

There remains to consider the state of health, frequency of disease, etc. Naturally there are no adequate statistics on this subject, since during the whole trade period no physicians were in the area. On the other hand, the traders were called upon in emergencies and so were in a position to take note of the state of health among the native population. However, their testimony agrees that the Indians were a healthy lot. On the other hand, we are told that colds and pulmonary disorders were not unknown, and since these were observed by the early visitors, it seems unlikely that all of them were introduced through white contact. However, there is no evidence for tuberculosis at this time, nor for severe epidemics, though occasionally a number of individuals would be observed to die from similar ailments. Naturally we assume that infant mortality was very high, since such is the case among all "primitive" peoples from whom we have adequate data, but there is no reason to believe that the death rate in infancy was any higher among these tribes than any others.

Dr. Richardson, of the Sir John Franklin Expedition (1819), observed goiter to be prevalent among the Sarsi. Strangely enough, he attributed this disorder to their water supply, which was from the river fed by melting snows in the Rocky Mountains. His chief reason for this was that none of the other tribes were troubled with this disorder except a few Indian women who resided at the Indian trading posts on the Upper North Saskatchewan, using water from the river. However this may be, the prevalence of goiter among this tribe was reported from time to time until about 1870.

It is generally assumed that the first contact with Europeans introduces new and fatal diseases to the native population. The Indians of this area did not escape such diseases, probably the most disastrous of which was smallpox; since this disease was prevalent in Europe, it was inevitable that it should reach even the Indians of this isolated area. So far as known, its first appearance here was about 1780, though it had previously ravaged the Indian tribes of the Mississippi valley. Anyway, in 1781 and 1782 this scourge raged over the northern Plains reducing all tribes, in some cases more than 50 percent. That it reached the Blackfoot we know, but have no definite information as to their losses. According to Umfreville, the Gros Ventre suffered severely. Henry states that there was a second outbreak about 1790 which greatly reduced the Piegan, so that they now numbered but 150 tents. The same writer states that smallpox attacked the Gros Ventre again in 1795. It is certain that from this time on there were more or less periodical scourges of this disease, and we have compiled a table from the available sources giving the dates when this disease was reported as serious among the Blackfoot and their immediate neighbors. However, it is difficult to estimate the actual losses. If the deaths had been as frequent as some writers indicate, it is difficult to account for the number reported as surviving. On the other hand, Henry and other observers frequently remark on the rapidity with which these tribes recuperated their losses. It seems probable that both statements are in part true, namely, that the losses from smallpox were not as great as reported, and secondly, that these tribes were able to increase in numbers when the food supply and other conditions were favorable.

The traditions of these tribes suggest that early in their experience with smallpox they developed a technique for checking the ravages of the disease, for, as soon as the disease appeared, the practice was to scatter widely in small camps. This is probably why we find it stated in the literature of the times that the Indians of the Plains, particularly those of the northern Plains, suffered less than others. Hence, it is probable that, though the introduction of smallpox threatened the continued existence of these tribes, they soon adjusted themselves to the situation, to the end that it was no more fatal to the increasing of their population than to the European. Since settlements did not encroach upon the Blackfoot until after 1850, they were not especially troubled by the usual run of children's diseases common among Europeans. Certain it is that after 1850 we have frequent reports indicating that measles, whooping cough, etc. appeared at intervals, and in some cases with disastrous results. Yet on the whole, except for the introduction of smallpox, the fur trade period seems to have been marked by a condition of good health, the indications being that the mode of living followed by the Blackfoot of this period was sufficiently well adjusted to the environments to enable the population to maintain itself and to increase in numbers to the natural limits of the culture pattern. We have previously attempted to answer the question why the Blackfoot population did not increase rapidly and enter upon an era of expansion after the introduction of the horse and the beginning of the fur trade. We suspect the answer lies in the adjustment of their mode of life to the particular geographical and ethnical setting in which they found themselves. All of the factors noted above took their toll in deaths, but since these natives seemed able to recuperate their losses from smallpox, we suspect that the factors limiting the population are a part of the total environmental and cultural complex.

When considering the loss of adult males in this population we noted that the chances of life were greater for females. Hence, the question may be raised as to the relative number of the sexes in this population and the

TABLE 1.2. Smallpox

Jenness cites *Four Centuries of Medical History in Canada*, vol. 1, J. J. Heagerty [Toronto, 1928], pp. 251–252, [that] Smallpox appeared on the Atlantic in 1635. 1738, had reached west of Winnipeg.

> 1691—Mooney [1928:12]—In Texas, etc. 3000 Caddo die.
>
> 1778—Mooney—" " " "
>
> 1781—Umfreville—Struck Fall Indians [Gros Ventres]. First great attack. Not so bad in the Plains.
>
> 1782—Bryce—Swept Assiniboine and down the Missouri.
>
> Mooney [1928:12]—cut fur trade for two years.
>
> 1790 approx.—Henry [1897:722]—Piegan reduced to 150 tents.
>
> 1795—Henry [1897:531]—among the Fall Indians [Gros Ventres]. Approximate date.
>
> 1801—Mooney [1928:12]—Over all the Plains area in the United States.
>
> 1836—Hale—Heavy loss—reduced to 1,500 tents (?) Blackfoot, Gros Ventre, and Sarsi
>
> 1837–38—H.B. [Hudson's Bay Co.]—Blackfoot losses.
>
> 1842–43—Grinnell—Blackfoot.
>
> 1845—Grinnell—Blackfoot.
>
> 1857–58—Grinnell—Blackfoot.
>
> 1861—Not suffered much from smallpox—(H. and V.)
>
> 1869—Outbreak followed military defeat.
>
> 1870—Severe outbreak—1,400 deaths.

Perhaps the best account of the smallpox scourge is by Thompson who was in the country a few years later. Near Eagle Hills on the North Saskatchewan in 1786 he saw a camp full of sick and dying Indians. Apparently this was another outbreak.[1] The great scourge began in 1780 among the Chippeway [Ojibwe (Anishinaabeg)] and the Sioux and thence spread rapidly westward and northward over the whole interior of Canada. More than one-half of the natives are said to have died. The traders collected furs from the tents and cabins of the dead as well as from the sick. The Piegan claimed to have the first smallpox from a camp of Snake Indians they raided. It is further claimed that there was a shortage of deer and bison the following year and that the number never reached the former level (Thompson 1916:320-325). In-how-far these statements are accurate we cannot determine, but Thompson was a careful observer.

---

1. Editor's note: Wissler misread Thompson here (Thompson 1916:320–323), and apparently did not see Tyrell's footnote correction on the date (320, note 3). Thompson was quoting Mitchell Oman, another trader, although he fails to indicate where Oman's story ends. Tyrell, editor of the 1916 publication of Thompson's Narrative, said in a footnote that the year must have been 1781, not 1786.

bearing of this upon the ability of the tribe to recuperate. As stated, the observed ratio was in excess of four females to three males. As expected, these tribes were not strictly monogamous, plural marriages being the rule for chiefs and prominent men. However, the female population of all tribes in this area was constantly augmented by captives, since in raids and war excursions the rule was to kill all males of arms-bearing age, but to take captive all young women and female children. All traders visiting this area were struck by the number of young captives in every camp. It is obvious that in this way the excess of females would be augmented, which would supplement the excess due to the greater hazards incurred by males in hunting and in war. Here may lie the secret of the apparent elasticity in this population, by which it could recuperate heavy losses from disease or war. It is interesting to note that this excess of females declines gradually after 1850, but even in the census of 1910 the full blood statistics for the Piegan reservation in the United States shows 640 females to 573 males. Whether this long persistence in the excess of females is due to the same causes operating in the fur trade period is a question we are unable to answer. However, it is clear from the data that there has been a steady decline in the excess ratio since 1850.

TABLE 1.3. Health

1750–1850—Health reported good
Trained to endure hardships.
    1809—Some venereal disease reported—colds and cough.
    1819—Goitre; 1861; peculiar to Sarsi.
    Smallpox; 1782, 1790–5, 1836; temporary losses only.
    Prosperity might have brought great increase, if not checked by smallpox.
1850–1885—H. and V. (1861) healthy, not suffered much from smallpox.
    1870—Smallpox severe.
    Eye disorders common.
    Unusual diseases of children rare; but measles in 1864. (Smith)
    Some tubercular reported (1879).
    1883–4—Grinnell, 1/4 the population starve. (600)
1885—Children's diseases appear—measles, etc.
    Bronchial ills.

Standard of Living

An important question at this point is as to whether the Blackfoot standard of living was in any way changed by the fur trade. In the first place, the earlier introduction of the horse must have affected the standard of

FIG. 3. Blackfoot camp at Two Medicine Lake. Credit: Marquette University Archives, Bureau of Catholic Indian Mission Records.

living by increasing mobility, making possible larger living quarters and increasing the bulk of transportable equipment. Since horses were used for gathering firewood, transporting meats, etc., the possible consumption per family must have increased. It is to be noted that during this period there seems to have been a marked development in the art of painting skins and decorating clothing. It seems reasonably certain that the characteristic art-style came in with horse culture, or that its development was due to the greater leisure among women released from the bearing of burdens. The early visitors to this group remarked a contrast between these Plains people and those of the woodlands to the east, not only in the richness of their equipment but in their superior standards of cleanliness and artistic appearance. Great pride seems to have been taken in beautiful tents, costumes, and horse equipment. This was further reflected in parades of mounted men and in the symmetrical arrangements of large camps (Fig. 3). Presumably these are all aspects of an increased standard of living due to the introduction of the horse as an improvement in transportation.

It is probable also that the horse is responsible for the tendency of tribes in this area to filter into each other, maintaining at times sufficient freedom to exchange ideas and information. While we cannot be sure as to the situation before 1750, there is ample evidence to show that during the fur trade period news could travel rapidly from tribe to tribe. For example, in 1806, Henry visited the village Indians of the Upper Missouri river, where he heard from visiting Crow (?) Indians that Lewis and Clark had found their way to the Pacific and on their return had some difficulties with the Indians in what is now Montana. The information as recorded by Henry is substantially correct, but we mention it here as an example of how information was rapidly diffused from tribe to tribe. It is quite likely that the possibility of receiving such information widened the geographical consciousness of these tribes to such a degree that the desire to keep fully informed stimulated long journeys and intertribal visiting. In a way this may be considered an item in the standard of living, namely the desire for travel and acquaintance with events in distant areas. Insofar as a similar condition held for the early period of indirect trade, it is difficult to estimate the amount of stimulus and the new ideas that may have reached the Blackfoot before direct contact with whites. It may be useless to speculate upon this, but upon the other hand, recognition should be given to the possibility of such a stimulus to culture change.

Naturally, trade introduced new objects, the possession of which would change the standard of living because of their labor-saving functions. As previously stated, the chief objective in the minds of the Indian customers was to secure firearms, and, while these were wanted primarily for war, they did nevertheless contribute to the security of the Indians in camp and thus take an important place in the standard of living. The other objects greatly prized by the Indians were metal cutting tools, the knife, and the ax. These were great labor-saving devices, especially the latter, since by its use the labor of women in gathering firewood, in making tent poles, etc., was greatly lessened [Editor's note: axes were also used in butchering large game]. Another important object was the kettle. Pottery is scarcely practical to a people frequently on the move. It is generally observed that pottery is to be found in the Plains only[15] among those Indians who tend to live in villages, and further, Strong reports that in prehistoric village sites along the Platte River pottery begins to degenerate when horse bones appear. Hence, there is every reason to expect a great demand for kettles, which again would increase the standard of equipment. As to just when practically every Blackfoot household came to be equipped with these few necessary articles cannot be definitively stated, but in 1809 Henry observes that many Blackfoot families are still destitute of axes and kettles, suggesting that the possession of these objects created certain social distinctions among these tribes. In 1833, Maximilian saw at Fort Mackenzie the greater part of the Blackfoot tribes and precipitately states that they were equipped with kettles and, for the most part, with tin dishes. This suggests that some time between 1809 and this date these Indians were sufficiently prosperous to thoroughly equip themselves in accordance with this standard.

So far, we have considered useful objects only, but trade did introduce a few luxuries. Most important seem to have been vermilion and a few other pigments. To this list should be added ribbons, beads of china and glass, mirrors, buttons, and shell ornaments. Cloth was not particularly valued by these people and it was not until after 1859 that textiles held an important place in the traders' stock. Naturally, these objects should not be considered as necessities, but they would play a considerable role in the standard of living, since every important family would desire them.

Two other important articles of trade were liquor and tobacco, yet for the most part these commodities were demanded as presents rather than as payment for goods. Nevertheless, the trader saw to it that he was fully compensated when it came to actual trading.

Apparently, there can be no doubt but that a marked change in the standard of living came by the end of the fur trade period, and in turn these new demands must have stimulated native production, which in turn should lead to corresponding social changes.

It was apparent to the trader that the multiplicity of wives increased the wealth of the Indian family. As previously noted, two important items in Blackfoot trade were pemmican and hand-tanned robes, all the work of women. Further, the easing of women's tasks by the introduction of the horse and metal tools made possible the production of surplus pemmican and robes without placing special strain upon the leisure of the women. Larpenteur remarks that a prominent man among the Blackfoot may be expected to have five or six wives and bring yearly to the trader goods to the value of some $2,000. He is thus a man of importance, usually owning a herd of horses and possessing luxurious camp equipment. In contrast Larpenteur states that a man with but one wife is usually observed as relatively poor in equipment and possessing no social prestige. All this suggests that in part at least the increased standard of living encouraged an excess feminine population, which in turn greatly increased the productive labor of the tribe. Of course, it is apparent that the male members of the tribe were also subject to new responsibilities in killing the necessary amount of game to produce this surplus of trade goods, and also charged with the necessity of defending their property against the covetous members of neighboring tribes and sometimes resisting the attempts of their less fortunate among their own tribe members to divest them of their property. The picture we get, then, of the fur trade period is one of increasing standard of living, beginning with very simple trade objects and progressing to a standard calling for an expendable amount of goods approaching a value of two or three thousand dollars per year. Of course it is not to be understood that every Indian family would succeed in acquiring such an income, but that this was not only the ideal, but it represented the level attained by a fair percentage of the population.

Dependence upon Trade

Whether this change in Blackfoot life is to be considered good or evil is an open question and one that is inappropriate to our present objective. We can, however, consider the question as to whether the introduction of trade goods and the corresponding change in the standard of living tended to increase the independence and self-sufficiency of the tribes concerned, or whether it tended to place them in a relation of dependence. This is possibly one of the most important phases of the contact between "primitive" peoples and civilized. For example, the introduction of the horse was not only beneficial to the Indian by placing in his hands for the first time a useful, large, domestic animal which he could propagate and control without assistance from without. When our definite knowledge of the Blackfoot begins in 1750, these tribes were apparently prosperous and quite able to maintain themselves under a rising standard of living, though it is possible that the saturation point in horse culture had been reached by this date.

The acquisition of firearms presents a sharp contrast for awhile. The Indians became entirely dependent upon this equipment to protect themselves from their enemies. They could neither manufacture the weapon nor the ammunition. Thus, they were solely dependent upon trade. To a slightly less extent they were dependent for metal tools and kettles. Conceivably, they could at any time have dispensed with other trade objects, but not without marked economic and social disturbance. What the trader sought was to occupy all the spare time of both men and women in the production of furs and other trade goods, while he, in turn, would supply them with this new and better equipment, thus eventually destroying many of their arts and crafts. At the same time the more intense hunting and trapping tended to reduce the game supply, a situation which the traders met in part by supplying cereals and other readily transported foods. However, the Blackfoot did not at any time during this fur trade period find themselves seriously disturbed by declining fauna. They were, however, rapidly moving toward a dependence upon trade for the maintenance of their standard of living, insofar as it related to equipment for the household, travel, and war. Yet, so long as the food supply remained adequate, and a sufficient amount of trade goods could be readily produced, the Blackfoot were in a state of relative prosperity. In fact, all the evidence we have indicates that this century of fur trade was a period of prosperity. Many observers testify that the natives were seldom in want of food for more than a brief period, and that they themselves repeatedly stated that they were rarely in want of food. On the other hand, they never lost an opportunity when visiting traders to orate eloquently on their impoverished condition in respect to the goods kept in stock by the traders. This is consistent since it indicates the high ideal of material well-being and luxury in equipment over and above the ordinary necessities of life. According to civilized standard this might be considered a highly satisfactory situation, except that the Indian was largely dependent upon imports to maintain his standard of living.

The Effect upon Tribal Discipline

The first observers of the Blackfoot and Gros Ventre remarked upon the excellent organization of their camps and the efficient discipline of the head chief and his associates. At that time this seemed in marked contrast to the condition observed in the tribes east of Lake Winnipeg. Further, there is reason to observe that this effective discipline was the chief factor in their culture, making possible the observed standard of living under horse culture. Again, the fur traders of the time seemed to have sensed the importance of maintaining this state of affairs, perhaps because at the outset no trading post could be set up and maintained within tribal territory without, when at a post for trade, one or more leading chiefs took the Indians in hand and compelled them to observe such procedure and regulations as previously agreed upon between the trader and themselves. It also appears that among these Plains tribes the traders sought to increase production on the part of the mass by appealing to the chiefs in authority, resorting to the questionable expedient of handsome presents, etc. We have noted that the traders were opposed not only to settlement by whites, but also to the entrance of white trappers and itinerant traders, the restrictions upon which did to a large extent preserve the original discipline of the chiefs. It is true that toward the end of the fur trade period the rivalry between traders reached such a state that the less responsible men of the tribe would be encouraged to disregard the orders of the chief, especially in respect to trade. However, the data at hand do not show any definite tendency for this influence to break down the original control.

   We should not confuse the constant struggle between the younger and older generations with a real breakdown in tribal discipline. For example, Henry, in 1809, comments upon the tendency of the young Blackfoot to disregard the advice and authority of the chiefs [e.g., Henry 1897:546], apparently assuming that a breakdown is in progress. On the other hand, there is ample evidence that the control and prestige of the chiefs continued effective until the end of the period. We conclude, therefore, that trade in this area did not seriously interfere with tribal organization and discipline, and it is quite possible that the increase in standard of living and enhanced wealth of the tribe tended to increase the efficiency and importance of this control.

Drain Upon Natural Resources

We have previously suggested that this population was living upon a close margin in the game supply and that the standard of living was gradually rising, thus creating a greater demand for the products of hunting. Naturally the question may arise as to in how far these increased demands could be met by the natural resources in game animals.

We previously estimated the annual consumption of buffalo at 150,000 per year. This makes no allowance for the pemmican and tallow consumed by the fur trade, nor do we at present have data upon it to make an estimate. However, Henry states:

[Editor's note: Wissler leaves a blank page here, with no indication of where in Henry's journals this information is to be found. My own search through Henry 1897 (Coues's edition) failed to find any figures on Blackfoot consumption of bison, although there are copious details on animals killed or brought in to provision the traders, and lists of skins traded to them. Pages 490–507 describe great numbers of bison seen and hunted during Henry's journey from Cree country, central Saskatchewan, to Fort Vermilion in Alberta where Blackfoot traded. Page 690, dated January 13, states that the Blackfoot chief Black Bear "made a pound near Red Deer river for the purpose of supplying us [the trading post] with buffalo" and on page 675, dated February 1, "Black Bear and others beyond Red Deer river, who are coming slowly, with lean horses loaded with fresh meat." Coues in footnote 15, page 276, explains "taureaux" are "raw-hide bags to hold about 80 pounds of pemmican; also, such a quantity of pemmican," Henry noting for June 10, 1806, that he provisioned canoes with one taureau per man (Henry 1897:276). Thus, the trade consumed both fresh meat killed for the posts and voyageurs, and previously killed meat made into bagged pemmican and traded.]

We have assumed that the increase in the standard of living was accompanied by an increase in the size of tents and household equipment, all of which would tend to demand more buffalo skins. A rough estimate of these demands can be made upon the basis of the standard of household equipment as reflected in the standardized culture of 1880. For example, we find that fourteen buffalo skins were considered necessary for the covering to a tent of average size. The life of such a tent did not exceed two years. Assuming that during the fur trade period the number of tents for the Blackfoot group was approximately 1,200, the annual consumption of buffalo skins for this purpose alone would amount to 8,400.

The other uses for buffalo skins in accordance with this culture pattern and the estimated consumption per capita is as follows:

Moccasins . . . 2
Robes . . . 1
other purposes . . . 3
total . . . 6

This would call for a consumption of approximately 50,000 skins per year, making a total of less than 60,000, which is considerably less than the number of buffalo needed for food and which leaves a large margin for trade. Of course, it should not be overlooked that the condition of the animal killed determined the value of the skin, and that the fur traders declined all but cow skins in prime condition. Nevertheless there is no reason to believe that at any time the Indian was under the necessity of killing buffalo merely for the sake of their skins.

We have given no consideration to the skins of elk, deer, antelope, and mountain sheep, all of which were used for clothing and which would be necessary to complete the equipment indicated above. On the basis of the culture for 1880, the annual consumption of such skins is roughly estimated at 20,000 per type of animal. It is also evident that the killing of these animals would furnish a considerable amount of food, which might call for a reduction in the number of buffalo killed. Yet since, in our estimate of the number of buffalo consumed, we based the per capita consumption upon an observed minimum under conditions favoring economic use, it is therefore probable that the additional support from the killing of deer, etc. would merely be sufficient to meet the average standards of living.

These estimates can be checked further by taking into consideration the labor required to dress all of these skins. Later culture studies indicate that all such labor was performed by women, and if 60,000 buffalo and 20,000 deer skins were to be tanned each year, it is plain that the amount of labor involved is considerable. In the population as estimated the total number of women able to work on skins certainly did not exceed 3,000. Upon this assumption the consumption of 80,000 tanned skins would demand that on the average each woman dressed from 26 to 27 skins, or at the rate of a little more than two per month.

It is difficult to estimate the number of hours required for the proper dressing of such skins, but the process is completely described in the later literature. Stretching and drying are far more important procedures and, while it appears that several days may elapse between the first and final stage in dressing a skin, the actual time required in the form of labor is much less. In three cases observed by the writer no precise time record was kept, but he is sure that the total working time need not have exceeded four hours.[16] Granting that this is a correct estimate and that the above requirements for the year would call for something more than for each woman to complete two skins per month, the total task could not have placed any particular hardship upon the women, nor would it have seriously interfered with their other domestic duties. Further, it is obvious that the number of skins tanned could be doubled without hardship, thus allowing a fair margin for trade in accordance with the increased standard of living. Our original question, however, referred to the balance between these new demands and the existing supply. From all the information at hand the natural supply was adequate to sustain a population of this size in accordance with the standards of living reflected in the culture as of 1880. There is no reason to believe that this standard was higher during the fur trade period. On the one hand, it is not clear that the production of skins for trade could have increased beyond a total consumption for all purposes of 100,000 skins per year without seriously cutting down the available supply of buffalo. On the other hand, we doubt whether the women could have increased the production of dressed skins to this amount without greatly lowering the standard of living.

Standard of Conduct

It is frequently stated that when European traders enter a territory occupied by primitive peoples or by oriental civilizations, they introduce new standards of conduct and precision. Commerce is calculating and exacting, calling for exact records, methods of estimating quantity and value. Since contrast between the culture of the fur trader and the Indian was great, especially since the Indian had developed nothing in the way of writing and almost as little in the development of measurement, the fur trader would at once introduce into Indian culture a number of new ideas and points of view. The literature of the time usually assumes that all effects of white trade were detrimental, that the Indian was exploited and defaulted. There is a great deal of truth in these charges, but on the other hand, from the first, traders adopted a credit system that seems to have been thoroughly understood by the Indians and which worked satisfactorily among many tribes. However, we have no evidence to the practice of such a credit system among these Indians until the very end of the fur trade period. Most of the trade was on a cash basis, that is, the Indians delivered the goods and received other goods in exchange. We assume this due to the unwillingness of these Indians to trap beaver, even if they were outfitted by the trader.

The best statement of the effects of the fur trade upon the Indian are given by Denig, himself a trader:

> The Indian trade does not admit of competition. The effects of strong rival companies have been more injurious and demoralizing to the Indians than any other circumstance that has come within our knowledge, not even excepting the sale of ardent spirits among them. This we could easily prove, but as no monopoly can be allowed by the nature of our government it is useless. When the American Fur Co. were alone in the country a trader's word or promise to the Indians was sacred, the Indians loved and respected their traders, and still do some of the old stock, but since corruption has been carried on we look in vain for that reliance on and good feeling toward traders which was once the pride of both Indian and white. [Denig 1930:458]

Denig may have overestimated these influences, but there can be no doubt but that the Indian acquired new ideas of procedure and developed a new pattern of conduct to govern his intercourse with the trader. Further, the traders employed Indian hunters and an occasional laborer in and about the posts, and, while but a few individuals were so brought in contact with the trade, they nevertheless acquired a new pattern and perhaps a new conception of productive labor. Nowhere in the culture of 1880 do we find a conception of labor and wages in any way comparable to that of the European during the fur trade period. Also, the increased standard of living among the Indians and the idea that trade goods could be had as the indirect products of labor must have had some influence in developing ideals of industry.

As to the charge that the traders debauched the Indians, we must take into consideration the culture patterns of the Indians themselves. The taking of Indian women by white traders was regarded by the Indians as legal marriage and so could not have had the immoral effect usually attributed to it. Further, the trader in charge of the post was usually a man of power and personality and, though he might on occasion defraud the Indian, nevertheless would stand as an exponent of the virtue and morality of his own culture. It seems impossible but that some of these ideals and standards of conduct should have been recognized by the Indians and to some extent observed in their intercourse with the whites. In any case they were forced to recognize certain superiorities in white culture, and such recognition is usually followed by some degree of imitation.

Another important influence might come through the marriage of Indian women to the traders, even though the numbers were insignificant.[17] The wife of a trader would automatically step into a standard of living more like that of the European than that of her own people. She would adopt new standards of dress, cleanliness, and industry. In no case would she break her social ties with her relatives and hence would be frequently under their observation, thus standing as an example for social betterment and a totally different ideal of living. However, further comment on this influence will be offered under another head.

Friction with the Whites

During the early part of this period no white man entered Blackfoot territory excepting those in the employment of the large trading companies. However, by 1800 independent trappers and traders were operating on the Upper Missouri and occasionally in the eastern part of the Saskatchewan area. We have observed the disinclination of the Blackfoot to trap beaver and as time went on the trading posts visited by the Blackfoot became less and less willing to accept other furs, or to increase the demand for buffalo skins. In fact there are data to indicate that this pressure was deliberate, the idea being that if the pressure was strong enough the Blackfoot would be forced to produce beaver. It was not long until the Blackfoot discovered that independent beaver trappers were exploiting the Upper Missouri and the adjacent mountains and so developed the practice of killing and robbing these trappers, taking their beaver skins back to the trading posts in their own territory. The literature gives no indication that these practices were in any way discouraged by the traders of the Saskatchewan, in fact we are led to infer that they were encouraged. It is also evident that these same traders encouraged the Blackfoot to discourage all independent white traders from entering their own territory. As a result the Blackfoot assumed an intolerant attitude toward all whites except their own traders, and soon acquired a reputation for hostility. The increase of white settlements on the Upper Missouri by the end of the fur trade period developed friction between the Blackfoot and the whites which threatened to take the form of open and perpetual warfare.

Like other Plains Indians, the Blackfoot were notorious raiders for horses, originally against other Indian tribes, but naturally when white settlements came within reach, they raided them for horses. Toward the end of the fur trade period, trade in horses among the Canadians increased so that the traders of the Saskatchewan were able to dispose of a number brought in by the Indians. Again, there is reason to suspect that raiding for horses was stimulated by the traders, but in any event the Blackfoot now found it profitable to raid white settlements for horses. In other words, the development of trade along these lines was rapidly bringing the Blackfoot into serious conflict with both the government of Canada and that of the United States. At no time during this period, however, did the Blackfoot suffer; on the other hand, they were always the gainers. The number of settlers on the frontiers was not great enough to cope with the situation.

Mixture of White and Indian Blood

We have previously commented upon the intermarriage of Indian women and white traders, but it is difficult to form a satisfactory estimate of the amount of white blood introduced during the fur trade period. In the first decade of 1800 the number of posts was approximately [13 in the Northwest Country department of the Northwest Company (Henry 1897:282); there were in addition a larger number of Hudson's Bay Company posts, and unauthorized "pedlars'" posts—Editor]. We note that in 1805 Henry estimated the so-called white population as 2,615 [Henry 1897:282]. Obviously, Henry, in this enumeration, counted the Indian wives as white, including also their children. Further, the names of employees and accompanying remarks by Henry lead one to suspect that many of these were of mixed descent—Cree, Ojibway, and the "breeds." In any case, it is clear that a considerable amount of white blood had been introduced by 1805 and that, while the rate of increase of this population as given by Henry is less than among full-blood Indians, it nevertheless signifies that these mixed-blood descendants of Indian women and white men will rapidly increase. Also, count must be taken of the increase in the number of trading posts, and the intrusion of independent traders, all of which will increase the white and mixed population.

How far the Blackfoot group were affected by this mixture is difficult to determine. Independent traders were kept out of their country, but once these individuals married into the Assiniboine or Cree they would be able to pass as Indians. It is further possible that some white traders also married into the Blackfoot group. On the other hand, the employees of the post seemed to have married Cree and Assiniboine rather than women of the Blackfoot group. In short, while it is plain that some white blood must have found its way into the Blackfoot group during the fur trade period, the end of that period should have left them much purer than either the Cree or the Assiniboine. The chief source of white mixture of this group may have been marriages with mixed blood Cree and Assiniboine.

However, in considering the influence of such mixture upon the culture of the tribe it is reasonable to expect that a few capable individuals will suffice for important culture changes. Thus, Maximilian mentions a Blackfoot mixed-blood by the name of Bird, who was a great power and influence because of his linguistic ability and intimate knowledge of fur trade methods [Maximilian 1906:135]. The same writer mentions a Mr. Berger, a white man, who was familiar with the Blackfoot language [Maximilian 1906:146]. Yet these citations about exhaust the literature of the period. About 1840 we note a few Blackfoot marriages, as Malcolm Clarke, Joseph Kipp, etc., individuals destined to play an important role in the next period of Blackfoot history, but these serve to indicate that the introduction of white blood and consequent mixed-blood leadership did not rise to a high level during the fur trade period. Hence we doubt that any important cultural influence can be assigned to this cause except insofar as it was a minor element in white contact as developed through trade. As we have previously noted, the presence of traders were attempts to control Indian production; the negotiations of rival traders, etc., may have played a large part in stimulating culture change.

The Treaty Period: 1850–85

The Blackfoot groups do not come into close contact with the governments of Canada and the United States until after 1850. This period is marked by the making of definite treaties with these governments and thus committing each to a policy. From the first, the British government, in laying claim to territory in North America recognized the territorial rights of each independent Indian group. In accordance with this policy the tribal claims to specified lands were accepted as valid insofar as they were confirmed in the first treaty. Further, the policy was to compensate the tribe for all lands the titles to which they relinquished. Consequently nearly all treaties specified sums of money to be given to the Indians in the form of annuities or in goods.

The first treaty in which the Blackfoot group participated was the treaty of Laramie in 1851, but since we must consider the acts of two governments, it seems advisable to discuss the Canadian treaties before proceeding with those made by the United States. Later we shall consider the peculiar situation in which the Blackfoot group found itself because it claimed territory both in Canada and the United States. Long before the opening of this period these Indians had become acquainted with the advantages and disadvantages of dealing with two rival nations, each with somewhat different sets of laws covering trade.

So far as we know, the first important treaty between this group and Canada was one known as the Blackfeet Treaty Number 7, concluded September 22, 1877, between Canada and the following tribes: Blackfoot, Blood, Piegan, Sarsi, and Stonie Assiniboine. In this treaty the boundaries were defined as west on the international boundary line Cypress Hills to the Rocky Mountains; thence northwest along the boundary of British Columbia to a point due west of the source of the main branch of the Red Deer River; thence southeast and south, following on the boundary of the tracts ceded by treaties number six and four, to the place of commencement.

It appears that the northern and eastern boundaries to this territory were down the Red Deer River to the outlet of Buffalo Lake, then east 20 miles, then on a straight line southeast to the mouth of the Red Deer River, roughly southward to the Cypress Hills and the international boundary. (See map in Canadian Handbook.) In accordance with this treaty the Blackfoot relinquished their title to about one-third of the land claimed by them according to Henry in 1809. It is interesting to note that the land so relinquished had been accredited to the Plains Cree, the Wood Cree, and the Assiniboine of the Saskatchewan by the treaty of 1876. This suggests that during the period from 1800 to 1850 the Assiniboine and Cree were expanding into this territory—an area of 1220,000 square miles—while the Blackfoot were drifting southward. Further, by the treaty of 1876 these Indians secured title to all the territory drained by the north branch of the Saskatchewan and the valley of the south branch, and all the territory in the province of the Saskatchewan north of the south branch. The eastern limit to this territory was approximately at Cumberland Lake.

The territory south of the south branch and eastward to Lake Winnipeg was released by the Cree, Ojibway, and others (?) in 1874. This implies that the Assiniboine had not only abandoned this territory before that date, but had ceased to claim it.

Apparently, the conditions of the Blackfoot treaty were that the lands to be permanently reserved for the Indians were to equal one square mile for each family of five, or in proportion thereto. Further, that a cash payment of $12.00 per capita and for an indefinite time an annuity of $5.00 per capita be paid. Each recognized chief was to receive $15.00 per annum and each subordinate chief $15.00.

TABLE 1.4. Treaties

Blackfoot claimed all territory in Montana east of mountains and north of Missouri.

1801—Northwest Company made a trade agreement with Blackfoot, Gros Ventre, Sarsi, Kutenai (?)

1851—Fort Laramie treaty confirmed this claim.

1855—Certain hunting rights formally conceded to the Flathead and Nez Percé.

1868—Southern boundary pushed back slightly.

1873—A reserve established across northern Montana, north of Missouri and Sun River.

1874—Southwestern boundary raised to Marias River. Lands taken away without consulting the Blackfoot. Agent and chiefs go to Ft. Benton to make peace with Assiniboine.

1875—For hunting area—ceded a new area south of Missouri, east of Musselshell River.

1880—Forced Blackfoot to give up 1875 concession.

1887—A separate reservation created including present lands.
Gros Ventre also given a separate reservation.
Blackfoot to receive $150,000 a year for 10 years.

Treaty of 1855

Recognize allegiance to U.S.
Remain within their territory.
Not molest U.S. citizens passing through.
Assent to garrisons.
To refrain from crossing to Canada or have any communication with British.
Not fight other tribes.
Indians to give up nomadic habits.
Deliver all of their own number committing crimes against whites.
All captive whites to be released.

It seems unnecessary to go into full details at this point since the general outline of the policy developed by the Canadian government is revealed. Further, it was not until 1877 that the Blackfoot group entered into a definite treaty relationship with Canada.[18] Further note should be taken that the Gros Ventre are not mentioned in any of the Blackfoot treaties, indicating that long before this date they had ceased to claim lands in Canada.

At no time did the Sarsi claim lands within the United States, though in company with the Blackfoot and Gros Ventre they frequently visited trading posts in this area. Consequently, in discussing treaties with the United States we are concerned only with the Blackfoot and Gros Ventre.

TABLE 1.4. Treaties (continued)

For this to receive:
$35,000 in goods per year for ten years.
$15,000 spent by U. S. in schools, agriculture, etc.

1887—Treaty of the Judith.

Called for education program—nothing done.
Indians request *coffee* and *rice* be omitted and *corn* substituted.

Laramie Treaty

May select 320 acres for farming.
Receive seeds, implements, guidance.
A suit of clothing issued each year for 30 years.
Cloth for all children.
$10 for each man per year.
$20 for each man if he gives up hunting and settles down to farm.
Each farm, a cow and yoke of oxen.
$500 prize for each of ten Indians growing the best crops.
Lands held free from settlement.
(Summary by Robinson, Dakota Historical Society, Vol. 2, p. 383.)

Addenda to tables:

Treaty 1855—10 yr. Annuities.
Pressure on Piegan to cease war—keep peace.
Continued peaceful until 1867.
1867—Short of horses and poor.
Other Indians raided them.
Friction—onslaught of troops 1869.
Smallpox in 1870.
1871—Whiskey trade intense.

As stated, the first treaty with these tribes was in 1851, which treaty involves all the Indian tribes of the Upper Missouri and was designed to bring about a better understanding between these tribes. One of the terms to which the various tribal delegations subscribed was that intertribal war should cease. It is true that before 1851 more or less informal agreements were made between the Northwest Fur Company and the Blackfoot, Gros Ventre, Sarsi, and Kutenai, especially in 1831. However, since these were trade agreements they belong to the period of the fur trade.

The 1851 treaty deserves detailed study because incorporated in it is the outline of an Indian policy which the United States attempted to follow for many years. A few of its stipulations may be noted here. (1)

The encouragement of agriculture. Each adult male Indian was accorded the privilege of selecting 320 acres of land for farming. If he did so, the government promised to give him the necessary implements and advice. Also, for each farm a cow and a yoke of oxen. Further, a prize of $500.00 for each of ten Indians producing the best crop in any one year. (2) All lands within the boundaries to Indian claims established by this treaty were to be held free from white settlements. (3) To encourage European dress. Each year for thirty years each man would be issued a suit of American clothing and each woman provided with cloth for a complete outfit. For each child, suitable cloth. (4) Annuities. Each adult male to receive ten dollars per year; if he gives up hunting and settles down to farming $20.00 per year. Apparently the Sarsi were also invited to move into United States territory, whence they would receive the same benefits.

As may be expected, the treaty of 1851 was soon amended by separate treaties with the tribes concerned, a list of which in so far as they affect the Blackfoot, is given in the accompanying table.

The first important treaty with the Blackfoot was in 1855. An observer described how,

> each day, the Indians, including men, women, and children, several thousand in number, would assemble and seat themselves in a semi-circular group on the ground [See Plate 3] and patiently listen to each section of the treaty as it was read to them by the Secretary [James Doty] and repeated to them by the interpreter. . . . While the council was in progress other bands and squads of Indians on horseback and on foot and gaily decorated were parading and chanting their Indian songs about the treaty grounds. . . . After the reading of the treaty was concluded, it became the Indians' turn to speak, which many of them did. It was surprising to listen to the eloquence that flowed from the untutored mind of the so-called savage Indian, who had never before mingled in common with the whites. As well as the Commissioners and others who were present, I was greatly impressed with the oratorical efforts of Chief Little Dog and Bear Chief who spoke on the part of the Piegan and Blackfeet tribes in general. On the last day of the Council and before its adjournment, Chief Little Dog, in making his appeal to his people and urging them to strictly observe the provisions of the treaty, spoke for six consecutive hours. All of the palefaces who were present were astonished when the sound logic and eloquence flowed from the tongue of this uneducated orator, while the efforts of Bear Chief were not lacking in logic and rhetoric. Commissioners Cumming and Stevens declared that the

oratorical powers of Little Dog and Bear Chief would have done credit to a Roman Senator. [Kennerly 1982 (written 1912–13):50]

The chiefs entered into an agreement to restrain their Indians from war; neither attacks nor raids for horses were to be made upon other tribes or upon the whites. Similar obligations were laid upon their neighbors in the United States. In return for this good behavior they were to be placed under the guidance of an Indian agent. Apparently, the annuities and other promises made in the treaty of 1851 were now forgotten, but in their place the Blackfoot tribes and the Gros Ventre were to receive an annual grant of goods to the amount of $35,000.00 for a period of ten years.

In the 1855 treaty, the extent of their lands in the United States was defined as follows:

> bounded on the south by a line drawn eastward from the Hell Gate or Medicine Rock passes to the nearest source of the Musselshell River, down that river to its mouth, and down the Missouri to the mouth of Milk River; on the east by a line due north from the mouth of Milk River to the forty-ninth parallel (the Canadian border); on the north by this parallel; and on the west by the Rocky Mountains. [Ewers 1958:217]

According to the treaty they were not to leave this territory, but all their hunting and roaming was to be within its limits, which is of course consistent with the agreement not to engage in war. Further, they were not to molest citizens of the United States passing through their territory unless trespassing; to permit the construction of military forts and roads; in case any of their number committed crimes against white men their tribe was to submit them for punishment; all whites now held captive to be released, etc. One agreement was that the government of the United States would spend $15,000.00 per year in establishing schools and developing agriculture. Finally, the one item in the treaty of especial interest to us was that these Indians were forbidden to cross back into Canada, or have any communication whatever with the citizens of that country or England. From the standpoint of present knowledge this is a stupid requirement, since a large part of the Blackfoot were at that time living in Canada, and in part at least trading at Canadian posts. Further, they were regarded by Canada as Indians for whom she was responsible and expected that they remain within her territory. (When was the boundary line established? [Editor's note: 1846]) At that time the boundary line was not definitely defined, at least not so that the Indian could know when he had passed from one country to the other. Anyway, the whole question must have been unintelligible to the Indian, because we have noted that in 1876 their rights to certain territory were established by the Canadian government. It is not clear whether the treaty of 1855 contemplated treating the Sarsi as a part of the Blackfoot, but presumably so.

Before we proceed with this discussion it is necessary to note that in the course of the next few years the international boundary line separated the Blackfoot group, the Gros Ventre becoming subject to the United States, together with a large portion of the Piegan, while on the other hand the remainder of the Piegan, Blood, Blackfoot, and Sarsi withdrew to Canada. These relations conform in large measure to the original habitats for these tribes and therefore represent their historical positions, but it was not until after 1870 that these tribes ceased to roam indiscriminately in Canada and the United States. In fact, it was some years later before they gave up this habit. It seems that the international boundary line cut through the territory of the Piegan and that some time previous to 1870, because of the unusual size of this tribe, it began to operate in two divisions ultimately known as the North and South Piegan. It seems that after the treaty of 1855 the South Piegan regarded themselves as belonging in the United States, and so far as our information goes refrained from temporary residence in Canada. Naturally, since the line passed through their territory, individuals and bands did cross over. On the other hand, it is clear that neither the Blood nor the Blackfoot at any time seriously considered allegiance to the United States, though they did not hesitate to roam and hunt within its territory and to visit trading posts on the Missouri. Hence, our discussion from this point on is concerned chiefly with the main body of the Piegan residing in the United States territory.

Conflict with the Whites

No one can review the United States records of its Piegan agency without realizing the great responsibility which the chiefs of that tribe incurred in the treaty of 1855. They not only agreed to prevent their own tribesmen from engaging in intertribal war and trespassing upon citizens of the United States, but were expected to control the Blood, Blackfoot, Sarsi, and Gros Ventre. Obviously, this was impossible. Nevertheless, it is apparent that the chiefs not only accepted this responsibility, but did their best to make good. Naturally, the surrounding tribes did not take the treaty seriously, nor did the Gros Ventre show any disposition to regard it. The Crow, Assiniboine, and others in the United States continued to raid Piegan territory for horses and scalps. The Cree, Ojibway, and Assiniboine of Canada also crossed the lines to prey upon Indians as well as whites. Neither the Blackfoot nor the Blood were on too friendly terms with Piegan to prevent their young men from occasional raids for horses. Thus, the Piegan chiefs were attempting to prevent their own men from retaliation for these raids and, insofar as they were successful, stimulating further activity on the part of their enemies. It is not to be supposed that the Piegan chiefs were able to suppress all raiding parties among their own people, and under the strain of this effort to break with the traditions of the past it is not surprising that the tribal discipline of the Piegan broke down about 1870.

For one thing the United States government, as represented by its agents, did not understand the situation, nor did the chiefs receive any sympathy or support from the white settlers in Montana. The conditions of trade were chaotic. Grinnell designates 1860–75 as the period of the whiskey trade. This is an apt designation of a regime of lawlessness characteristic of early western frontiers. The Journal of Granville Stuart is a good source of information for this period. Stuart's Journal opens in 1863 and continues through the treaty period. A few citations from his journal are appropriate. *1861*—The Blackfoot and other Indians are charged with stealing horses from the whites; the head chief of the Blackfoot killed two subordinate chiefs and civil war is expected. *1862*—The Gros Ventre and the Piegan are at war. *1863*—Stuart notes that the whiskey trade is debauching the Indians. *1868*—some Blackfoot Indians are charged with killing white people and escaping to Canada. *1869*—Blackfoot charged with killing white man.

During this same period the Piegan agent reports: *1858*—The Crow and Assiniboine are raiding the Piegan. *1859*—The chiefs are trying hard to keep faith with the treaty. *1862*—Piegan disturbed at the increasing encroachment of the whites. *1867*—Blackfoot from Canada raid into Montana. *1868*—Raids from Canada have become so frequent that white people attempt to kill Piegans on sight; Piegans retaliate. *1869*—The situation becomes tense and [on January 23,1870] United States troops make a raid into the Piegan country killing 120 men, 53 women and an indefinite number of children.[19]

It is not difficult to see that the events briefly outlined in the above are in part due to the influence of unprincipled white men both in the United States and Canada. The selling of liquor to the Indians was illegal in the United States and attempts were made to restrict it in Canada. The bootleggers, as they were called at the time, were national outlaw traders. However, no efforts were made by the local authorities to suppress their activities. Since these Indians did not produce a great quantity of furs, and since they were under some obligation to take their furs to the regular trader, the bootlegger was in the main forced to trade in horses.

He encouraged the Indians to steal horses from both whites and Indians. When operating in the United States the horses thus secured were run into Canada and sold, and vice versa. The Canadian Indians soon learned the trick of crossing the line and stealing horses and sometimes cattle, all of which could be readily sold in Canada. Although the white settlers in Montana were really aware of the situation, the majority of them profited by the trade and so were disposed to lay the whole blame upon the Indian. The important point is, however, that the whiskey traders entered the Indian camps and actively instigated the young men to disobey the orders of their chiefs by going on raids for horses. These acts, together with the usual amount of intoxication in the camps, is probably sufficient cause for the breakdown of tribal discipline. Also, the terrible punishment at the hands of United States troops in 1869 [January 1870] was followed by a severe outbreak of smallpox, so that the year 1871 finds the Piegan thoroughly demoralized. Even under these circumstances the chiefs, in council with their agent, declared their intention to maintain peace with the whites and to do what they could to observe the obligations of the treaty. But the reports of the agents indicate that the years 1871–74 show no improvement. In the latter year the situation became so desperate that the Indian agent advised the Piegan chiefs to kill the whiskey traders on sight, but the chiefs showed good judgment in declining. At the same time the reports from Canada show an equally deplorable condition; in fact, we are led to believe that there was far less effective control of white traders, that the regular fur trade was disorganized, and that the situation was dominated by "the most reckless white men on earth" (Agent's report 1874). This condition in Canada seems to have continued to nearly the end of the treaty period, since we are told that in 1880 and 1881 the raiding of Canadian Indians and whiskey traders reached such a state that 3,000 cattle were made away with in one season. Accordingly, the white settlers of Montana began an active campaign against the whiskey trade and instituted an effective control of the Canadian line. But before these steps were taken the chiefs of the Piegan were in part rescued from their impossible position.

Restoration of the Chiefs

Our chief authority for the breakdown of tribal control is Agent Wood, who seems to have been appointed in 1875. His own statement reads: "knowledge of the value of organization and government" prevailed until incursions of White homesteaders and businessmen after 1863, when dispirited Piegan began "to have no purpose in life except to hunt and procure robes and peltries for the traders" (Wood 1875).

Wood seems to have been an unusual person, possessed of a genius for understanding Indian life, and with an intelligence decidedly above that of the usual agency procedure. His method seems to have been to inform himself as to the former culture of these Indians, and in particular respecting the form of tribal government which had been functioning. Thus, he states that there were formerly 33 bands of Blackfoot, each independent of the other, but recognizing the tribal council in which each band was represented, and also the authority of the head chiefs as recognized by the council. His notes on this subject and his general review of Blackfoot culture are in agreement with the literature on the subject.[20]

When wholly informed, Wood called a council. It is not clear from his statement whether the Canadian Indians were fully represented, since the organization which he set up was to function among those residing in the United States, and since most of these were Piegan it may be assumed that he was concerned with these only. These deliberations were highly successful in that the original type of government was reorganized and a council designated on traditional lines. Wood seems to have made clear to this council that he and the government of the Untied States were back of them. The point of departure in their deliberations seems to have been the brief treaties, but in addition the council drew up a list of laws to be enforced. Some of this legislation applied to suppression of the liquor traffic, traffic in women, the abandonment of polygamy, punishment for theft and assault, and finally a death penalty for murder. The council designated three head chiefs to be charged jointly with the agent in the administration of these laws. The functions of Age Societies were rehabilitated in the form of tribal police, to execute the orders of the head chiefs.

It is interesting to note that the United States Indian Inspector, making his routine visit to this agency, remarks that while the procedure set up by Agent Wood is not legal it nevertheless works justly and efficiently.

In 1876, Agent Wood reports that the chiefs have suppressed the liquor traffic, that no crime was committed, and that though there were a few cases of insubordination among the young men, these cases were satisfactorily handled by the chiefs. He further states that while one-third of the population at the agency resides near his headquarters and is consequently under his direct control, the other two-thirds roam at large under the control of the chiefs.

This is the year during which the friction between the Sioux and the government of the United States came to a head. Many Plains tribes were friendly to the Sioux and so were placed under restrictions, yet throughout this struggle the Piegan council remained loyal to the United States, regarding the Sioux as their traditional enemies. For example, the Sioux called a council of all Indians in the northern Plains to meet at Cypress Hills. A large body of Piegan attended but withdrew from the conference when the other tribes present had decided upon simultaneous war with the United States. It seems that while the conference was in progress, a Santee [Sioux] Indian shot a Piegan, which occurrence angered the Piegan to such a degree that upon their return to the agency they offered to join the whites in war against the Santee and other hostile tribes.

It is worth while noting at this point the unintentional injustice of the Indian Department in Washington in making regulations of universal application. For example, the Indians opposing the whites and taking part in the Custer affair were armed with most approved breech-loading guns. Accordingly a sweeping order was made to the effect that all breech-loading guns were to be taken up, or that at least no ammunition for such guns should be given by the government or sold by traders. This order seems to have embarrassed Agent Wood and to have somewhat shaken the confidence of his Piegan council. Apparently, the agent protested and took no steps to enforce the regulation, hinting that his Indians could secure such arms and ammunition from Canadian traders. Like other Indian agents subject to rapid turnover, Wood gave up his office in 1876. John Young, Wood's successor, reports that the tribal government is functioning as well as ever and that the Piegan are equal to the Sioux in courage and would be able to hold the border against all other Indians. We also note that by 1879 not only had the Blood and North Blackfoot ceased to camp in the United States, but that the North Piegan had come to regard themselves as belonging in Canada. Young seems to have continued in office until 1883 and throughout his administration regarded the tribal government as functioning satisfactorily, the Indian police as efficient in preserving order, and the general situation satisfactory.

In conclusion, we note that the administration of Agent Wood marked a distinct turning point in the adjustment of the Piegan to the United States and so far as we know is one of the most constructive examples of efficient government service to be found in the history of Indian affairs. If Wood had not come upon the scene at this time it seems probable that disintegration would have become complete and that subsequent oppression and misunderstandings would have reduced the Piegan to a pitiable remnant. What we see instead is a recovery in morale and the normal functioning of a dependent tribal group led by native chiefs in whom their followers placed implicit confidence. Many difficult situations subsequently arose but we note that the council and the chiefs worked hand in hand with their agent to the end that these Indians were, in 1900, at least in a fair way to achieve a satisfactory adjustment. We should not forget that during this period a number of excellent white men and mixed bloods were closely identified with the tribe, thus contributing a background that must have greatly strengthened the tribal council and its chiefs. Another important point is that one of the three head chiefs, White Calf, continued in office until 1901; all who knew this chief testified to his remarkable ability and his fine personality. At the time of his appointment the other two chiefs were older men shortly to be replaced, but tradition indicates that they also were unusual persons, nor can it be said that successors were greatly inferior to White Calf, and so whatever may have been the causes leading to the appointment of these great full-blood native leaders, it is certainly due to their presence that the Piegan surmounted the many difficulties in which they found themselves.

During Agent Young's administration, a contractor building a new trading post faced what he later recalled as the first labor strike on record in Montana. With Young's permission, the contractor, Charles Aubrey, hired Indian men to erect the log buildings, supervised by a white carpenter, and then selected twelve young men to chink the logs with mud. He recalled,

> The Indian workers, while awkward, were steady and constant at their tasks. Pay day was every Saturday. . . . Three large holes were dug in the ground and three men put to each hole. The other three men I put on the roof to apply the mud, paying them $1.50 per day. Mortar men and water men were paid $1.25 per day, 10 hours constituting a day's work. I employed 20 women to apply the mud to the chinking, paying each 75 cents per day of eight hours. All went well the first day, but the second morning . . . I found the Indians sitting in the mortar holes smoking.
>
> I said to them, "Boys, the women are waiting on you. Why aren't you making mud?" One of them replied that they would talk when they had smoked out that pipe. . . . In a few minutes the men came out of the mortar holes and the spokesman, named Shine-in-the-sun, who was boss of the roof men, much to my surprise, told me that they wanted $2 per day all round or they would not work—a strike was on.
>
> Shine-in-the-sun set forth their grievances in a most eloquent and earnest manner. The work, he said, was very hard and the pay small. Work on the roof was very dangerous, since in getting their feet muddy they might slip off the roof. The hod carriers might slip off the ladder and be killed (the climb being 10 feet). They asserted further that they were expert workmen, deserving

of the increased pay they demanded. I was very much interested and somewhat amused at the earnest manner and odd appearance of the strikers. Most of them were dressed in short calico shirts and breech-clouts, bare-footed and bare-legged, the better to enable them to mix the mortar.

I told them that while their work was satisfactory for Indians, that six white men could do all of it. The Blood Indians had often asked for work, and that I would hire them. One of the Indians, Laughing Dog, replied that the Blood Indians had gone north three days before, and that there were no white men in the country to take their places. This was all true, too. I then informed them that I would allow them the advance in wages which they asked for that day if they would go to work, which they did at once.

The women workers were much interested in the outcome of the strike, and I was waited on by two of the older women, one of whom, Two Stars, demanding $1 per day for the ladies on the job. They asserted that the work was very hard and that they cut their hands on the rough logs. I told them that there were too many women wanting work, but that if they would select 12 women from their number who could do the work the men were doing, I would pay them $1.25 per day, beginning with the next morning. I enjoined them to be on hand early, before the men came.

In the morning the 12 women were on hand long before the men, and they started work promptly. Pretty soon Shine-in-the-sun and Laughing Dog came to me, complaining that the women had taken possession of the mortar holes and refused to give them up unless I told them to do so. I replied that I had hired the women to take their places. "The women cannot do the work as well as we can," said Shine-in-the-sun. "Tell them to get out of the mortar holes." I declined to do so, and later the boss of the women, Diving-to-the-Shore, came to me complaining that the young men were throwing hard mud balls at them. I then hired two guards, Running Eagle and Crow Face, to protect the women, which they did.

That evening the ousted men workers came and offered to go to work at the same wages I had paid them before. I finally agreed to let them do so. The next morning the strikers and the strike-breaking women were working together harmoniously, and the job was soon finished. That ended the first strike I ever heard of in Montana. Years later I met Shine-in-the-sun with a band of Piegans, and he remembered me as soon as he saw me.

He told me of the poverty which had befallen his people. [He was] an Indian of much native ability. [Aubrey 1919]

Dependence upon the Buffalo

It is frequently stated that the troubles of the Plains Indians began when the buffalo ceased to supply their food, and further, that the sudden disappearance of this animal brought about a state of economic collapse. This seems to hold true for some of the Plains tribes, but does not seem to have been the cause of tribal breakdown among the Piegan. At the time when the authority of the chiefs failed, the supply of buffalo was reported as adequate. It is true that some rations were given out by the government, but the policy involved was that of compensating these Indians for the restrictions imposed by the treaties. We note that the Piegan were operating in mobile camps until 1882, the agent stating in his report for that year that the winter hunt for buffalo of the previous year was not satisfactory, and in consequence the Indians remained within the reservation during the winter of 1882. We note further that during this year an epidemic prevailed among the Indian horses, greatly reducing the supply and, while not so stated by the agent, such a loss would interfere with active buffalo hunting. In the 1870s the Piegan were accustomed to spend part of the winter in the valley of the Musselshell River. We note that previous treaties of this tribe confirmed their rights to hunt buffalo in this region. However, in the 1870s cattle ranching among the whites developed rapidly and encroached upon the buffalo ranges of the Musselshell. According to Stuart, after cattle became numerous the Indians were charged with illegal killings and theft. These charges were indignantly denied by the Indians and by the government agents. The thefts were said to have been by irresponsible white men and roving Indians from Canada. Naturally, this situation led to friction and an insistent demand that the Piegan be confined to their reservation. In 1880 the Piegan pitched their winter hunting camp in the Judith Basin south of the Missouri. The white settlers complained of the usual depredations, while the Indians protested innocence. Yet in response to this situation the government ordered troops to round up the Piegan and forcibly return them to their reservation. The long midwinter march back to the reservation was a severe trial to the Indians, and carried out with such dispatch that both the Indians and their horses were completely exhausted. It is reported that many horses died on the way, as did many of the aged and sick Indians. Agent Young regarded this proceeding as wholly unwarranted and unjust. Naturally, the Indian council took the same view of the situation, and for a time chaos threatened. The agent hence regarded this as a probable setback in the heretofore promising development of tribal government. However, the Indians seemed to have taken the matter philosophically, recognizing that they could no longer leave the reservation to hunt buffalo, but must content themselves with the supply upon their own range. For some time the Indians had recognized the possibility that the buffalo would entirely disappear and so had given ear to the various recommendations of their agents that other methods of supplying food be taken up.

So, as we have said, the Indians faced the winter of 1883 depending entirely upon game taken on their own lands and food supplied by the government. As the buffalo were now failing, the Indians began to feel hungry. The government had introduced cattle to the reservation and naturally these were stealthily killed by hungry Indians. To make matters worse, the Cree of Canada actively raided the Piegan reservation, carrying away more than 200 horses. The Piegan were bound not to retaliate. In brief, the outlook was dark and the Indians entered upon the winter of 1884 with no buffalo in reach. The government had made no preparation to meet this difficulty, having only a small amount of food in store. It is not strange that this was a famine winter. The chiefs and agents did what they could to relieve the situation by conserving the food in storage and making frantic appeals to Washington. Railroad connections at that time were not the best, and further the lack of adequate highways made it almost impossible to transport supplies to the reservation. How many persons died of hunger is not stated, but the death rate is regarded as excessive.[21] It is stated that the Indians ate horses and were finally reduced to eating the bark of cottonwood trees. By 1885 sufficient rations were on hand to prevent actual starvation, but still the Indians were reported as hungry and the illegal killing of government cattle proceeded as before. However, during this year the government adopted a policy of purchasing beef cattle and erecting a slaughterhouse from which regular issues could be made to the Indians.

Notwithstanding these calamities and the danger of demoralization the tribal government seems to have remained intact and to have functioned satisfactorily.

The Piegan were in an advantageous position for maintaining themselves in part by hunting. Their reservation was bounded on the west by the Rocky Mountain chain, a region that later was made a natural forest and is now for the most part included in Glacier Park. Since the Blackfoot owned and occupied the land into the foothills of this range, there was never any encroachment of white settlers from that direction. The full effect of this upon the subsequent history of the Piegan is difficult to estimate, but as the buffalo supply began to weaken there was still free hunting in the foothills into the mountains. Also, the information at hand indicates that during the winter months there was a migration of elk and deer to the foothills and often far out on the reservation. Naturally, the supply of game in this mountain region declined under the hunting regime of the Piegan, but still the supply was sufficient to enable the Piegan to make a more or less gradual adjustment to new conditions. That considerable trapping was engaged in is indicated by the government reports of income from sales of fur; thus, in 1876 these sales amounted to $60,000.00, gradually diminishing to 1885, when but $500.00 was reported. It is impossible to tell from the record what part of these sales were buffalo robes, but no doubt other furs made up a considerable part of these sales.

Two Medicine River, which passes through the reservation, is bordered by trees of cottonwood, aspen, etc., but in the main the wood supply of the Piegan was from the foothills and the mountains. This was no small factor in the welfare of the tribe, since the winters are severe.

Isolation from white contact was enjoyed by the Piegan perhaps to a greater extent than any other tribe of the Plains. Not only were the mountains west of them, but the Canadian border on the north merely separated them from their Canadian relations, and for a long time their territory eastward was continuous with that of the Gros Ventre and Assiniboine. Nor was there great pressure from the south, since the land between the south border of the reserve and the settlements of the Missouri was unsuitable to agriculture. Again, the mountains west of the reservation were a real barrier to westward travel, the chief bases being at Banff in Canada and Missoula in the United Sates. Thus, the waves of white migration passed by rather than through Blackfoot territory.

Experience in Agriculture

It so happened that practically all the Indian tribes of eastern United States were in part agricultural, hence it is not strange that the Indian policy of the United States should be set upon inducing all Indians to live by farming. This was also the basic industry of the whites and, naturally, if the Indians expected to survive as communities under white control, they would be expected to conform to that pattern.[22] It seems from the literature that the wisdom of this policy as applied to the roving Indians of the Plains was never questioned. Consequently, in the Laramie treaty promises were made to equip the Indians for farming at the earliest possible date. Strangely enough, the Piegan seemed to have accepted the idea in theory and to have shown some enthusiasm for the experiment. Since they were totally ignorant[23] of agriculture the government set up an experimental farm in 1859 on Sun River, about 75 miles from Fort Benton. Strangely enough, a few of the head chiefs of the Piegan took up residence near the farm for at least a part of the year. According to reports of the government farmer, the experiment worked well for a season or two, after which prolonged drought and the ravages of insects destroyed the crops.

Considerable livestock was accumulated, but this served to tempt roving Indians, who began stealing stock in 1862. The climax came in 1865 when a party of Blood Indians from Canada raided the farm, drove away or killed all the stock, and carried off or destroyed the entire equipment. Accordingly, the Agent recommended the abandonment of the farm, chiefly on the ground that the climate and other conditions were unfavorable. Nevertheless, the farm was reestablished, and when the agency was moved to the present reservation the experiments were continued. It soon became a fixed procedure for each Indian reservation to be provided with a farmer, with equipment for a government farm, and with definite responsibilities looking toward the training of Indians to farm. However, the new boundary to the Piegan reservation, as established in 1874, enclosed land even less favorable to agriculture than the valley of the Sun River and, while some agriculture has been practiced by these Indians up through the present time, conditions have been so unfavorable that the produce of their fields formed but a small part of the necessary food supply.

Progress in farming is indicated by the following statistics: From 1878 to 1884 the average number of families trying farming was 55. In 1885, after the period of famine, 200 families were reported as experimenting in agriculture, but in 1911 only 120 were actually practicing some agriculture. We have no definite information as to the status of these farming families, but there is good reason to believe that most of them were of mixed blood, and in many cases the head of the household a white man. In 1892, Grinnell, who was thoroughly familiar with the situation, stated that the region was so unfavorable that the normal expectation would be one crop in four or five years. In 1908, the government developed an irrigation project for this reservation, hoping by the introduction of an artificial water supply to offset the continued drought. This project seems to have been poorly handled in that the main ditches were run through gravel deposits and so failed to carry water. On the other hand, the climate is such that severe frosts may be expected in all the summer months and so the crop possibilities are limited. Hay can be raised, however, the only difficulty being that the Piegan reservation is so far removed from a market that the produce cannot be sold at a profit. Further, we are informed that many of the farms taken up by white settlers to the east and south of the reservation are being abandoned because they find it impossible to make a living by their operation. These facts have practically convinced the Indian department that the Piegan can never maintain themselves by farming.

Horses and Cattle

These Indians were familiar with horses and continued to propagate them throughout the reservation period. At first the stock was somewhat inferior, though well-suited for Indian purposes. Once the Indians were confined to the reservation the government provided better breeding stock, and with the hearty cooperation of the Indians greatly increased the marketable value of their horses.

The reports of the government indicate the number of horses as fairly constant from 1855 to 1881. During the next few years when the Indians were short of food, the number of horses rapidly decreased. No doubt many of them were eaten. Also in 1882 an epidemic carried off more than half their horses. Thus, according to the reports, the horses of the Piegan decreased from 4,000 in 1881 to 1,100 in 1885. Later on, the government took steps to increase the number and quality of Indian horses, to the end that in 1901 the number rose to 17,006, or about eight per capita. From this time on a considerable part of Piegan income was from the sale of horses.

Both Indians and whites anticipated the disappearance of the buffalo, and as early as 1858 the chiefs expressed concern over the encroachments of white hunters. After the farm was opened on Sun River, the chiefs urged the government to equip them for raising cattle. However, no progress seems to have been made by the Indians themselves until 1890. For the most part, all cattle before that date were maintained by the government as a government herd. Difficulty was experienced in preventing Indians from killing these cattle, and especially were they subject to raids from Canadian Indians. The famine of 1884 practically wiped out all cattle. However, by 1890 we find a well-developed program for cattle raising by the Indians, and for a time everything went well. In 1901, 18,600 head were reported. In 1911, the number of cattle owned was somewhat less, but sales for that year amounted to $64.00 per capita. Later, the decline in prices, coupled with unusual periods of drought, practically disorganized the cattle industry of the Piegan. However, this is probably but a temporary setback, because their reservation is on the whole well adapted for grazing.

Like all other Indians, the Piegan had difficulty in learning to milk and to properly care for their cows. It is an interesting observation that all the Plains Indians were disinclined to use milk and some tribes still show an aversion to it. Of course in their wild state they possessed no domestic milk animal except the horse, and in no case have we any information that any Indian tribe practiced milking mares. For many years the cattle introduced to reservations were intended to produce beef rather than dairy products. However, the white culture patterns for the Plains did not include the development of dairying; for many years the statistics for Montana showed that the state exported more cattle than any other state and imported more dairy products. The herding of cattle on the Plains did not include milking in its pattern, so the Indian is not to be blamed for showing a dislike to this occupation. Another disturbing factor in developing the use of milk was the migratory habit of the Piegan. They might on occasion be induced to care for their cows during a few weeks, but then a family finding itself disposed to go on a long visit would leave their cows to shift for themselves, expecting to go on with the milking when they returned. Of course, such treatment soon stopped the milk supply. In other words, the raising of cattle for beef did not conflict with the important culture patterns of the Piegan and so was a possible industrial substitute for buffalo hunting.

Income

Once settled on the reservation the government attempted to provide labor and other profit-making activities so as to develop the income-producing habit. Even as early as 1870 the agent of this reservation adopted the policy of employing Indians wherever possible. We note in the reports of that period that a few Indians were receiving wages for assisting in building cabins and other work necessary to improve the agency quarters. In 1875 the agency was removed to a new site and most of the entire tribe, women as well as men, were employed in tearing down the old buildings, transporting materials to the new site, and in their reconstruction (Fig. 4). The reports of this activity are not explicit, but information gathered by us from the Indians relative to the moving of the agency in 1875 and again in 1877 indicates that a great deal of enthusiasm and satisfaction prevailed among the Indians because of their participation in these activities. It is reported that the women transported a large part of the material on travois. This would conform to the tribal pattern because the travois was the property of the woman and used by her exclusively. These are the only instances on record where Indian women were employed by the government, and we suspect that the agent in this case was reprimanded from Washington and that instructions were issued to

Fɪɢ. 4. Old Agency (on Badger Creek), in the early reservation period.

employ men only. This may have been wise in the long run, but there is every reason to believe that the tribe might have been happier and made better progress if the agent on this reservation had been free to employ women for certain types of labor.

The building of fences forms an important item in all reports from 1876 to 1890, at times more Indians applying for work than would be accommodated. Further, it was necessary to haul by wagon all goods shipped to the reservation, the shipping point being Fort Benton. Sometime before 1880, a sufficient number of Indians were supplied with wagons[24] to undertake this service, for which they were paid at the regular rate. Also, during this period a sawmill was set up by the government and operated by Indian labor. The report of 1881 indicates that 385 men were employed during the year, and in 1911 we are told that the total wages paid out to Indians amounted to $68,704.00.

In 1910 we are told that 40 percent of the men were engaged in gainful occupations, together with 6 percent of the women. What these occupations were may be indicated by the following:

Tᴀʙʟᴇ 1.5. Occupations

Farm Laborers	Farmers	Stock Raisers	Herders
10	12	275	10

The few women gainfully engaged are listed under stock raisers, 37 in all; this probably means that 37 women owned respectable herds of cattle and horses.

Some general statistics on income indicate that in 1907 a total of $204,417.38 was reported, and in 1913 the per capita income was $117.74. The accompanying table gives the comparative incomes for the tribes in Canada.

TABLE 1.6. Income—Canadian Indians (Abbott [1915:82])

			1913	
	Blood	Blackfoot	Piegan (Canada)	Piegan (U.S.)
Population	1140	752	457	2842
Per Capita income	$54.10	$76.59	$80.08	$117.74
Horses	2458	1871	1434	6100
Cattle	3279	1085	1060	12,106
Sheep	—	—	—	3,600
Hogs	—	—	5	510
Acres Farmed	1737	36	1824	5,000
Administrative cost	$7,500	$6,400	$5,020	$25,302

Housing

The tipi of the Plains Indian stood in such sharp contrast to the type of housing for white culture that from the first every effort was made to induce the Indians to construct and occupy a log cabin. The theory seemed to be that if the Indian could be induced to give up the tipi he must necessarily abandon his roaming habits. As may be expected, the transition proceeded slowly, in fact the Piegan has not to this day [1933] entirely given up the tipi habit. From the standpoint of white sanitary ideals, the tipi is to be preferred, and some critics of our Indian policy have maintained that the decline in Indian population and general health was due to their living in cabins for at least part of the year. While it is obvious that the tipi was more sanitary and better ventilated, it does not necessarily follow that the cabin was responsible for all their ills.

In 1870 the agent reported ten log cabins apparently occupied by Indian families employed at the agency, yet in 1873 and 1875 the report states that but three Indian families lived in cabins. However, after this date a few cabins were built each year, usually by the agent, to the end that in 1881 82 cabins were reported as occupied. From this date until 1890 an average of about 200 cabins were occupied. From this time on the number increased rapidly until somewhat stabilized as approximately

700 cabins. It is fair to assume, however, that these were occupied only during the few severe months of the year, the remainder being spent in tipis often pitched at great distance from the cabins of their owners. That these cabins were often primitive is indicated in the report for 1911, where it is stated that 576 cabins were without floors, while 540 were provided with floors. The great increase in houses occurred between 1880 and 1890 and the statistics on population indicate that the tribe was at its lowest level during that and the next decade, after which there has been a rapid increase in population. Whether this increase can be definitely correlated with improvements in housing is not clear, the probabilities being that housing was an unimportant factor in this result.

An important culture pattern conflict should be noted in this connection, since in former times it was the custom of the Piegan to abandon the tipi in which a death occurred. According to traditional information they often avoided the abandoning of the tipi by carrying the dying person out of doors or into a hastily improvised shelter. The building of a primitive house increased the difficulty, since it was inevitable that a person should die in a house and thus automatically require its abandonment by the family and preventing its use by anyone else. This conflict, however, seems not to have been as violent as in the case of the Navajo, since the Piegan seemed to have gradually adjusted themselves to this new condition by dropping the taboo against a dwelling in which there had been a death.

Observations made on the reservation 1902 to 1905 revealed considerable range in the costs of housing. Some of the mixed-blood families maintained large frame houses conforming to the ideal of the period. A number of well-to-do full-blood Indians owned cabins of two to three rooms, handsomely furnished, but in which they rarely lived. One of these cabins examined by the writer was equipped with a brass bed and a full accompaniment of bird's-eye maple furniture, a hanging lamp, lace curtains, etc. There were two rooms, the other being a combination of dining room and kitchen, equipped according to the ideal of the time. Everything seemed quite new, although according to our information the furnishings had been in place for at least three years. Upon inquiry it was learned that neither the owner nor his wife had ever slept there, nor cooked a meal in the house, but that during the whole time they had lived outside in a tipi or improvised shelter. The motive, as indicated by the owner, was to possess an equipment as good as that of a white man in order to advertise his social status. While this is an exceptional case it merely represents what was looked upon as desirable by a large number of these Indians. Further, parallel cases could have been observed on other reservations, for example, among the Pawnee of Oklahoma.

Citizen Dress

The white man has always shown a disposition to force his costume upon all types of native peoples. In fact, this is the first culture change he insists upon. Regulations were adopted compelling the native who appeared among white people to clothe himself accordingly. Naturally then, we find corresponding pressure upon the Piegan to adopt what is termed official [officially termed?—Ed.] citizen dress. As late as 1855 we are told by Indian traders that the Piegan "bought no dry goods," they being well provided with skin clothing, which was in fact better adapted to their mode of life. In accordance with the treaty of 1855, among the annuities was included a large quantity of calico, but we find the Indians protesting in 1858 that this material was useless to them, but expressing a willingness to take shirts and blankets instead. It is not always clear what an Indian agent means by citizen dress, for Indian men continued to wear blankets long after they adopted shirts and trousers. Perhaps in this case they were reported as citizen dress in part. The original costume for women was sufficiently like that of white women to require no change, though as skins became scarce cloth was substituted. So we infer that the numbers reported by agents as adopting citizen dress are usually males, though in some cases they specifically mention women. For example, in 1878 the agent reports 70 men and 120 women as in citizen dress. This seems to have been the maximum until about 1890 when practically all adults were reported as in citizen dress in whole or in part. Since the supply of skins practically ceased by 1900, it is evident that citizen dress with certain slight modifications would from then on be universal. For example, in 1903 the agent states that nearly all the men wear trousers, but a few old men still wear leggings made of cloth. Most of them use the blanket and all wear hats and shirts.

Shoes and boots were the last to be adopted. Even as late as 1910 most of the Indians wore moccasins of their own making. In many cases the women and children were entirely without shoes, while the men were usually provided with a pair of boots to wear when needed.

We lack specific information as to the rapidity with which underclothing was adopted by these Indians, nor do we have satisfactory data as to standards of cleanliness. Presumably, the Piegan suffered as other native peoples are supposed to have done from the diseases encouraged by improper attention to this new type of costume.

Education

Before 1873 no schools were available, nor were there resident missionaries. In the brief treaties the government had pledged itself to provide schools for all Indian children, but naturally little could be done until the Indians were settled upon their reservation and ceased to roam about. Even as late as 1907 the school attendance report was 124; it is safe to say that these were for the most part the children of mixed-bloods and of those few Indians living at the agency. The following table shows the number eligible for attendance and those actually attending school:

TABLE 1.7. School Attendance Report

	Eligible	Attending
1911	833	281
1921	974	623
1931	1,173	986

It thus appears that the Piegan have not been enthusiastic about sending their children to school and that even now [1933] a considerable number do not attend.

One primary object in establishing schools was to teach them to write and to speak English. In 1882 the agent reported six Indians able to speak English, but by 1900 the number had increased to 1,200. The most complete information is given in the census of 1910, which reports 810 as unable to read; of those over 19 years of age 58 percent were reported as unable to speak English. (The census report for school attendance disagrees with the report of the agent, indicating that there were 789 of school age, of which 192 are in attendance.)

From the start the Piegan strenuously opposed permitting their children to attend non-reservation boarding schools. It seems that the first experiment of this kind was unfortunate, as a considerable number of the children died during the first winter. Another point to be considered is that the Piegan population is widely scattered on the reservation, rendering it difficult to provide satisfactory day schools. Further, the well-to-do mixed-blood families are usually able to send their children away to private white schools and are consequently not themselves interested in providing adequate schools.

Health

The data on population indicates that there was a rapid decline among the Piegan from 1860 to 1890, after which the numbers increased, at first slowly and then more rapidly. Probably this decline was due to certain calamities discussed in the preceding text, but on the other hand we note the reports for the presence of certain diseases apparently introduced after the establishment of the reservation. Medical attendance seems to have been provided before 1875, and in the '80s children's diseases became prevalent, such as measles, mumps, etc. It is also interesting to note that a large percentage of medical treatments were listed as eye troubles, though trachoma was not reported until later, as for example, 153 cases in 1911. Tuberculosis did not become alarming until after 1910. In the early reports, wounds and deaths from violence were prominent, but after 1890 these ceased to occupy an important place. Thus, on the whole it appears that aside from tuberculosis and trachoma, the health conditions of this reservation were favorable. Later reports show an active campaign against trachoma, so that this disease is now well in hand. Further, it is interesting to note that notwithstanding the alarming reports, the number of blind Indians is about what would be expected among the white population.

Henry reports [Henry 1897:416] that one of his posts in the Red River district was on short rations from May 28 to August 10 [1806], a period of 74 days. There was a scarcity of game in the surrounding country, so that during this period Henry states that only 14 buffalo, a few deer, and a few bags of pemmican were available. The number of persons is given as 54. According to his statement all were suffering from hunger, though obviously not starving.

> This establishment is now in a miserable condition; they have neither flesh nor fish—nothing but some old musty beat [pounded dry] meat, and no grease. They have had but 14 animals, including cabbrie [antelope], since the departure of the canoes in May last, and a few bags of pemmican—a mere trifle for so many mouths—say 3 clerks, 1 interpreter, 3 laboring men, and 47 women and children, or 54 people entitled to regular rations. . . . The Indians are starving all over the country, no buffalo being found. [Henry 1897:416]

If we accept Henry's former estimate of four hundred pounds of meat per animal, the food supply would have amounted to 5,600 pounds, or approximately 1.3 pounds per capita per day. Naturally it is assumed that some additional food was available, but the significance of this statement is that an average consumption of something more than one pound of meat per day was inadequate.

Drinking

"We do not mix our liquor so strong as we do for tribes who are more accustomed to use it. To make a nine-gallon keg of liquor we generally put in four or five quarts of high wine and then fill up with water. For the Crees and Assiniboines we put in six quarts of high wine, and for the Saulteurs eight or nine quarts" (Henry 1897:542). [High wine was rum or brandy.]

TABLE 1.8. Whiskey

1755—Henday says, Piegans had gone to la Corne: when he came there the custom of making Indians drunk was in vogue. Not likely that drink could have reached them before.

1782—Cocking mentions no drinking.

1784—Umfreville complains of degeneracy from drink.

1809—Henry—Not so strong for Slaves [Blackfoot]—5 quarts of high wine to 9 gallon keg (water). Drink all day and to midnight: the next day trade and depart (1897:653–54).

Will not trade for drink: demand that free (1897:723).

Piegan noisy when drinking but not insolent (1897:574, says his men when drinking "make more damned noise and trouble than a hundred Blackfeet").

Later—Liquor now dominates them—as bad as the Cree (1897:723).

They say drink, wars and women sole delight (1897:724 "war, women, liquor, and horses are all their delight").

1819—Richardson—in a camp saw one Cree who would not drink; others ridiculed but he rejoined that all would be better off (Richardson p. 111).

1862—Decried by Stuart in Montana.

1868—Whiskey trade strong—demoralizing.

1860–1875—Grinnell: the period of the whiskey trade.

1873—Agent reports many liquor deaths.

1876—Agent reports liquor selling checked.

1880—Protective Association to stop whiskey trade (Stuart).

Denig [1930], p. 530—Crow Indians not going to drink. ["They all drink whenever they can get it—men, women, and children—except the Crow Indians, who will not taste it."]

Umfreville—Seems to affect Indians differently than whites—become violent, roll on ground, bite.

1854—Denig—Assiniboine. Drink not harmful—total deaths in 20 years not a hundred (Denig 1930:465).

Since from day to day Henry records the issuing of liquor to those around him and comments upon the quarreling, fighting, etc., it seemed worthwhile checking over these accounts to get an estimate of the frequency of murder and assault due to the use of liquor. We find that for the seven years, 1800–1807, we have the following citations:

TABLE 1.9. Alcohol Related Offenses[25]

Year	Drinking	Killings	Stabbings	Shootings	Beatings	Bites	Burns	Fights
1800	19	1	2	1	2	2	1	1
1801	6	1	0	2	0	0	0	0
1802	4	4	2	0	0	0	0	0
1803	13	1	4	1	1	1	1	2
1804	8	3	1	1	2	1	2	13
1805*	2	1	0	1	0	0	0	1
1806	3	2	0	0	1	0	0	3
1807	22	2	0	0	0	0	0	0
Total	77	15	9	6	6	4	5	20

*Change of policy on liquor.

1800, brought out 90 gal. high wines. There is no way of estimating the population engaged.

L.R.R. [Lower Red River district] white 175 Indian 600

U.R.R. [Upper Red River district] white 190 Indian 4870

Henry does not state the quantity of liquor stored at his post, but for the year 1800 states that 90 gallons of high wine was brought in. At the usual rate of dilution this would amount to at least 1,000 gallons to drink.

It must not be assumed that Henry enumerated all murders and assaults connected with drinking, but only those directly under his observation. It is not clear how many of these offenders were Indians proper and how many were employees of the post. In many cases Henry names the culprit and checking these with his list of employees we note that three are Indians. An indefinite number are employees of the post, but whether white or Indian can not be determined.

In 25 cases Henry gives the names of the aggressors and we note that three murders were committed by the same man and that three other men are credited with two assaults each. However, we think the data sufficient to give a picture of drinking behavior during the period. The number of murders and assaults recorded by Henry as not in any way connected with drinking is ? [difficult to determine—Ed.][26]

There is no way of estimating the population affected, since Indians were coming and going. We note, however, that the estimate for the total Upper Red River area served by Henry's post is given for 1805 as 4,870. If allowance is made for children, this would indicate a fairly high rate of murder, since many such occurrences must have escaped Henry's observation. Henry's table shows 36 serious assaults, or an average of five per year.

For 1805 Henry [1897:282] gives a table of Indian and white population for the whole northwest. Apparently he uses the term *Fort des Prairies* to cover the whole Saskatchewan drainage, since this is the use made of the term in other parts of the work.

Another term needing explanation is *Upper Red River,* which is equivalent to the Assiniboine River, while his term *Lower Red River* applies to the Red River in Canada and the United States below the mouth of the Assiniboine.

Accordingly Henry's table gives the following population data:

TABLE 1.10. Population

	White	Indian
Fort des Prairies	298	64,361
Upper Red River	190	4,870

Apparently, the Fort des Prairies estimate for Indians is meant to include Cree, Assiniboine, all the Blackfoot group, and a few Indians of various tribes introduced into the area as trappers.

Also, it is interesting to note that the Indians for Fort des Prairies are classified as follows: males, 4,823; females, 13,632; and children, 45,906. It will be noted that there are approximately 2.0 women to each man and 3.3 children to each woman. While the excess of women may be correct, it is higher than other estimates, and the number of children is much higher.

One check on this statement is Henry's later estimate for the Assiniboine, Cree, and Blackfoot group, which gives 4,910 men, or warriors. It will be noted that this is approximately the same as his estimate in 1805. We have previously commented upon the excess of women, but since Henry gives no actual count we cannot check the other items. Yet, insofar as his estimation of males is concerned, the two accounts agree fairly well. Another reason for regarding his estimation of children as too high is that in other parts of his table for 1805 the ratios of children per mother are 2.4 and 2.9. Also the excess of women as given is 1.7 and 1.8. However, these are woodland Indians and so not strictly comparable to those of the Plains.

Area of the Northern Plains

A new calculation was made of the Plains area in Canada. First we note that the total area is:

Alberta 255,285 sq. miles
Saskatchewan 251,700 sq. miles
Manitoba 251,832 sq. miles

Only a small part of this total area is south of the Saskatchewan, constituting the Plains.

The Blackfoot area as defined by Henry comprises 70 to 80 thousand square miles.

The Plains in Saskatchewan comprise about five-sixteenths of the total area, or approximately 78 to 80 square miles. The Plains of Manitoba are estimated at [10,800].

[Quotes from] Henry, page 209:

> But the Indians totally neglect their ancient customs; and to what can this degeneracy be ascribed but to their intercourse with us, particularly as they are so unfortunate as to have a continual succession of opposition parties to teach them roguery and destroy both mind and body with that pernicious article, rum? What a different set of people they would be, were there not a drop of liquor in the country! If a murder is committed among the Saulteurs, it is always in a drinking match. We may truly say that liquor is the root of all evil in the North West. [Henry 1897:209]
>
> Oct. 3d [1803, Pembina River Post] This caravan demands notice, to show the vast difference it makes in a place where horses are introduced. It is true they are useful animals, but if there were not one in all the North West, we should have less trouble and expense. Our men would neither be so burdened with families, nor so indolent and insolent as they are, and the natives in general would be more honest and industrious. Let an impartial eye look into the affair, to discover whence originates the unbounded extravagance of our meadow gentry, both white and native, and horses will be found one of the principal causes. Let us view the bustle and noise which attended the transportation of five pieces of goods to a place where the houses were built in 1801–02. . . . Antoine Payet, guide and second in command, leads the van, with a cart drawn by two horses and loaded with his private baggage, cassetêtes [tomahawks, but perhaps a play on *cassette*, small box], bags, kettles, and mashqueminctes [editor Coues "cannot make out" this word—it is an Ojibwe term for a large wool paisley shawl (Cory Wilmot, personal communication, Nov. 24, 2011)]. Madame Payet follows the cart with a child

a year old on her back, very merry. Charles Bottineau, with two horses and a cart loaded with 1½ packs, his own baggage, and two young children with kettles and other trash hanging on it. Madame Bottineau with a squalling infant on her back, scolding and tossing it about. Joseph Dubord goes on foot, with his long pipe-stem and calumet in his hand; Madame Dubord follows on foot, carrying his tobacco pouch with a broad bead tail. Antoine Thellier, with a cart and two horses, loaded with 1½ packs of goods and Dubois' baggage. Antoine La Pointe with another cart and horses, loaded with two pieces of goods and with baggage belonging to Brisebois, Jasmin, and Pouliot, and a kettle hung on each side. Auguste Brisebois follows with only his gun on his shoulder and a fresh-lighted pipe in his mouth. Michel Jasmin goes next, like Brisebois, with gun and pipe puffing out clouds of smoke. Nicolas Pouliot, the greatest smoker in the North West, has nothing but pipe and pouch. Those three fellows, having taken a farewell dram and lighted fresh pipes, go on brisk and merry, playing numerous pranks. Domin Livernois, with a young mare, the property of Mr. Langlois, loaded with weeds for smoking, and old worsted bag (madame's property), some squashes and potatoes, a small keg of fresh water, and two young whelps howling. Next goes Livernois' young horse, drawing a travaille [travois] loaded with his baggage and a large worsted mashguemcate belonging to Madame Langlois. Next appears Madame [John] Cameron's mare, kicking, rearing, and snorting, hauling a travaille loaded with a bag of flour, cabbages, turnips, onions, a small keg of water, and a large kettle of broth. Michel Langlois, who is master of the band, now comes on leading a horse that draws a travaille nicely covered with a new painted tent, under which his daughter and Mrs. Cameron lie at full length, very sick; this covering or canopy has a pretty effect in the caravan, and appears at a great distance in the plains. Madame Langlois brings up the rear of the human beings, following the travaille with a slow step and melancholy air, attending to the wants of her daughter, who, notwithstanding her sickness, can find no other expressions of gratitude to her parents than by calling them dogs, fools, beasts, etc. The rear guard consists of a long train of 20 dogs, some for sleighs, some for game, and others of no use whatever, except to snarl and destroy meat. The total forms a procession nearly a mile long, and appears like a large band of Assiniboines. [Henry 1897:227–228]

TABLE 1.11. Peaceful Attitude of Piegan Chiefs

1809—Henry—Piegan most peaceful to whites. Piegan oppose Gros Ventre hostile to the post. Thinks chiefs have lost some in control—apparently speaking of Bloods and Blackfoot.

1833—Maximilian—Piegan seem to be trusted more. Gros Ventre and Blood considered bad. Piegan chiefs seem to have better control.

1855—Piegan chiefs feel bound by treaty and try to hold men in line.

1861—Head chief kills two chiefs—internal trouble. Canadian discipline good. Piegan try to keep peace with U.S.: at war with other Indians. Horses taken from whites—Canadian Indians?

1862—Increase of whites disturbs Indians. War with Gros Ventre.

1863—Chiefs' control breaking—whiskey trade a menace.

1865—Annuities stop.

1866—Rations issued.

1867—Short of horses—production of furs lessened. Whiskey trade responsible? Increase in raiding whites for horses. Canadian Indians also. Rising friction.

1869—War.

1870—Smallpox. Chiefs decide to hold for peace with U.S.

1873—Chiefs for order and peace, but not able to cope with whiskey trade.

1874—Agent advises chiefs to "kill traders"—afraid. Canadian situation bad.

1875—Agent Wood.

1881—U.S. tries to stop Canadian Indians at the line.

     U.S. Blackfoot Agents

1855—A. J. Vaughn—jovial, bad drinker, took an Indian wife, hand and glove with the traders. Through 1859.

1861—Hiatus in RCIA (Reports of the Commissioner of Indian Affairs), due to burning of shipment on riverboat.

1862—Henry W. Reed.

1866–1867—S. B. Wright.

Editor's Note: At this point in his manuscript, Wissler begins excerpts from Agents' reports and related documents but had not written a text. We follow his outline notes from these reports to develop a narrative history, assuming such was his intent. The text following is written by Kehoe.

Reports of the Commissioner of Indian Affairs and of Agents to the Blackfeet

RCIA FOR 1853

The Blackfeet have the reputation of being a large and powerful nation, and are a terror to all the tribes in this agency, save the Sioux. Their number has been largely exaggerated. From the very best information that I can derive from intelligent men who have resided amongst them for years, I learn that there are three different bands, numbering about alike, and all speak the same language. The entire number of their lodges do not exceed 1,200, averaging nine souls to a lodge. The Gros-ventres of the prairie, and who are called and known as the "Falls Indians," inhabit the same country as the Blackfeet, and number 420 lodges, averaging the same number to a lodge as the Blackfeet. The only difference between them and the Blackfeet is their language, which is altogether different— the Gros-ventre speaking the same language[27] as the Arrapahoes, who reside on the Arkansas.

The Blackfeet are a wild, roving, reckless people, committing murder and stealing everything that falls in their way. They inhabit an extensive country lying between the head waters of the Missouri and the waters of the Hudson Bay; extending their war expeditions as far south as the river Platte, and in former years as far as the valley of the Great Salt Lake [p. 356].

They possess a large number of horses, many of which they raise themselves, but a much larger quantity are stolen from their enemies. Each individual's wealth is estimated by the number of horses he has in his possession. These animals being so essentially necessary for their convenience and comfort, for the accumulation of which (like many white men for money) they will go to any length. There are but few of these Indians that have less than two wives; the common number is four, and many have ten. At times many jealousies exist among them. They are generally employed about the drudgeries of the lodge, (save one who is more highly favored than the others,) performing the hardest labor, more so than is required from our slaves by the hardest of masters [356–357].

The larger portion of the Blackfeet nation is composed of women; the result of this has been caused by so many of their young men having been cut off by their enemies in their war expeditions [357].

Great dread of the Blackfeet he found to prevail with the Indians for a long distance west of the mountains, which had caused many to leave their accustomed resorts, and had led to the abandonment of the St. Mary's village, west of the Jesuit missionaries, and the traders who had succeeded them [458].

All these Indians are properly American Indians, wintering for the most part on American soil—on the Teton, Marias, and Milk rivers. They range in the summer on British territory, as well as on both sides of the Missouri; and only a portion of the Blackfeet tribes of the Blackfeet nation have their winter homes in the vicinity of the British posts. The Gros-ventres have more permanent abodes—scarcely ever leaving Milk river—and

could easily be induced to till the soil. This is somewhat the case with
the Piegans, though they are excellent as guides and hunters. The Bloods
and Blackfeet will require more time and patience; but I doubt not, under
good direction, all those Indians would in a short space of time, be equal
to the Cherokees [459].

On the 27th July we came up with a large camp of Assinaboines, consisting of about one hundred and forty lodges [457].

RCIA for 1854

Report of Isaac I. Stevens, Governor and Superintendent of Indian Affairs, on his "exploration from the head of navigation of the Mississippi
river to the Pacific ocean" (1855:184).

Before he reached Blackfoot country, Governor Stevens met parties
of Red River Hunters (Métis). Discussing their right to hunt in Manitoba
and North Dakota, Stevens concluded, "I was very favorably impressed"
with their claims for hunting rights and citizenship for their children
born on the United States side of the boundary. He recommended, "Our
government could obtain the whole of these people as citizens. We might
thus protect the frontier, and always have in this vicinity a controlling
check upon the Indians. . . . The virtuous mode of life of these interesting people, their industry and frugality, and their adaptation to frontier
life, make them eminently deserving the attention of our government"
(1855:193–194).

Turning to "The Blackfeet Nation," Stevens gives its country as: "beginning on the north where the 50th parallel crosses the Rocky mountains; thence east on said parallel to the 106th meridian; thence south to
the headwaters of the Milk river, down said river to the Missouri, up the
Missouri to the mouth of the Judith; thence up the Judith to its source;
thence to the Rocky mountains, and north along their base to the place
of beginning. . . . The Piegans occupy the country between Milk and Marias rivers, upon Marias river and the Teton, and between the Teton and
the Missouri. . . . The country between the Missouri and the headwaters
of the Yellowstone is unoccupied. It is the great road of the Blackfoot
war-parties to and from the Crows, Flatheads, and Snakes. It is also the
hunting-ground of the Flatheads and the Indian tribes generally of Washington Territory east of the Cascades, who resort hither at all seasons of
the year to hunt buffalo" (1855:194).

Stevens presented a table of Blackfoot population prepared by James
Doty, who "had the opportunity of making an actual count of more than
half these Indians":

The Bloods	350 lodges	2,450 population	875 warriors.
Blackfeet	250 lodges	1,750 population	625 warriors
Piegans	350 lodges	2,450 population	875 warriors
Gros Ventres	360 lodges	2,520 population	900 warriors
	1,310	9,170	3,275

(Stevens 1855:194)

Stevens explains that after a disastrous attack by Crows forty years earlier, the decimated Gros Ventres were "in a manner adopted" by the Blackfoot, so he includes them in that group (1855:195). He notes that the artist with his party, John Mix Stanley, had estimated Blackfoot population at 1,330 lodges and 13,300 souls, and that his own estimation, "consulting all reliable sources of information in the upper Missouri," gave a total of 14,400 (1855:194). It is important to note that Blackfoot, along with the other nations of the northern Plains, had suffered severe decimation in the smallpox epidemic of 1837–38, less than a generation previous (Sundstrom 1997:309).

The governor relied upon Alexander and Natoyist-Siksina' Culbertson to prepare a Blackfoot delegation to wait upon him at the American Fur Company's principal post, Fort Union. Culbertson was a partner in the American Fur Company, and his wife, usually called Natawista by her American friends, was a member of a prominent Kainai (Blood) family, daughter of Two Suns, sister of Seen-from-Afar, aunt of Red Crow and cousin to Little Dog of the Piegan. Stevens described "Mrs. Culbertson, who had fully adopted the manners, costume, and deportment of the whites, and who, by her refinement, presents the most striking illustration of the high civilization which these tribes of the interior are capable of attaining, rendered the highest service to the expedition, a service which demands this public acknowledgment." She went upriver with the party to Fort Benton, where the council with the Blackfoot and Gros Ventre would be held, explaining, "'My people are a good people, but they are jealous and vindictive. I am afraid that they and the whites will not understand each other; but if I go, I may be able to explain things to them, and soothe them if they should be irritated. I know there is great danger; but, my husband, where you go will I go, and where you die will I die'" (Stevens 1855:196). (A noble sentiment, although in 1869 after they had spent most of the fortune they had accumulated, she left Culbertson to return to her Kainai people. For biographies of Natoyist-Siksina', see Wischmann 2004 and Carter 2003.)

Camping beside the large gathering of Indian people, Stevens noticed that "[i]t is a great mistake to suppose the Indians to be the silent, unsociable people they are commonly represented to be. I found them to be on ordinary occasions the most talkative, gossiping people I have ever seen." His honest observations impelled him to contend with his own party, with whom he "found too much prevailing a contempt for the Indians as an inferior race, and a too confident reliance upon our physical superiority. I found it necessary to expostulate personally with my men upon this subject" (Stevens 1855:196).

John Mix Stanley served not only to graphically record scenes, but also as an assistant to Stevens. In September 1853, the governor sent him north of Fort Benton to contact Piegans and invite them to the council there. Stanley met the band of about one hundred lodges led by Low Horn and Little Dog in the present Blackfeet Reservation. After a day spent feasting Stanley in one lodge after another, with "profuse quantities" of a favored dessert of boiled bison blood mixed with dried berries, the camp packed up to travel. First describing the travois, Stanley wrote that it "serves for the safe transportation of the children and infirm, unable to ride on horseback, the lodge [cover] being folded so as to allow two or more to ride securely. The horses dragging this burden, often of three hundred pounds, are also ridden by the squaws, with a child astride behind and one in her arms, embracing a favorite young pup. Their dogs, of which they have a large number, are also used in transporting their effects in the same manner as the horses, making with ease twenty miles a day, dragging forty pounds. In this way this heterogeneous caravan, comprised of a thousand souls, with twice that number of horses, and at least three hundred dogs, fell into line and trotted gaily until night; while the chiefs and braves rode in front, flank, or rear, ever ready for the chase or defence against a foe" (Stanley in Stevens 1855:201–202).

On September 21, 1853, Stevens formally met with Piegan, Blood, and Blackfoot delegations at Fort Benton. "On this occasion, the chiefs and warriors were all richly caparisoned. Their dresses, of softly prepared skins of deer, elk, or antelope, were elegantly ornamented with bead-work. These are made by their women, and some must have occupied many months in making. The other articles of their costume were leggings, made of buffalo-skins, and moccasins, also embroidered, and a breech-cloth of blue cloth. Their arms were the northwest guns, and bows and arrows. On all solemn occasions, when I met the Indians on my route, they were arrayed with the utmost care. My duties in the field did not allow the same attention on my part; and the Indians sometimes complained of this, saying, 'We dress up to receive you, and why do you not wear the dress of a chief?'" (Stevens 1855:201).

It was Stevens's purpose to persuade the Indian nations to forgo war, in order to facilitate American trade and travel. Low Horn, principal

Piegan chief, told Stevens that Blackfoot had, years ago, agreed to a treaty of peace with nations west of the mountains, and there had not been conflict, he said, between the hunting parties on the Missouri Plains. But, he continued, "their young men were wild and ambitious, in their turn, to be braves and chiefs. They wanted by some brave act to win the favor of their young women, and bring scalps and horses to show their prowess. He added, 'The Blackfeet are generous and hospitable. They always forgive injuries. Some years since, after a Blackfoot had been killed by a Gros Ventre, several Gros Ventres fell into our hands. These Gros Ventres all expected to be put to death; but we fed them, treated them kindly, and gave them horses to carry them home.' I [Stevens] then interrupted him, and said, 'I know this to be true, for the Gros Ventres told me of it themselves. . . . Why is it that you have two or three women to one man? Is it not because your young men go out on war parties, and thus the flower of your tribe is cut down? And you will go on diminishing every year until your tribes are extinct. Is it not better that your young men should have wives and children, and that your numbers shall increase? Won't your women prefer husbands to scalps and horses?' . . . While in the council, Low Horn, the principal chief and speaker, made all his replies without rising from his seat, and in a quiet, conversational tone. After the council, he assembled his braves and resumed the lofty bearing of a chief. He addressed them with great fervor and eloquence; commanded them to cease sending out war parties henceforth, and threatened them with severe punishment if they disobeyed. I have since learned that these chiefs were faithful to their promises, and continued to make great exertions to prevent their young men from going on war parties." The council concluded with distribution of gifts, to the value of six hundred dollars, "with which they were greatly pleased" (Stevens 1855:202–203).

Stevens devoted several pages to describing the Blackfoot he observed. On several points, his notes differ from conventional later descriptions. For example, so far as he saw, women wore their hair "flowing" loose, parted in the middle, and cut "barely to the shoulder." "The women carry their children in their arms, or in a robe behind their backs; when traveling, the children are placed in sacks of skin on the tent-poles [poles tied together were yoked to horses to be pulled like travois—Ed.] . I saw no cradle of any form." An "ordinary-sized lodge," he said, "will accommodate as many as twenty-two persons—men, women, and children. . . . The lodges are often neatly and quite tastefully arranged. The cooking-utensils are simply a shallow vessel of tinned iron, purchased from the traders, and a rude tripod for hanging this vessel over the fire. The food of these Indians consists principally of buffalo-meat . . . relished . . . by the typsina root [prairie turnip, *Psoralea esculenta*, Blackfoot *mas'* or in Métis

French, *pomme blanche*] and dried berries. . . . Living so much upon animal food, any vegetable food is esteemed by them a great luxury. Hard bread is eaten with avidity, and no more palatable feast can be provided for these Indians of the plains than a dish of boiled rice sprinkled with sugar. Most of these Indians have never tasted whiskey, and only know of it by their traditions of the white man's fire-water. The manners of these Indians in their intercourse with each other are kindly and cheerful. The men treat their wives with great kindness and familiarity, and are very fond of their children; a constant laughing, chatting, and gossiping is going on in their lodges. The principal amusements of the Indians are their dances . . . and games of mixed skill and chance, upon which they bet very heavily." He describes the hoop-and-pole game, upon which "horses, dresses, and arms are staked," and "the game of the bullet. . . . It is played by men standing up in a circle with arms extended above their heads. The bullet is passed from hand to hand, and the point of the game is to guess in whose hands the bullet is. In this game there is much action and gesture. It is always accompanied by a beating of drums. Few scenes in Indian life can be more picturesque than a party playing this game at night, and illuminated by fire-light, which brings into full relief the excited faces and wild gestures of the players" [this game is similar to today's handgame, also called stick game—Ed.] (Stevens 1855:204–205).

In accord with United States policy, Stevens wrote that he "deem[ed] it of the highest importance that an agency and farm should be established in the Blackfoot country" (Stevens 1855:205). He asked James Doty, son of the governor of Wisconsin Territory, to assess the potential. Doty recommended a set of agency buildings costing $12,000, constructed of adobes, and a staff of one interpreter, one farmer, one blacksmith, and three laborers in addition to the agent. To operate, the agency and farm would require: "three yoke of oxen, with yokes; two heavy wagons; six log-chains; two whip-saws; two cross-cut saws; one chest of carpenter's tools; two dozen Collins's axes and handles; half a dozen shovels; two steel breaking-ploughs, 14-inch cut; six cast cross-ploughs; one double harrow-frame; four grain cradles and scythes; one dozen scythes and snaths [pole on which scythe is mounted]; one dozen steel hoes; one dozen pitch-forks; one grindstone; half a dozen spades; one dozen scythe-stones" (Doty in Stevens 1855:205–207). The best location, given the need for agricultural conditions and not too distant from "the head of navigation on the Missouri" (Fort Benton), seemed to be on the Sun River at its junction with the Missouri, and this was the site chosen for the farm. Doty recommended that, the first year, the farm would plant a variety of grains and vegetable, and the second year, expand but plant only those crops that had done well previously. "Mr. Clarke," presumably Malcolm

Clark, a trader and rancher married to a Piegan woman and living near present-day Helena, was recommended to erect the buildings: either he or Mr. Harvey, another trader, "can underbid any one out of the country" (Doty in Stevens 1855:206).

Alfred J. Vaughan, a career man in the Indian Service married to an Indian woman, held the Central Superintendency of the Upper Missouri in 1854. His dispatches from Fort Pierre, in Lakota country, recount constant harassment of the Crow by Blackfoot "who murder indiscriminately anything that comes within their reach" (Vaughn 1855:85). Two groups of Lakota, the Honepapas [Hunkpapa], and Sioux Blackfeet (no connection to the Montana-Alberta, Algonkian-speaking Blackfoot) refused to accept annuity gifts, indeed slashed up the gifts piled for them and tossed a keg of gunpowder into the river, then shot their guns at it. These two groups, he states, "are constantly violating all the stipulations of the [Laramie] treaty. They are continually warring and committing depredations on whites and neighboring tribes, killing men and stealing horses. They even defy the Great Father the President, and declare their intention to murder indiscriminately all that come within their reach. They of all Indians are now the most dreaded on the Missouri. Something must be done, as the lives of your agents, and of all others in this country, are daily placed in jeopardy" (Vaughn 1855:87). The Assiniboine, in contrast, he reported to be strictly observing the peace provisions of the treaty (Vaughan 1885:83–84). To the Crow, in council, Vaughan "explained fully the wishes and desires of their Great Father, . . . and the designs of the government in sending them these presents. I told them their Great Father did not wish their country in return, (an idea many of them entertain;) that he did not ask of them one spire of grass for the whole; but that he only wished his red children might live in peace with the surrounding nations." They should defend their homes against enemies attacking in their own country, he agreed, to which the Crow replied that peace "was impossible under the existing state of things" (Vaughan 1855:85).

Vaughan hints at a political reality his government doesn't want to acknowledge. Indian people were quite familiar with traders, the competition between trading companies, and the efforts of independent entrepreneurs. Giving gifts to leading men was conventional practice by traders in Indian country. Piling up several hundred dollars' worth of gifts in the center of a council ground, giving a portion to every household in a camp, as the government's agents did, didn't make economic sense. When Indian people hold giveaways, someone is being honored by the giving and particular persons are singled out to receive the gifts, according to the respect or friendship they have earned. Wholesale giving away, in large quantities, indiscriminately, had to seem suspicious. Was

Vaughn lying when he assured the people that the United States did not want their country? George Manypenny, the Commissioner of Indian Affairs, had explicitly instructed Isaac Stevens that in his councils with the Upper Missouri nations, he should seek "the establishment of well defined and permanent relations of amity between the Indian tribes of that region and the United States, and a general pacification of the Indians among themselves . . . and to have proper regard . . . to the general policy of the government and *the future growth of the population of the United States in that direction*" (Manypenny 1856:14; our italics).

In his 1854 report, Vaughan foresaw the disappearance of the bison herds:

> The migration of both Indians and buffalo is westward, and the few herds of these animals left are surrounded and killed in the winter on the banks of the Missouri. The enormous destruction of these animals for their hides, meat, &c., by accidents in crossing rivers on the ice, where thousands sink, by becoming imbedded in mud and snow, by storms, and wolves killing the small calves, must, before many years, end in their entire extinction, or at least render them so scarce as to be inadequate for the subsistence of the numerous tribes of Indians who now live by hunting. [Vaughan 1855:83]

Denig and Catlin had envisioned the same calamitous threat. Vaughn urged this plan:

> It is certainly due to humanity, to our national honor, as a free, rich, and enlightened people, that some foundation should be laid in time for the future welfare of the red man. It is certainly discouraging to commence agricultural operations among people whose confirmed habits are at direct variance with such pursuits; but were a mission formed among them on the principle of manual-labor schools, the young could be brought up in industrious habits and knowledge, which many of the grown Indians could be induced to realize the benefit of, and pastoral employments joined with a certain amount of agricultural labor. To effect this, the Indians, or at least a portion of them, must become stationary; the Indian agent reside with them constantly; war be entirely stopped by treaties or otherwise; good teachers, farmers, and mechanics employed, and suitable amounts appropriated to meet these expenses. This is at least worthy of thought, if not of trial. [Vaughan 1855:83]

We need to put these reports and recommendations in context. The "government policy" stipulated by Commissioner Manypenny did, since Thomas Jefferson's presidency at the beginning of the 19th century, assume Anglo colonization inexorably pushing westward, ultimately to the Pacific (Prucha 1986:50–51). War with Mexico was launched in 1846 to take California, securing the Pacific region. In between the two colonized regions were the Plains, mountains, and the Great American Desert (Great Basin). The United States needed to secure routes linking its two regions, both wagon roads and railroads. Aside from this need for transcontinental routes, the interest of the United States in the western Plains was primarily to allow its traders to purchase and ship out furs and bison hides. Soft-tanned hides were in strong demand for robes and winter wear, and after the Civil War, for industrial belting as the eastern United States built its Industrial Revolution (McHugh 1972:253). Thus, the indiscriminate wholesale slaughter of bison was an integral component of America's transformation from producer of raw materials to manufacturer. This mid-19th-century transformation exploded in the Civil War showdown between slave-based agribusinesses and free labor factories. Catlin, in the 1830s, saw heavier predation on the bison as Eastern and Midwestern Indian nations were displaced to west of the Mississippi; he knew that bison, once common east of the Mississippi to the Appalachians, had disappeared in his own lifetime (Roe 1951:228–256). (George Washington had shot a bison in Ohio in 1770 [Roe 1951:232]). Denig and Vaughn knew the market for robes and meat and watched escalation of bison slaughter. Indian nations of the Plains knew only of an insatiable demand for hides. All this talk for peace was reasonable, considering how often traders were attacked and how raids jeopardized their intake. But why the generosity with presents?

Major Vaughan was told by Blackfoot that "they are a great and powerful people, but the whites are few and feeble. If the white men are so numerous, why is it the same ones come back to the country year after year, with rarely an exception?" Vaughan submitted that this sensible question could be dramatically refuted if annually, for five or more years, a party of fifteen or twenty leading men were taken by steamboat to spend the winter touring the States (at that time, all east of the Mississippi). Such an experience of the "magnitude" of the United States would, he was convinced, do far more than annual annuities unloaded from a single steamboat to persuade Blackfoot they were facing an immensely formidable power (Vaughan 1860:119–120).

Blackfoot were, in the mid-fifties, probably most advantageously situated of the Plains nations. The Rockies, "the Backbone" in Blackfoot, were at their backs, British Canada claimed their northern territories and

demanded less from them, and Fort Benton, head of steamboat navigation on the Missouri, lay in their southern territory. Aggressively defending their land by remorseless raids upon Crow along the Missouri and
Cree and Assiniboin on their eastern flanks, Blackfoot had little reason to
expect extinction of bison on the rich grazing they controlled. Still relying
on the piskuns (corrals) (Fig. 5) they had been building for many centuries along rimrocks and in coulees, now adding to the bison harvested
there, those they shot from horseback with guns and bows (first a volley
of gunshots, then follow-up with rapid firing of arrows), Blackfoot easily
provisioned their lodges in spite of the decimation of their young hunters
by war.

In 1856, the Commissioner of Indian Affairs had an agent, E. A. C.
Hatch, for the new Blackfeet Agency, apparently located at Fort Benton.
Hatch was to supervise the Gros Ventre as well as the three Blackfoot
groups. He outlined U.S. Blackfoot territory as:

> On the west and south by a line commencing at a point where
> the main range of the Rocky mountains intersects the forty-ninth
> parallel; running thence southerly along said mountains to Hell
> Gate Pass; thence in an easterly direction to the nearest source
> of the Muscle Shell river; down said river to its mouth; and
> thence down the Missouri river to the mouth of Milk river. On
> the east by a line running directly north from the Milk river. . . .
> their country extends far north into the British possessions. The
> country . . . contains about fifty thousand square miles within the
> territory of the United States. That portion of it adjacent to the
> Rocky mountains is good soil, covered with a luxuriant growth of
> vegetation, well watered by spring streams, and capable of sup-
> porting a dense agricultural population [!] but nearly the whole
> country is covered with the short nutritious buffalo grass and
> well adapted for grazing. [Hatch 1857:74]

The Gros Ventre, he said, occupied the land between the Milk and Missouri rivers, as far west as the mouth of the Marias. Piegan held the southern portion of the outlined territory, even hunting on the south side of the
Missouri during the summer, but members of the three groups "are often
found camping and hunting together."

Hatch enumerated the three Blackfoot groups as about 350 lodges
of Piegan, 250 lodges of Bloods, and 200 lodges of Blackfoot. The Piegan were led by Lame Bull, Low Horn, Middle Sitter, Mountain Chief,
Little Grey Head, and Little Dog; the Bloods by Ouís-tag-sag-nate-que-
im "the Father of All Children," Calf Shirt, Feather, Heavy Shield, and

Fɪɢ. 5. Bison drive site in Cut Bank Valley near Browning. Archaeological crew of Blackfeet are excavating the ancient buried corral as a curious bull of today peers over the edge of the drop. Credit: Thomas F. Kehoe.

Nah-tose-ous-tah; the Blackfoot by Three Bulls, Cootenais [Kootenay], Hair Collar, Bull Turning Around, The Swan, The Sun, and Stum-uk-dris-pee-my. There were an average of ten horses per lodge, some households owning as many as two hundred (Hatch 1857:75–76). He noted that the office of "chief" [Blackfoot: *akóxkina*, "head chief," and *ninaa*, "leader"] is hereditary, and the lesser role of "band-leader . . . depends upon the bravery of the individual and his success in war" (Hatch 1857:74).

The next year, 1857, Major Vaughan again reported for the Blackfoot, writing from Fort Benton. His superior, Alfred Cumming, stated:

> By the provisions of the treaty of the Judith, liberal arrangements are made for the advancement of the Blackfeet nation in education and other useful employments; no portion of that fund has yet been expended. . . . The Blackfeet are intelligent and tractable, and could they enjoy the benefits of a similar institution [to the Jesuit mission at St. Mary's in the Bitterroot Valley] would become equally distinguished [as the Nez Percés and Flatheads there who "are highly educated . . . (and) intelligent, moral, and observant of the forms of Christian worship"]. The most desirable point for the establishment of a farm, schools, &c., for the Blackfeet, would be near the base of High mountain, ten miles south of Fort Benton [Cumming 1858:118–119]

Cumming was already urging (ibid.) that the nations displaced to Kansas and Nebraska be relieved of "superfluous territory," reduced to 15 square mile reserves allotted to families "but patents should in no instance be issued to any of these Indians." If this was not done, he believed, the settler population would soon drive out the Indians, reducing them to vagabonds. The next year, Commissioner Charles Mix urged the same policy; it would not pass Congress until 1887. Cumming recommended linking the Missouri and Columbia rivers between Fort Benton and Walla Walla to create a transportation and emigration route across the West; Mix reported that in 1858, Yanktonai Sioux complaining that some of their territory had been taken away in the 1851 treaty, refused to meet for a conciliatory council or to accept the $21,000 worth of goods appropriated by Congress to ameliorate them (Mix 1858:15).

Vaughan had little to say in 1857 because he had only recently arrived at Fort Benton when he realized he had to dispatch a report with Major Culbertson, about to leave downriver, if it were to be received in Washington by its due date. Having met only with Gros Ventre and one Blood band, Vaughan forwarded on their request that corn be given in place of the rice and coffee customarily included in the annuity "presents": "coffee they care but little about."[28] To pad out this meager report, Vaughn rhapsodized on his "astonishment and delight . . . .When I reached the point where the Marias and Teton unite their pure and crystal water . . . it truly struck my fancy with pleasure and amazement" (Vaughan 1858a:122). The next year, 1858, Vaughn inspected the High Wood valley south of Fort Benton and the Sun River location recommended by Doty in 1853, agreeing that the Sun valley fifteen miles above its mouth seemed most favorable to agriculture—although Vaughn mentioned an inauspicious August storm leaving snow on nearby mountains, and in 1859 informed his superintendent that severe drought would bring poor yield from the farm's first crop (Vaughan 1860:116). Two Jesuits from St. Mary's and the Indian agent for the Flatheads accompanied Vaughan, confirming the potential of the location from their over-mountain experience and agreeing to build a mission and school for Blackfoot near the farm (Vaughan 1858b:78–79). A. M. Robinson, the superintendent of Indian Affairs for the Upper Missouri, repeated his predecessor's reminder that stipulations in the Judith treaty for education and other benefits for the Blackfoot had not yet been carried out, that the Blackfoot were "anxious," and that diminution of the bison herds demanded establishment of agricultural production (Robinson 1858:76). Vaughan concurred in the strongest, if flowery, language:

> Allow me to refer again to a matter of the utmost . . . importance to the life and well being of the red man. The gigantic buffalo, which has forever heretofore been to him, in truth, the "staff of life," . . . is slowly but surely year by year decreasing . . . fast passing away. . . . [T]he cupidity of the whites [by whom it is] ruthlessly slaughtered that its furred robe may demand its price from the trader. Were these inducements for its speedy extermination withdrawn—this price upon its scalp no longer offered—the buffalo would again increase . . . and the red man once more become proudly independent, as his fathers were before him. [Vaughan 1858b:83]

"The obstinate and unconquerable tenacity with which these prairie Indians hold their purpose" and "the restless solicitude and anxiety" with which they roamed over their hunting grounds could protect the herds only at the expense of unremitting war, yet although the Blackfoot "never can be conquered or subdued. They are unconquerable. The spirit of many of them is stronger than life; yea, stronger than death!" Their leaders strove to adhere to their treaty agreement at the Judith in 1853 (Vaughan 1858b:79).

Of immediate practicality, Vaughan urged, in 1858 and again in 1859, that the annuity "presents" purchased for distribution to Upper Missouri nations be "selected for its intrinsic worth alone, always preferring plainness and durability to cheapness or beauty." Discontinue, he urged: calico, because it is so flimsy; half the amount of bread and coffee sent, because the bread arrives dry or rotting and coffee is difficult to prepare with the Indians' utensils; fish hooks, lines, mirrors, combs, thread, none of these being used by the Indian people; substitute Chinese vermilion (red paint) for inferior American vermilion. In place of these unwelcome products, Vaughan asked for shirts, bed ticking (a sturdy fabric), flour, one-point blankets, gunpowder and balls, and "about three dozen plain and substantial saddles suitable for the prairies . . . for the chiefs" (Vaughan 1858b:82). We notice that fur trade staples such as glass beads, metal awls used by women in sewing hides, metal kettles, knives, and guns are not requested; the government's "presents" should not compete with traders' business, particularly considering the agent lived at the trading post. An invoice of Piegan annuities for 1858 does, nevertheless, list quite the range of goods usually carried by fur traders (Ewers 1958:230).

"Unremitting" efforts were made by Vaughan during 1858 to prepare an accurate census of Blackfoot, producing this table:

TABLE 1.12. Census of Blackfoot, 1858

Band	Lodges	Men	Women	Children	Total	Horses [1860]
Piegans	460	900	1,200	1,600	3,700	3,980
Blood	300	500	800	1,100	2,400	2,400
Blackfeet	150	260	400	540	1,200	1,200
Gros-ventres	265	400	700	1,000	2,100	2,320
Total	1,175	2,060	3,100	4,240	9,400	9,900

The disproportion in numbers between men and women he attributes to the many hazards encountered by men in war, winter cold while on war journeys or hunting, and accidents in hunting. Men commonly having more than one wife, "reaching to five or more," he suggests represents adjustment to the disproportionate numbers of women to men (Vaughan 1858b:80–81). We may add some figures to Vaughan's: for the Piegan, each household (lodge) housed an average of two men, 2.6 women. 3.5 children, or all together, eight persons. These figures counter the often-repeated impression of considerably more women than men, perhaps given by men's being more seldom seen at their lodges, while women liked working in small groups. The average number of horses per household was little more than one per person, 8.7, and would include both men's riding mounts and women's travois and pack horses; John Ewers's exhaustive research on Plains horse use came up with a similar figure for the period before the nations were forced to settle on reservations, after which hay was raised and herds of hundreds of horses maintained by some ambitious people (Ewers 1955:29). The average from Vaughan's table does not reveal disparities in number of horses owned by families, but disparities in ownership were overridden by expectation that wealthy families would lend horses to poor ones (Ewers 1955:30). In effect, successful households were patrons of the less fortunate in their bands.

With all the 19th-century warnings of decline of bison, and 20th-century analyses of the herds' extinction, little attention has been given to competition for forage between bison and horse herds. Ten thousand horses kept on the best grazing lands in Blackfoot territory meant less pasture for bison herds. John Ewers quotes a 1942 report by the agricultural agent for the Montana Blackfeet Reservation, that 1,822 range horses not used for work consumed grass that would have supported 6,000 cattle (Ewers 1955:21–22). McHugh states that bison and cattle eat roughly the same amount of forage (McHugh 1972:222), so by the 1942 agent's figures, 10,000 horses would have displaced nearly 33,000 bison. Indian ponies may have eaten somewhat less than the larger 1940s reservation stock, but they grazed year-round on native grasses. The pre-reservation ratio of one horse per human was not extravagant, yet human-bison ecological effects shifted after horses were adopted in the mid-18th century. Humans now camped *on,* rather than *near,* prime pastures. Their camps would be more prominent in the landscape, more vulnerable to enemy raiders, and the necessity of retaining good horse pasture heightened sensibility of territory control. Horses were more than a sign of wealth; substantial herds were signs as well as means of territorial domination. We don't seem to have Blackfoot discussion of competition between horse and bison herds.

Eighteen sixty was a turning point in Blackfoot economy: there was a Blackfeet Farm. Major Vaughan headed his annual report from "Blackfeet Farm," and appended to it the report of the official farmer, Daniel F. Paris. With obvious glee, Vaughan wrote,

> It affords me unfeigned pleasure to inform the department of the complete success of the Blackfeet farm this year, which places the matter regarding the fertility and productiveness of the soil beyond all cavil and doubt forever. [Had he never heard of decline of fertility after initial cropping on virgin soil?] . . . with genial showers this season . . . I am now cutting as fine wheat, I think, as ever was raised in any State . . . the best of Indian corn

and vegetables of all kinds and varieties in profusion, which the Indians are getting very fond of, especially corn and potatoes. [Vaughan 1860:83]

Notwithstanding the marvelous crops, Vaughan passed on requests from Blackfoot that $10,000 worth of cattle be purchased for the Sun River valley range. He boasted that "the main chief of the nation," Little Dog, was living on the farm, awaiting "a small farm" Vaughan promised to "open and cultivate for him" ten miles from the Blackfeet Farm. That 180-acre farm, "well fenced," employed, in addition to the farmer, an interpreter and four laborers, two (probably brothers) born in France and two in Germany.

A one-year hiatus, due to disruption of communication from Fort Benton when the boat with annuity goods burned, left only census figures in the 1861 Report of the Commissioner of Indian Affairs. The figures are identical to those in the following year, 1862, report, and oddly discrepant with Vaughan's carefully prepared table from 1860:

TABLE 1.13. Census of Native Americans, 1860

Band	Men	Women	Children	Total	Horses [1861, 1862]
Piegans	1,700	2,000	3,700	[7,400]	3,980
Blood	1,050	1,350	2,400	[4,800]	2,400
Blackfeet	530	670	1,200	[2,400]	1,200
[Total Blackfoot	3,280	4,020	7,300	14,600	7,580]
Gros-ventres	900	1,200	2,100	[4,200]	2,530
[Total	4,180	5,220	9,400	18,800	10,110]

It seems unlikely that the human population approximately doubled within a year, nor does the statistical table in the commissioner's annual report indicate source for the 1861 figures, given that he tells us no communication was received from Fort Benton (Dole 1861:18). The statistical table does list, for the Blackfeet Agency, its annual appropriation for annuities and other stipulated benefits, $35,000 (RCIA for 1861:213).

Invasion

Remote as Blackfoot country was, and still functioning independent of the United States, it was entangled in the U.S. Civil War. Major Vaughan, a Virginian, was replaced with a Northern man, Henry Reed. Suspicions of disloyalty ran rampant. The Commissioner of Indian Affairs' Report for 1862 recorded,

On the 29th of August, 1862, honorable J. R. Giddings, United States consul general in Canada, addressed a letter to the Secretary of State, in which he said: "There is little doubt that the recent outbreak [August 18] of the Chippewa Indians [in fact, Santee Dakota] in the northwest [Minnesota] has resulted from the efforts of secession agents, operating through Canadian Indians and fur traders." . . . As early as the 5th of August last, the superintendent of Indian affairs in Utah wrote to the Commissioner of Indian Affairs that several prominent chiefs were endeavoring to effect a general rising of the tribes in that region, to exterminate the white settlers. On the 26th of August the agent of the overland mail company telegraphed the Postmaster General that "general war with nearly all the tribes of Indians east of the Missouri river is close at hand." Rev. P. J. De Smet, an intelligent Catholic priest, in a letter to the Commissioner of Indian Affairs, dated September 5th, stated: "Whilst in the upper plains of the Missouri river last June and July, at Fort Barthold [Berthold], among the Gros Ventres, the Ricarees and Mandans, at Fort Union, among the Assinaboines, and at Fort Benton, among the Blackfeet Indians, I heard it frequently stated by American traders that the Indians of the plains had been greatly tampered with by the English traders along the boundary line, and expected to assist them in the then expected war between Great Britain and the United States. This excitement took place when the news reached the upper country of the difficulties created between the two countries by the arrest of Slidell and Mason.[29] A great number of Indians of the various tribes had been induced to come and trade their furs on the British side of the line, and were promised that they would be provided, in due time, with all that was necessary to expel the Americans from their Indian country. . . . Many of the Indians were dissatisfied with the treaties by which they had agreed to part with their lands. They complained that they had been deprived of their hunting grounds and of the means of subsistence. They also complained of alleged frauds on the part of Indian agents and traders. [Dole 1862:4–5]

Blackfoot would have been surprised that the commissioner apparently believed they had "agreed to part with their lands." Agent Reed reported that 120 "principal men" met him at Fort Benton to express their concern that with an unprecedented number of white men in the Upper Missouri country [five or six hundred by Missouri steamboat, many others overland, going to gold mines discovered in southwestern Montana], "there might be some design of getting their lands from them, which they could not consent to, as this had been their home as well as that of their fathers, and they hoped to make it the place of their graves and the home of their children." Reed "assured them that there was no such intention . . . that the whites now had by far more land than they could cultivate or knew what to do with" (Reed 1863:179). Whether Reed believed this, who can say? The unprecedented number of white men "constantly passing through the country, especially from Fort Benton to the mountains, besides the whites resident in the country," led Reed to urge that one or two companies of U.S. soldiers be stationed at Fort Benton, not so much to patrol against Indian depredations as to give "care and attention" to the "many whites who . . . cannot be tolerated in any civilized society" (Reed 1863:180). This is the first official notice of lawless whites, and, Reed adds, their "introduction and sale of liquor."

And the farm? Rivers ran unusually high that spring of 1862, enabling the steamboat to travel rapidly upriver all the way to Fort Benton, but at the same time flooding a good part of the Sun River farm. Only five acres of corn, out of sixty planted, three acres of wheat and oats, and practically no potatoes or vegetables survived to harvest. Vaughan had recommended, in 1860, spending $2,500 to construct irrigation for the farm to overcome drought; the 1862 farmer, James Vail, only bemoaned the overabundance of water that year. Again in 1864, the river inundated the planted fields (Vail 1865:299). Agent and farmer alike considered even the lower Sun River valley best suited for grazing cattle, not crops. Little Dog, for whom a farm of eight or ten acres had been made four miles below the Blackfeet Farm, saw the futility of cropping and went back to his camp (Reed 1863:180).

Gold fever drew 30,000 whites into what was quickly set up, in 1864, as Montana Territory. One thousand tons of freight was carried through Fort Benton by boat, a great deal more transported overland to the mountains to service the prospectors and miners. Bear in mind that the gold seekers were pouring into Indian country while millions of other men fought the Civil War. Lawless though the Montana horde might be, they were not battling the Union but expanding it; hence, Lincoln's general John Pope declared in 1862, "It is my purpose utterly to exterminate the Sioux . . . destroy everything belonging to them and force them out to the plains. . . . They are to be treated as maniacs or wild beasts, and by no means as people with whom treaties or compromises can be made" (quoted in Prucha 1986:145). Many Minnesota Dakota fled north, squatting in Manitoba and Saskatchewan until small reserves were given to them. Meanwhile, the United States Congress passed, in 1862, the Homestead Act enabling a settler to own 160 acres after five years' use: 15,000 claims were occupied under this law *during the Civil War years*! All told, in the Civil War years, 1862–65, approximately 300,000 whites traveled from the Mississippi River frontier west across the Plains, to find gold in the Rockies or California, to homestead, or to make money provisioning emigrants, selling liquor, or continuing export of furs and buffalo robes (Morison and Commager 1942:702–703). Between 1865 and 1870, more than 20 million dollars' worth of gold dust was produced by placer mining along the mountains in southwestern Montana; then these sources were exhausted. Some prospectors went south to newer discoveries of gold in the Black Hills, many went back East, and others settled as ranchers (Stuart 1925:II, 33–36). In 1870, the first ranching operation east of the mining zone brought a thousand head of cattle into the Sun River valley. More and more cattle were driven onto the eastern Montana grasslands, allowed to range with little supervision or notice of railroad, homestead, or Indian land boundaries, until a severely cold, snowy winter of 1886–87 killed so many that ranchers reformed their practices, hiring herders and providing shelter and hay. Stock numbers rebounded quickly. A legal inquiry into the 1887 treaty cession of the eastern half of the Blackfeet Reservation established that at the date Congress ratified the treaty, "there existed . . . a demand for the subject lands in large tracts for the purpose of grazing livestock" (Indian Claims Commission 1967:266–273).

In 1859, Blackfoot had told Major Vaughan that they doubted his nation was really so great as he was boasting—why did they see only the same few men again and again? Now, in 1864, the Blackfeet Agent, Gad Upson, could say, "The great number of whites, together with the expedition of General Sully, that have shown themselves in this country, has had a beneficial influence upon [the Blackfoot], and some have foresight enough to perceive that their power over the whites is fast passing away to return no more forever" (Upson 1865:300). In 1865, 250 wagons, pulled by multiple yokes of oxen, were in the business of freighting goods and immigrants between Fort Union and Fort Benton. Thousands of oxen ate a great deal of pasture, displacing bison from the Missouri bottomlands. Add to them, and emigrants' and settlers' horses and mules, the new industry of cattle ranching: in 1860, about 200 head of cattle were raised around Fort Benton, rapidly increasing after 1863 to feed the thousands traveling into or through Montana. In 1866, a herd of 600 was driven from Texas to fatten in Montana (Stuart 1925:II, 97–98).

Upson's report for 1864 contains a paragraph foreboding a terrible event. The agent went to inspect Blackfeet Farm and found "the worst management and the grossest neglect." Mr. Malcomb [*sic*] Clark lived there as government farmer, supposedly appointed by "one Robert Limon" by authority of the former agent, Henry Reed. Upson doubted this, and in any case, could see that Clark was using the farm buildings, already "dilapidated," as hotel and trading post for his own private gain. Clark was dismissed, replaced by James Vail, an honest farmer (Upson 1865:294). Five years later, 1869, Clark would be killed by a party of young Piegan men, his wife's relatives, avenging humiliation he had callously inflicted upon one of them. Meanwhile, Vail left and the single laborer remaining was powerless to prevent a raid by Blood men. All the stock was run off and tools taken. The laborer took all he could salvage to Fort Benton, hoping that at least the crops—wheat, barley, oats—could be harvested, but "some evil-disposed person," Upson recounted, destroyed the fences to let his wagon train animals feast on the grain. That, said Upson, ended the experiment of persuading Blackfoot to farm (Upson 1865:513).

Clark couldn't resist the lure of quick money from the deluge of prospectors heading for the gold field of southwestern Montana. The 1855 treaty made at the Judith River expiring after ten years, Congress wanted a new treaty that could facilitate settlement under the Homestead Act; $15,000 was appropriated to set up a treaty with the Blackfoot nation to cede "their right to occupy" any land south of the Missouri and upper tributaries of the Teton Rivers. (Note that the Commissioner of Indian Affairs, D. N. Cooley, carefully phrases what is demanded: not the territory that the United States already claims through the Louisiana Purchase, but the First Nation's right to occupy that portion of the territory [Cooley 1865:31]). Agent Upson begged, as he had begged previously, that the commissioner send Army troops, then discovered with dismay that the contingent stationed at Fort Union, at the junction of the Yellowstone with the Missouri (on the Montana-North Dakota border) protected only the traders and army sutlers colluding with them (cf. Larpenteur 1933:357). Specifically, the commandant had held up the boatload of annuity presents for the Blackfoot; when Upson convinced the man that he had to release the substantial shipment, it was too late to take it upriver by boat, so a wagon train had to be engaged to freight the lot, a two-months' enterprise that would bring the annuities at the beginning of winter instead of early summer. The bands were very seriously inconvenienced by failing to receive the expected supplies, and then by the burden of traveling in dangerous and difficult weather (Upson 1865:513).

More than takeover of their southern territory, exacerbated by the delay in annuity distribution, afflicted the Blackfoot in 1865. The year began with a measles epidemic. Upson wrote that 280 Piegan, 1,500 Blood and Siksika Blackfoot, and 160 Gros Ventre died (out of 1,870 Piegan, 2,150 Blood, 2,450 Blackfoot, 1,800 Gros Ventre [Cooley 1865:30]). Fifty lodges, one-sixth of the band's households, stood in the winter camp after surviving families moved out on the spring hunt: each lodge sheltered the corpse of a man who had succumbed to the disease. The people suspected that white traders or government agents had put poison in the previous year's annuity "presents" to kill them off. Upson brought together Gros Ventre, led by "Far-ma-see" ("Sitting Squaw"), and Piegan led by Little Dog, concluding an agreement to cease war upon each other (Upson 1865:301). Blood and North Blackfoot had not shown for this conclave, and Upson argued the latter really resided in British territory. Whether the huge increase in whites, with their freight wagons and stock, passing through the southern portion of Piegan and Gros Ventre country persuaded these two nations to ally, does not appear in the record. Upson engaged Blood and Siksika Blackfoot to meet in November at Fort Benton with him, Piegan, and Gros Ventre, to sign the new treaty authorized by Congress. It was the will of the Congress that the Indian nations should "release and relinquish" all land south of the Missouri and Teton, in return to hold exclusive right to their acknowledged country north of these rivers, except that they should permit United States citizens and employees to travel through, and roads to be constructed for them. For 20 years after signing the treaty, the Indians would be paid $50,000 annually, not in money but in goods decided upon in Washington, particularly agricultural implements, livestock, and mechanics to maintain the farming tools, and in clothing (American type) and provisions. In other words, the "payments" would be the means by which the United States would dictate to the First Nations a new mode of life. Signing the new treaty would stipulate "acknowledgment to be made by the Indians of their dependence upon the United States, and obligation to obey . . . the direction of the superintendent or agent" (Dole 1865:251). The November 1865 meeting did occur, and the treaty was signed. In January, Major Upson left to carry the document to Washington, journeying from Montana via San Francisco (it was common to go by ship around South America between the eastern states and California, rather than overland). Upson died in March in California, and by the time his papers were received in Washington, Commissioner Cooley decided to shelve the document.

Far from acknowledging dependence upon the United States, in 1866 the Blackfoot declared they would kill every white intruding on their country. Bull's Head with a group of his North Piegan men burned the buildings of Blackfeet Farm, revenging Sun River prospectors' murder of four North Piegan men who had happened to stop nearby. Then and elsewhere, Blackfoot murdered ranchers. In June, Little Dog, who had endeavored to accommodate the Whites, brought twelve horses stolen by young men of his band in to Fort Benton, for the agent (Hiram Upham, Upson's deputy) to return to their white owners. Four miles from Benton City on his return journey, Little Dog and his son were killed by their own people (Upham 1866:203). Such an unequivocal repudiation of a policy of accommodation meant, the whites inferred, war.

Fort Benton had been incorporated as a municipality, Benton City. Situated on the north bank of the Missouri, even under the unratified 1865 treaty it lay in Blackfoot territory. Nevertheless, the new city's freighters and merchants argued that they did not come under the Interior Department restrictions designed to segregate Indians from unscrupulous white entrepreneurs. Under the 1834 Intercourse Act regulations banning liquor from Indian territory, liquor should not be brought into, nor sold from, Benton City—not even to emigrants on wagon trains or on the decks of steamboats moored to the north bank. Benton City businessmen resented the privilege of established licensed fur traders. They hated Indians, convinced every man stole horses from whites. Their reasoning seems to have been that if there were no Indians they would be totally free to exploit emigrants' needs, most definitely including selling cheap liquor, plus they could homestead good ranchland. In 1867, Indians coming to Benton City to purchase provisions were shot without warning. Newly appointed agent George Wright repeated his predecessors' request for an agency separate from the traders' post, where he would no longer be "dictated to, as he now is, by old trading posts, merchants, thieves, and blackguards" (Wright 1868b:208).[30] His Blackfoot and Gros Ventre charges dared not come to Benton City even as officially invited delegations.

John Bozeman, a gold prospector who gained fame by identifying the Bozeman Pass route between Montana and Colorado, was murdered by a small group of Indians, said to be renegade Blackfoot disowned by their people, on the Yellowstone, April 1867. News of Bozeman's murder linked to a Bannock Shoshone's report that all Blackfoot women and children had traveled north into British country, their men readying an attack on whites in the Gallatin Valley. Granville Stuart, a pioneer businessman in Deer Lodge, said all the settlers in southern Montana responded with alacrity, bringing their own women and children into the towns from ranches while the men mustered into half a dozen companies of militia. By mid-May, it was reported that Sioux, Arapaho, Cheyenne, and Gros Ventre were allied for all-out war against the white invaders. Governor Meagher somehow fell off a steamboat at Fort Benton and drowned, July 1, 1867, and without him, the war fizzled. The militia companies were disbursed on October 23, 1867, having cost $1,100,000, of which less than half was finally paid to Montana merchants in 1872 (Stuart 1925, II:63–67). "Acting Governor Meagher's Indian war in Montana is the biggest humbug of the age, got up to advance his political interest, and to enable a lot of bummers who surround and hang on to him to make a big raid on the United States treasury," reported the agent for the Flathead. Traveling from his post west of Blackfoot country, down the Missouri to Illinois, he passed hundreds of whites on foot, horseback, or in wagons, none apparently anxious about Indians, nor did he see or hear of any boats fired upon, despite "the many statements made in newspapers to the contrary" (Chapman 1868:259).

Agent Wright wrote, "It might be argued that if there should be a repetition of Indian wars, the race would be . . . exterminated. . . . This theory may be, in contemplation, pleasant, yet practically it would meet with embarrassments, for . . . [t]his government is too humane to annihilate those who, from wrongs inflicted upon them, justly punished the white aggressor" (Wright 1868a:258). Once again, in September 1868, a treaty was presented to a council of Blackfoot leaders; they signed, but once again, the United States Congress failed to ratify the treaty. In consequence of no treaty with legal standing, no appropriation was made for annuity goods in 1869.

An 1868 census showed 4,200 Piegan, 2,380 Blood, 2,980 Blackfeet, and 3,000 Gros Ventre (RCIA for 1868:352). Agent Wright stated they had "been on the war path against the whites the past two years," yet he had been "constantly besieged by the Indians for food and clothing, which I gave them at general distributions, besides feeding them when they called on a friendly visit." Wright also got a former army surgeon, Dr. H. M. Lehman, to help "the many who were suffering from diseased eyes, ulcers and arrow wounds." Even the principal chiefs Mountain Chief of the Piegan and Father of All Children of the Bloods were "afflicted," and benefited, Wright said, from the doctor's attentions. From this experience, Wright "earnestly" called for a physician to be appointed to serve the Indian people, "in return for their general cleanliness and high regard for virtue, as unchastity is severely punished by them." A successful doctor, he observed, "is looked upon as more than mortal, and his advice on general Indian topics is respected, and often results in good" (Wright 1868b:206).

At last, an agency was constructed for the Blackfoot, on the Teton River near present-day Choteau, 75 miles north of Benton City. Besides the log-walled agency with its residence, stable, and storage buildings, houses were to be constructed for Indians, now counted as 6,000 Piegans, Bloods, and Blackfeet (RCIA 1870:461). Acting agent F. D. Pease told his superiors that his charges suffered from scarcity of game, and their leaders expressed willingness to settle on the promised farms, once they were furnished with tools, seeds, stock, and provisions until crops could be harvested; but the Blackfoot had found out that the 1868 treaty had not been ratified by Congress and no annuities would be forthcoming, in spite of the Indians signing in good faith. Agent Pease observed, "The country south of the Teton River, ceded to the government under the late treaty [1868], is being surveyed and fast taken possession of by settlers. In this particular alone is the treaty being recognized by the government" (Pease 1870:300). "The Indian campaign of 1869," according to rancher Granville Stuart, started with ten Blackfoot driving off cattle and horses from a ranch in the Gallatin Valley. A troop of 40 soldiers from Bozeman, with 15 civilian vigilantes, overtook them after a 75-mile pursuit. The Blackfoot made a stand on a rocky hilltop that the troops were able to surround, killing them all while losing only one man from the troop (Stuart 1925:II, 85–87). The previous summer, Mountain Chief had traveled to Fort Benton to request the agent, then still residing there, to get rid of illegal whiskey traders operating on the reserved land. The dignified chief was beaten up by a couple of Benton citizens as he left the agency office, and when Wright tried to press charges, the sheriff refused to accept them (Dempsey 2002:20). In summer 1869, a brother of Mountain Chief and a teenage boy, carrying out an errand for trader Alexander Culbertson, were killed on the street, supposedly in retaliation for the deaths of a pair of cattle herders near the town. General Alfred Sully, Superintendent of Indian Affairs for Montana Territory, found he was as powerless as Agent Wright had been to prosecute the Benton assassins (Ewers 1958:246).

We have now come to 1870. Early on January 23, Brevet Lieutenant Colonel Eugene M. Baker with his companies of cavalry opened fire on a winter camp of Piegan. Their leader, Heavy Runner, rushed out waving his government papers. Baker's soldiers shot him dead. When the shooting stopped, Baker counted 173 Piegan bodies. Later investigations showed the majority to be women and children. Those who were able to flee into the bitter winter day saw all their possessions burned by the army. Baker had been marching to "chastise" Mountain Chief's band, where Malcolm Clark's murderers were believed to be (Mountain Chief's son Pete Owl Child and Black Weasel). Joe Kipp, son of a trader and a Mandan woman who was daughter of a voyageur, had followed his father's occupation, trading with Piegan. He was Baker's guide, apparently either confused over which of the winter camps on the Marias was Mountain Chief's, or perhaps unable to persuade Baker to hold off once a camp was sighted. Joe Kipp adopted one of Heavy Runner's young sons who had escaped, and married two of Heavy Runner's daughters (DeMarce 1980:142–143).

Outrage at yet another massacre of women and children flooded the Eastern press. (A similar unprovoked slaughter at Sand Creek in northern Colorado, by Colonel Chivington upon Cheyenne and Arapaho, in 1864, had raised an outcry and investigation that year [Prucha 1986:150].) Brigadier General de Trobriand, stationed with infantry at Fort Shaw, on the

Sun River west of Great Falls, testified that Baker had burned the camp because a smallpox epidemic was raging, which was true but no excuse for driving women and children into the snow. De Trobriand remarked that in any case, the Army lacked sufficient surplus rations to "feed that crowd" (de Trobriand 1870). General Sheridan had telegrammed General Sherman, Secretary of War, that "Colonel Baker had to turn loose over one hundred squaws. Had no transportation to get them in" (Sheridan 1870). Sheridan failed to mention that Baker's troops brought 300 seized Piegan horses to Fort Shaw. The bereaved remnants of families struggled north to British country, where Alexander Culbertson noted that "a very large number died" before they reached shelter (Dempsey 2002:49).

A partnership of Montana traders, Alfred Hamilton and John Healy, with about a half-dozen employees, had left Benton in December, promising to refrain from trading whiskey while traversing the Montana side of Blackfoot country. During their journey, they met a band of Bloods, led by Bull Back Fat, on the Marias, provided food to the people when they saw they had none, and traveled north with them. Crossing the line, the traders set up at the junction of the Belly and St. Mary's Rivers in southern Alberta, where Many Spotted Horses' band wintered. The partners presented the chief with 300 dollars' worth of goods, and Healy—with a wife in Montana—allied with Many Spotted Horses by marrying his daughter. (Hamilton apparently honored his marriage to the Piegan Iron Breast's daughter Lucy.) Late in January, an angry troop of Piegan led by Cut Hand rode up to retaliate for the Baker massacre by killing the traders. Bull Back Fat brought up his own soldiers, assured the traders that their kindness to his people would not be forgotten, and told Cut Hand he and his men could trade but must maintain peace. The Piegans sold Healy and Hamilton 1,600 bison robes, plus furs, in exchange for all the ammunition the traders would allow; with these, and trade from other Blackfoot afraid to go to Montana, the partners grossed $50,000 by May (Dempsey 2002:2, 49–52). Healy and Hamilton's post was nicknamed Fort Whoop-Up.

So began fifteen years that would be the most tragic for Blackfoot. Between a smallpox epidemic and a heartless massacre, half the Piegans' territory taken over by get-rich-quick gold seekers and their entourage of freighters, businessmen, and ranchers, game increasingly scattered, the nation knew it was in crisis. After the epidemic, there were 9,216 "Blackfeet" by their agent's count, including 3,240 Southern Piegan, with Gros Ventre listed separately in their own agency; 1,400 Blackfoot were estimated to have died from smallpox (RCIA for 1870:190, 333). A table of statistics for 1870 stated, in regard to "size of reservation," "No reserve" (i.e., no ratified treaty). Four acres were cultivated by Indians, one acre by

"Government." There were no frame houses, ten log houses. Two hundred bushels of potatoes and one hundred of turnips, each bushel valued at two dollars, and 20 tons of hay, valued at $400, had been harvested; one horse worth $150, no cattle were listed (RCIA for 1870:339). Lieutenant Pease, the agent, wrote that the "Indian War" with Blackfoot in 1869 had consisted of one "small war party" driving off a fine team of mules and then killing one and wounding one of a group of "Spanish hunters and trappers near Fort Shaw." This one raid served as pretext for calling all Blackfoot hostile, not permitting any licensed trader to traffic with them, and letting them be "indiscriminately slaughtered" (Pease 1870:197).

In July 1870, the Congress legislated that officers of the armed forces could no longer be appointed as Indian Agents. President Ulysses Grant, although himself the Union's leading general during the Civil War, adopted a "Peace Policy" repudiating War Department control of Indian affairs. Instead, under the Department of the Interior, Indian agencies were portioned out to established churches, as missionary fields (Clum 1872:20). That the policy might contradict the U.S. Constitution's First Amendment separation of church and state was ignored; as historian Francis Paul Prucha notes, the United States was caught up in evangelical fervor, hellbent to extend Christianity and the "Christian way of life" throughout the continent (Prucha 1986:152). A similar policy operated in Canada, where there was no constitutional obstacle to government selecting certain churches to carry out federal responsibilities. Consistent and continuing parallels between United States and Canadian policies and practices toward First Nations indicate it would be correct to say that the English-speaking governments of North America shared an Anglo culture, positing a wild and savage "Indian race" inferior to the blessed white race but capable of being tutored to live like semiskilled rural working-class families. Appropriate to this image and Justice John Marshall's extraordinary phrase, that they were "domestic dependent nations" (1831, *Cherokee Nation v. Georgia*), Indian people were considered to be childlike. This tenacious and self-serving ideology of superiority was particularly likely to pervade the thinking of men and women who had chosen to evangelize for their churches. Thus, a policy that looked humane and gentle had its roots in bias and blindness.

"Fort Whoop-Up" led a proliferation of whiskey outlets that the Superintendent of Indian Affairs for Montana Territory said was "the bottom of all Indian troubles and depredations in this Territory. . . . Robes, blankets, horses—everything—is sacrificed to whisky, and when reduced to utter poverty the Indian steals, and the result is war with the whites" (Viall 1872:409). The superintendent "found [whiskey traders] in all cases backed up by men of large influence and capital." Viall persevered and finally got two offenders sentenced to jail terms (eighteen and six months, respectively). "The hardest blow to their trade was the fact that the above men were convicted on Indian testimony" (Viall 1872:410). Another problem in Montana Territory, mentioned by the superintendent and agents but not perceived to be as dangerous as illegal whiskey, was the presence of approximately 6,800 Yankton, Santee, and other Sioux in eastern Montana, in the basin of Milk River, in territory meant to support Assiniboin, Crow, and Gros Ventre. Smaller numbers of Cheyenne and Arapaho, Cree, Ojibwa, and Saulteaux lived and hunted there, too (Simmons 1872:430–31). Thus, Blackfoot suffered heavy invasion on two fronts, white emigrants in southern Piegan country and eastern Plains nations on the east, adding to the pressure from their earlier First Nations neighbors. An estimate put the number of bison slaughtered in eastern Montana during the summer hunts at 50,000—"The buffalo are being rapidly killed off" (Simmons 1872:431).

The agency for the Blackfoot built on the Teton River was only a couple of years old, but already by April 1871, "neglected," "dilapidated," and filthy. Only a worn, broken mowing machine could be seen, no tools. Agent Armitage obtained nearly 6,000 feet of lumber from Helena, repaired buildings, and requested another freighting of lumber to build a schoolroom. Since he had to bring in breaking plows with teams, it was late in the spring before fields were prepared and crops planted: 10 acres of wheat, 18 of oats, 15 of barley, 12 of potatoes, 10 of turnips, 2 of onions, and about 8 acres of vegetables (beans, peas, corn, carrots, cabbage, beets, lettuce, cucumbers). Lacking rain, Armitage had a mile-long irrigation ditch constructed. At the end of August, he had distributed "a large amount" of the garden vegetables to his Indian charges, and was harvesting the other crops, although early frosts had injured the grains. A few families lived in tipis close to the agency, "raising and trading horses and tanning hides and furs"; everyone else depended on hunting for subsistence (Armitage 1872:428–429). The agent reported 2,750 Piegan in 550 lodges, 1,750 Bloods in 350 lodges, and 3,000 Blackfeet in 600 lodges, the last number probably unreliable since the Siksika Blackfoot, and many Blood, remained generally in British Canada.

"What shall be done with the Indian as an obstacle to the progress of settlement and industry? What shall be done with him as a dependent and pensioner on our civilization, when, and so far as, he ceases to oppose or obstruct the extension of railways and of settlement?" asked the new Commissioner of Indian Affairs, Francis Walker, in1872. "The feeding system" of "buying off the hostility of the savages, excited and exasperated as they are, and most naturally so, by the invasion of their hunting-grounds and the threatened extinction of game" was, Walker admitted, unfair in that it was applied only to First Nations large and well-armed enough to threaten the frontier. Smaller, less militant nations had to "gather a bare subsistence by hard work" (Walker 1872:3–4). The "present system allows the freest extension of settlement and industry possible under the circumstances, while affording space and time for humane endeavors to rescue the Indian tribes from a position altogether barbarous and incompatible with civilization and social progress" (Walker 1872:9). As Walker wrote, the Northern Pacific railroad [Duluth, Minnesota, to Puget Sound, Washington] was rapidly lengthening westward, soon to parallel the Union Pacific [Omaha, Nebraska, through Ogden, Utah, to San Francisco] to the south and create a pincer crushing the Sioux. The Northern Pacific would also quickly deploy troops to control Blackfoot territory along the Canadian border. "Every year's advance of our frontier . . . is bringing imperial greatness to the nation . . . [while] to the Indian it brings wretchedness, destitution, beggary." . . . [Indians are] "a people who have been impoverished that we might be rich" (Walker 1872:10–11). And Walker reminds Congress that because Indians were "expressly excluded by the Constitution from citizenship," Indian persons could not be given earned government pensions, for, not being citizens, they could not take the oath to support the Constitution, a requirement enacted the previous year, 1871 (Walker 1872:12, 105). Walker's successor, Edward Smith, in his report for 1873 railed against the "anomalous relation" of Indian nations, simultaneously sovereign powers making treaties, and wards of the United States. He urged "radical legislation" to recognize Indians "strictly as subjects of the Government," and an end to annuity payments as "presents": an Indian should be given a share of the payment for surrendered land only when he has labored, the payment then appearing as wages—no labor, no annuity payment (Smith 1874a:3–4). Smith would seem to not understand the concept of payment for ceded land, a surprising obtuseness in a highly placed American official. Both Walker and Smith advocated military enforcement of the bounds of reservations, not permitting an Indian to go out of his reservation unless allowed by his agent. Finally, in a short clause tacked onto the legislation appropriating funds for the Yankton, the Senate decreed that no treaties would henceforth be made with any United States Indian nation or tribe (Prucha 1986:165).

At this time, 1873, the government at last announced a reservation for eastern Montana, 17,408,000 acres (27,312.5 square miles, although the Commissioner of Indian Affairs' report for 1874 says 31,250 [Smith 1874b:49]) covering from the Missouri River on the south to the Canadian line on the north, and from the Sun River on the west to the Dakota territory line on the east. This included both the Blackfeet Agency and the Milk River Agency, so this at first glance generous reservation in fact had to sustain not only 7,500 Blackfoot (or at the minimum, half that number if the others remained in Canada), but also 19,755 Crow, Assiniboin, Gros Ventre, and Santee, Yanktonai, and Teton Sioux administered from Milk River. River Crow, numbering 4,100, with their own agency, were supposed to hunt south of the Yellowstone River. More than 27,000 Indian people would need to subsist on game, principally bison, from these 27,000 square miles; recall that population density here in the early 19th century has been calculated at six to seven square miles per person, meaning that 27,000 Indians should have 164,000 square miles, not 27,000. Blackfoot territory alone had been 20,000 square miles (Wood 1875:299). If, as calculated on page 12, each bison requires from two to four square miles of range, the reservation could sustain perhaps 9,000. One bison feeds 25 people for one day, so *each day,* 1,090 bison were needed for the Indian population, and 398,000 over the year. No one seems to have discussed quantities of prairie turnip normally harvested from natural or minimally cultivated fields in northeastern Montana, but these, too, must have been inadequate for a population seven times the region's historic density. Clearly, the reservation could not possibly support its Indian population, even if antelope, elk, and deer were also harvested. Clearly, packing all the northern Plains First Nations onto this reservation doomed the bison herds.

Bison hunting, both a subsistence and a source of cash, would no longer be reliable. There was nothing mysterious about the diminution of bison; there were too many slaughterers, and the reason was political, the eastern First Nations driven westward from their lands and their country, and southern Montana taken over by United States colonists. With vigilantes, militia, and federal troops consolidating the takeover, reservation nations had to find means to increase food supply and to lessen the intolerable predation on bison herds. Cattle ranching would seem the obvious answer, given that the reservation was nearly all grassland, but it was not a simple answer: cattle need winter feed and shelter, entailing raising hay, building corrals or cover, and they must be controlled with fences or vigilant herding. All this Indian people understood when they requested cattle from their agents. Unhappily, Anglo ideology insisted that breaking ground and planting alien crops was fundamental to civic morality (even cosmopolitan Thomas Jefferson idealized yeoman farmers, fancying himself one at Monticello). Farming physically expressed man's domination over the earth, a practice 19th-century Anglos believed to be prescribed by God. Farming—overturning earth with plows, inserting selected, foreign plants in unnatural monocrop fields, tightly controlling livestock, putting up fences—was an outward practice of the acceptance of discipline that made states possible. Ranching on the range was a frontier practice, too close to lawlessness, unable to foster a disciplined work ethic or tightly settled communities amenable to authority. Only farming, not ranching, would transform Indians into law-abiding American commoners.

The Blackfeet Agency report for 1873 said that the government farmer had cultivated 80 acres, Indians none, the government breaking 20 acres; 3 houses were occupied by employees, 3 by (non-employee) Indian families; there was one carpenter shop, one blacksmith shop; neither sawmill nor gristmill; 50 bushels of wheat were raised, 80 of oats, 3000 bushels of potatoes; 30 tons of hay cut; two horses, value $100, and 11 cattle, value $900. The 3,150 males and 4,350 females of the three Blackfoot nations had property (unspecified, presumably horses) valued at $40,000. A Methodist man and woman taught at the one school, located at the agency, with 10 boy and 15 girl pupils, these no doubt making the figure of 25 listed as "having learned to read." Ninety Blackfoot were killed that year by their own people, 42 by hostile Indians, and two white men were killed by Blackfoot (RCIA for 1873:No. 80, 338–339). Commenting on the statistics, Agent Ensign candidly admitted that the school, a novelty that year, had attracted about 500 children, with each disappearing as soon as their curiosity was satisfied, a matter of at most three or four days. The 25 students in the statistics table were white children of agency employees, with a few Indian youngsters willing to follow their example. He explained that grasshoppers had destroyed all the grain, turnips, and cabbages, only potatoes escaping their ravages. Whiskey traders were as disastrous, 32 Piegan killed "through the agency of liquor" in only one season. With reservation boundaries designated, Ensign hired a detective to direct a police force against this illegal trade (Ensign 1874:252).

Hardly had the 1873 legislation been announced, than Montana settlers agitated for a reduction in the reservation, moving the southern boundary north beyond the good grazing of the Teton River valley. A new agent, R. F. May (the salary of $1,500 per year was too low to attract competent or honest men, so turnover was high [Ewers 1958:267]), listened to Little Plume, a principal Piegan chief, protesting what May agreed was "a gross injustice . . . to take from peaceable, friendly Indians a very large portion of their best hunting and pasture land without consultation or remuneration . . . a violation of the wise and Christian policy of the Government" (May 1874:260). Withal, the influence of emigrant ranchers and businessmen prevailed, and the newer 1874 boundary stood along Birch Creek and the Marias River. Half of the 1873 Blackfoot territory had been snatched away. The remainder was home to 2,450 Piegan in 350 lodges, and claimed also 1,500 each, in 225 lodges, of Blood and Blackfoot, although Agent May said that neither of the latter had come south of the Canadian line, except for 13 on a raid who killed a white man near the

Sun River mouth. Of the total 5,450, May estimated 2,150 males and 3,300 females; he estimated an additional 175 "mixed-bloods" and 26 whites, of whom 12 were agency employees. May reported that two whiskey traders had been shot dead on Badger Creek, by a young Piegan man defending his father, an "entirely justifiable" deed in May's eyes. The 40 acres planted to oats, potatoes, turnips, and vegetables on the agency farm, and an acre each planted by "two old Indians," were all destroyed by grasshoppers. None of the Piegan were convinced that agriculture would be viable for their sustenance, especially considering hunting was still good (May 1874:29–260).

Statistics for 1874 indicate how little had changed in Blackfoot country. Furs to the value of $95,000 had been sold, and the number of horses owned by Blackfoot (combined three divisions), 6,000. Fifteen Indian families lived in houses. The day school, taught by B. W. Sanders (and his wife? two teachers are entered in the statistics table), enrolled 11 boys and 15 girls; four Indians are counted as able to read, two of them having learned that year, 1874. May believed many Piegan families wanted their children to receive schooling, but could not keep them in school when the families moved out to hunt; thus he advocated a boarding school. In spite of still living off the hunt, 1,500 Blackfoot usually wore Anglo clothing ("citizens' dress"). Medical treatment was provided to 350 through the agency. Reflecting the demonic effect of illegal liquor, 113 Blackfoot had been killed that year by other Blackfoot, 30 by "hostile Indians," and seven (directly, aside from whiskey traders' effects) by whites. Blackfoot had killed five whites, 35 whites had committed crimes against Blackfoot, and of these, two were punished (RCIA for 1874:104–105, 126). Agent May wrote that the northern divisions, Blood and (Siksika) Blackfeet, were in "deplorable' condition because "They are living in a country where there is no law, except that which is administered by bloodthirsty 'wolfers' [men who poisoned carcasses that wolves would eat, to get wolf skins to trade] and whisky-sellers" (May 1874:259). The end of lawlessness was, however, in sight: the newly formed North West Mounted Police came into Alberta in 1874 to wipe out the whiskey trade, while on the American side, Detective Andrew Dusold pursued whiskey traders, refusing to be intimidated by the territorial mercantile interests profiting from iniquity (Dempsey 2002:203–204).

Yet another agent was appointed to the Blackfoot, in 1875. John S. Wood had been city marshal for Ottumwa, Iowa. Probably he was the eighteen-year-old trumpeter, in 1864, in Captain Wisner's Company I, 22nd Regiment of Volunteers, from New York. If Agent May had proven himself a friend to the Piegan—perhaps the cause of his leaving the agency (Ewers 1958:273; Wissler 1971:25), John Wood would even more staunchly stand up for the people. First, he assiduously collected eth-nographic information from Blackfoot, noting that their own name for themselves is "Sakitapix" (his spelling of Niitsitapi?), divided into Pie-gan, Kanaan (Kainai) or Blood, and Siksikas or Blackfeet. Each band of each division was led by a band-chief or war-chief and a "mina maska" (ninámska, keeper of a medicine pipe). There had been 33 bands, allied in the "Exkinoya" (Akóxkina, meaning "top man," that is, head chief) "Great Council" (properly, Nínawa). The bands gathered each summer for the council, following a four-day ceremony, "mis-i-mam" (*misam* is an adjunct root meaning "long time," "long ago"; he may have referred to the Long Time Pipe bundle ceremony) . Of the seven grades of all-com-rades societies, he said, "the first four classes form the West Point educa-tion of the future warrior, while the last three prepare him for a statesman among his people." Wood was assured that this "knowledge of the val-ue of organization and government" had been practiced up until white settlement twelve years previously (1863). In contrast, when he arrived in January 1875, the people appeared "disorganized and spiritless . . . to have no purpose in life except to hunt and procure robes and peltries for the traders." They complained continually of the unjust seizure of their land, and distrusted appointed agents: May's vigorous efforts to rescind the territorial decree had raised hopes whose disappointment they laid to treachery on the part of the agent.

Wood used the ethnographic information he gathered for an extraor-dinary project, restoring the authority of the band chiefs and council. Group by group they traveled to the agency, until 5,000 were in atten-dance. Over several days, he reminded them of the fatal effects of whiskey, the inexorable growth of emigrant settlements, and the likelihood that the bison would become scarce in a few years. Finally, he convened a formal council in which Little Plume, White Calf, and Generous Woman were elected head chiefs. (Little Plume led the Worm band, Generous Woman the Grease Melters, both wintering along the Marias from the junction with Birch Creek and Two Medicine River, to the Sweet Grass Hills. White Calf was leader of the Skunks band, wintering on Blacktail Creek, a tribu-tary of Badger Creek [Ewers 1974:147; Schaeffer M1100-#135].) The coun-cil prepared and passed a code of laws: polygamy and traffic in women were abolished, the death penalty set for murder, and punishments for theft, assault, and brutal conduct established. Criers proclaimed the laws throughout the camp. Wood was impressed by the "strict sobriety and exemplary conduct of these people here," and particularly by the ensuing rigorous observation of the laws. Commissioner of Indian Affairs Smith quoted Inspector Watkins on Wood's unprecedented restoration of First Nations authority:

While there is no law under which such a tribunal can legally act, their decision is considered binding by the Indians, and every violation of the law which they have thus made is reported to the agent, and steps taken to bring the offender to justice—if an Indian, to be tried and punished; if a white man, to be turned over to the proper authority. I consider the code of laws eminently just and the practical working of the system very beneficial. [RCIA for 1875:47]

Wood claimed that,

Since the establishment of the laws not a single . . . infraction has occurred. No quarrels or intemperance; on the contrary, sobriety and kindness. . . . no thefts . . . the occupation of the whisky-trafficker is gone, as the Indians have declared against using his vile poison. [Wood 1875:301]

Next step for Wood was to relocate the agency, for the redrawing of the reservation boundary left the Teton River agency outside. He chose a site on Badger Creek, presently known as Old Agency. After his harangue on the threats they faced, "a number of chiefs" told him they would like to try farming, if they were given implements as the settlers used, and Wood promised this would be his project so soon as the new agency would be ready. His own farm, like those of his predecessors, hardly encouraged agriculture, for of his sixteen acres planted, turnips, cabbage, and vegetables were eaten by grasshoppers and the potatoes injured by frosts. He mentions that besides the railroad cutting through bison habitat, the emigrant settlers were hunting "to their most remote pastures," the herds displaced by the colonists' cattle. Statistics showed the value of furs sold as $48,000, half of the amount given for the previous year, and 3,000 horses, again half the number given the year previously. Eighty percent of Blackfoot subsistence came from their hunting, 20 percent from government supplies (RCIA for 1875). Wood seems not to have realized the hollowness of his assurance to the council that ten acres cultivated would feed ten people for a year.

Population given for 1875 is 3,000 males, 4,200 females, plus 215 mixed-bloods. Of the total, 2,500 "came under the civilizing influence of the agency." Somehow, only 25 were wearing "citizens' dress" (did Wood expect more complete outfits than May recognized?). Wood had a resident physician who treated 2,699 people, and recorded seven births and six deaths, these from old age or chronic disease. "Diseases of a filthy character" were "disappearing" with the curbing of whiskey traders.

Though lacking a church building or missionary, Wood used the school for Sunday services and Sunday school, and prayer meetings with Christian instruction on Thursdays. According to Wood, "pagan ceremonies" and "medicine-man" healings were seldom heard, the agency doctor resorted to instead. Scaffold burial or "tossing the body into a hole" had been replaced by coffins and a procession of the entire camp to the grave to listen, "with uncovered heads," to a Christian burial service. The school shone through Wood's efforts, for he "caused the children to wash and comb their hair before entering" and gave dresses to those without annuity clothing. A curriculum was regularized, including cutting and sewing clothing for girls, earnestly attended to, and singing hymns at the opening and closing of the school day; these "the children sang with great taste and correctness" (Wood 1875:300–301). Thirty-three boys and 47 girls attended, the boys more often called away to accompany their families on the hunt—as usual, the agent calls for a boarding school—and now 18 Indians can read. "Church members" total 15 (RCIA for 1875:113).

Then came the Custer War. The Battle of the Little Bighorn took place on June 25, 1876. Soon after, messengers went out to bring together leaders of all the Northern Plains nations. They met in the Cypress Hills, just north of the Canadian line, Yankton and Santee Dakota, Assiniboin, Gros Ventre, Mandan, Cree, Ojibwa, Little Plume of the Piegan, and Sitting Bull's Lakota. Only in May 1874 had Assiniboin and Gros Ventre, meeting in Fort Benton with a Government Special Agent, acceded to a treaty of peace with Piegan. Little Plume told Agent Wood, back at Blackfeet Agency, that when he heard the Sioux talking of wiping out the whites, he and his camp left. "The Sioux were their enemies, and . . . they would fight them if ever they came to this country, and . . . the whites were their friends, and they would help them whip the Sioux" (Wood 1876:86). Not only had Blackfoot and Sioux been enemies for many decades, soon after the Cypress Hills council, two Santee had killed a young Piegan out searching for strayed horses.

Retaliating for defeat at the Battle of the Little Bighorn, the Indian Affairs Office ordered that neither breech-loading guns nor ammunition for them be sold to Indians. Agent Wood protested that "nearly all the [Blackfoot] men are armed with a Winchester carbine . . . they have not used the primitive bow and arrow for many years, most of them never." Without ammunition for their rifles, the men could not hunt. They feared, too, that without means of defense they would be attacked by Cree, Assiniboin, or Sioux, nations with whom they had many bloody battles up until the 1870s. Wood told the Indian Affairs Office that the Piegan would be forced to go into Canada to trade for ammunition. The North West Mounted Police had stamped out most of the whiskey posts, some turning legitimate to remain in business, and with colonization encouraged by the presence of the police, new trading posts established. Bootleggers running liquor from Benton City even found some regular customers among the enlisted men of the police (Dempsey 2002:215). Bison had been plenty, enabling the Blackfoot to trade an estimated $60,000 of robes and furs. Still, Wood called attention to the ever-increasing pressure on the herds. Agriculture had failed again, once more all but potatoes devoured by grasshoppers. Other than that, Wood reported the school holding steady, 20 boys and 28 girls enrolled with an average attendance of 31, and ready acceptance of his physician's services: 1,363 treated, 66 births, and 25 deaths.

Blackfeet Agency on Badger Creek opened in November 1876, with a fenced cemetery adjacent. Wood was replaced by an agent less impressed by his charges, and especially disgruntled by the siting of the agency, in a valley with limited tillage and bordering hills that would make herding cattle difficult. A new site in the Badger Creek valley was selected in 1878, and the agency moved to it in 1879. Agent John Young had cleared (using Indian men and women for the labor) and fenced nearly 100 acres and broke 20, putting in potatoes, turnips, carrots, peas, and other vegetables, all flourishing when he wrote on August 1, 1877. He had Indians assisting agency employees in constructing an irrigation ditch, too. The winter hunt had been adequate, although only one-third as productive of robes as in the previous year, and the summer hunt was better. Leaders did agree with the agent that the numbers of bison must fail, and some band chiefs traded horses for cattle to ranch (3,400 horses, 150 mules, and 80 cattle were listed for Blackfoot). When an alarm of smallpox was heard in the spring, Piegan crowded in to be vaccinated, and no one fell ill; 2,586 received medical attention, with the physician recording 69 births and 10 deaths. There were now 260 mixed-blood and 23 white persons, in addition to the agency's nine employees, residing in Blackfeet Agency territory (RCIA for 1877:296–97), some of the mixed-bloods and whites former trading post employees who married Piegan women and settled with their wives' people, running a few cattle (Dempsey 2002:217). The all-comrades societies ("soldier bands," Young called them) were functioning well as police, as Agent Wood had expected. Young noticed that Piegan would "laugh immoderately at our mistakes in" speaking Piegan, and conversely, hesitate to speak English, not wishing to be ridiculed for mispronunciation; songs, however, were happily taken up, women singing hymn tunes while gathering firewood (Young 1877:131). New categories in the statistical tables list 30 "full-blood male Indians who labor in civilized pursuits," six mixed-bloods who did, and eight families, changing the subsistence figures to 10 percent living from "civilized pursuits," 50 percent from hunting, and 40 percent from government rations (RCIA for 1877:313).

The Era of Settlement

The middle of the 1870s was the turning point for Blackfoot life. The Office of Indian Affairs had accepted President Grant's appointment, in 1869, of an overseeing Board of Indian Commissioners who regularized the government's business with its First Nations. Purchasing was centralized, cutting opportunities for traders and agents to collude in skimming kickbacks, furnishing underweight, moldy, or shoddy provisions, and overcharging for freighting. Licensing for traders required bonds and publicly posting prices, so that Indians should not pay more than whites for goods, or receive less for robes and furs. Agents had to send in quarterly reports, including details on expenditures, and would not be issued unrestricted funds. With all the expansion of bureaucracy, funds for Indian Affairs dropped from $8,329,815 for 1874, to $4,733,875 for 1878, to provide for 250,000 Indians (RCIA for 1878:lxii–lxvi; Prucha 1986:158–160). This severe reduction pushed a policy of employing Indians rather than hiring white persons, a policy touted as progress to civilization by enabling Indians to earn their treaty annuities "In the sweat of thy face shalt thou eat bread," as Commissioner Oberly quoted the Bible in 1888 (Oberly 1888:lxxxix), and pragmatically beneficial in that it offered an alternative to trading hunt products for what had long been necessities—ammunition, knives, kettles, frying pans, tea, sugar, cloth, shirts, and blankets. That annuities were installment payments for ceded land, not gifts, escaped the memories of the commissioners, good bourgeois Protestants all.

For Blackfoot, the rapid escalation of Canadian colonization, marked by the Canadian bands—Kainai, Siksika, and Aapaatohsi-piikani— signing Treaty Number 7, September 1877, pushed the tendency of the Aamsskaapi-piikani (South Piegan) to rely on the Montana Blackfeet Agency. Their congeners received reserves in Alberta. Visiting and marriages across the 49th parallel persisted, true today, too, but economic and political possibilities were dichotomized. Ranchers, railroads, and federal law enforcement officers surrounding the reduced Indian lands ended wars between First Nations, for troops prepared for battle could no longer travel to their enemies' villages nor attempt to beggar them by running off their horses. Blackfoot still had bison to hunt, the herds that had been steadily exterminated along the westward-advancing frontier finding their last pastures in the Cypress Hills and in the center of the northern Montana reservation between the Sweet Grass Hills, Bear Paw Mountains, and Judith Basin. Drought in the early 1880s added to the herds' distress. The last few prey bison were killed in 1883. (In 1886, bison were captured in southwestern Montana to be kept in the National

Zoo in Washington, D.C., some ranchers kept a few, and in 1878 a Pend d'Oreille man transported six young animals over the Rockies to the Flathead Reservation, where they became the nucleus of the National Bison Range [Bartlett 2001].) Anglo imperialism had surrounded the Northern Plains nations by 1847, when the United States broke Mexican control of California, while Britain had outposts on the Canadian Pacific coast by 1821. Closing in upon the Northern Plains, this ring of business entrepreneurs, homesteaders, mineral exploiters, and transport routes mile by mile destroyed the ecology that had sustained Plains First Nations for millennia; their own complicity in slaughtering bison for Eastern markets sapped their resistance. The crux of their crisis was the decimating smallpox epidemic of 1869, the incredible debauchery of the whiskey trade between that year and the North West Mounted Police's closing illegal posts in 1874–75, and the final pinch of land grabbing when the reservation boundary was moved north to Birch Creek.

The future was clearly visible by 1878, when Agent Young could report, at last, a good harvest of potatoes, turnips, and other vegetables that he distributed to Indian families—he enjoyed seeing Blackfoot children munching on raw potatoes the way white children eat apples. About a dozen families broke land and put in crops, ten built wooden houses, more men were laboring at least occasionally for the agency or on their farms, 70 men and 120 women habitually wore "citizen's dress," the school had about 37 children in daily attendance, although, oddly, Young reported only four Indians could read (the previous year he said 18 could read). Two thousand bushels of oats and barley had been harvested, 19,200 bushels of vegetables, and 100 tons of hay cut. Still, there were 3,850 horses and only 100 cattle, $50,000 worth of robes and furs were sold, and 75 percent of the people's subsistence came from hunting, even though because annuity supplies had been shipped too late the previous year to reach the Blackfoot, two years' worth of provisions were distributed in 1878 (Young 1878, RCIA for 1878:288–289, 305–330). Young recognized eleven Piegan bands under these leaders: White Calf (principal chief since Little Plume's death in 1877), Three Suns (Big Nose), Running Crane, Fast Buffalo Horse, Horse Head, No Runner, Red Paint, Tearing Lodge, Four Bears, The Horn, The General, Big Lake, and Lodge Pole Chief (Ewers 1974:123–124).

According to the Commissioner of Indian Affairs in his report for 1879, "Hauling [freighting by wagon] is far more profitable than hunting ever was," because cash wages of $1.50 per 100 pounds were paid directly (alternatively, $1.75 per 100 pounds could be credited toward purchase of the wagon and harness) and traders, forbidden to deal in tokens, found Indian customers managing money with care. Indian Affairs had first contracted with Indians for freighting, providing wagons and harness, for Kiowa and Pine Ridge and Rosebud Lakota in 1875, then extended to Cheyenne and Arapaho in 1877, next to nearly all agencies, so that in 1879, 1,369 wagons and 2,500 sets of harness for four-horse teams were distributed and a policy of hiring Indians embraced. Savings of "several thousand dollars" were realized in part because Indians were paid less than white freighters, and in part because the Indians did not pilfer goods entrusted to them (Marble 1880:xii–xiii).

The commissioner wrote that in the spring of 1880, 500 head of cattle would be given through the Blackfeet Agency to people who were likely to care well for stock (Wissler remarked, "To [the Indian], cattle were but mongrel buffalo" [1971:49]). Meanwhile, over the winter of 1878–79, White Calf's band hunted bison around the Bear Paws, where numerous other Indian parties were congregated in an uneasy truce. Near the end of the season, some Sioux ran off Piegan horses toward Sitting Bull's camp in Canada, and when overtaken by Piegan, killed one. Six Sioux died in the battle, their comrades escaping with the stolen horses. Fast Buffalo Horse with his All Chiefs band had gone straight north to the Elk River to hunt, but found few bison and weather so heavy that their horses became very weak and a woman and child froze to death. They got back to the agency in "deplorable condition," prompting more families to ask for assistance in making farms. Running Crane and his Lone Eaters band led in developing farms. Two hundred ninety-six Indian men were "engaged in civilized pursuits," school attendance averaged 63 daily. Only $25,000 worth of robes and furs had been sold (Young 1879, RCIA for 1879:234–235, 254–255). The next year, Young happily reported 32 families with farms cultivating 80 acres in toto and living in wooden houses (a condition he made for assistance with seeds, implements, etc.), 320 Indian men employed in "civilized pursuits," an average daily school attendance of 75 children and 24 Indians who could read. The farms, including the agency farm's 80 acres, yielded 3,000 bushels of potatoes, 1,000 of turnips, 600 of oats and barley, 100 of carrots, and 300 tons of cut hay, the potatoes in particular having been important in feeding people over the winter. Government cattle—50, not 500—had been given to those families who were farming along Birch and Badger creeks. Work on the agency farm, and cutting and hauling firewood and lumber for buildings, was eagerly sought by Blackfoot men and women. Only $20,000 worth of robes and fur was sold (Young 1880:105–107; RCIA for 1880:246–247, 266–267).

Against this pleasing picture of "progress" that Agent Young presented, he had to describe a cruel setback. In July 1880, the president had rescinded the 1875 extension of the Blackfeet Reservation south of the Yellowstone into the Judith Basin. Bison herds were still to be found in the Judith Basin, so all the Blackfeet Reservation nations—besides the Blackfoot, Gros Ventre, Crow, and Sioux—rode there for their winter hunt. Sioux and Piegan still skirmished there, Sioux stealing horses, Piegan pursuing, ending with six Piegan killed and one Sioux. Then a merchant in Helena complained that Piegan had killed some of his cattle on the range, a "false complaint of interested parties," Young wrote. Agent Young and the Piegan said killing cattle was unlikely, because the hunt had been good and Indians much preferred bison meat. Notwithstanding the protests, a troop of United States soldiers was sent out to force the Piegan back to their (diminished) reservation. Winter weather was severe, many Piegan horses died from exhaustion and lack of feed, most of the bison meat had to be abandoned, and the people's lives were endangered. At the beginning of August, the Piegan held their Medicine Lodge. Young described this as much like the Jewish Feast of the Tabernacle (Sukkoth); "[I]ndeed, there are many customs among these Indians too like levitical law to be mere coincidences" (Young 1880:106). Four years among them had softened Young's attitude toward his charges.

A new category, diseases, was added to the Indian commissioner's annual report for 1879. Figures for the Blackfeet were:

TABLE 1.14. Disease Report, 1879–1881

For 1879
Zymotic diseases [infections]—300; Syphilis and gonorrhea—209
Constitutional diseases—28; Tubercular diseases—62
Parasitic diseases—5; Integumentary system—26
"Constitutional"—7 types; not named—431
Casualties—93; Births—60; Deaths—22 (RCIA for 1879:264)

For 1880
Miasmatic diseases—210; Syphilis and gonorrhea—205
Constitutional diseases—29; Tubercular diseases—59
Parasitic diseases—9; Integumentary system—54
Locomotive system—2; Special diseases (7 types)—345
Casualties—16; Births—44; Deaths—14 (RCIA for 1880:275)

For 1881
Zymotic diseases—366; Syphilis and gonorrhea—117
Diathetic (chronic or allergy-related) diseases—17; Tubercular diseases—20
Parasitic diseases—23; Integumentary system—42
Nervous system—3; Eye—154
Ear—1; Digestion—38
Urinary and genital—24; Violent diseases and deaths—97
Births—49; Deaths—28; Diphtheria and measles among children, most families (RCIA for 1881:310)

Medical statistics published in the Indian Affairs annual reports did not refer to the malnutrition afflicting northern Plains peoples. Beginning in 1882, more detailed tables were prepared, for example for 1882, 25 Blackfeet were treated for gonorrhea, plus 2 for gonorrheal ophthalmia and 1 for gonorrheal stricture of the urethra; 14 for catarrh, 7 for acute bronchitis; totals of 403 males, 207 females "taken sick or wounded" and nearly all "recovered" (RCIA for 1882:facing 366). The next year, 1883, 348 Blackfeet were treated for influenza (none the previous year), 25 for whooping cough, 16 for mumps, 10 for chicken pox, 7 for tonsillitis, 1 for diphtheria, 72 for acute bronchitis, 17 for inflamed larynx, 8 for inflamed lungs, 3 for inflamed pleura, 20 tubercular (16 of these scrofula), 37 skin diseases, 143 for conjunctivitis (inflamed eyes), 15 for burns or scalds, 6 for frostbite; a total of 283 males, 268 females "taken sick or wounded," with 8 deaths and 29 still under treatment, the rest "recovered" (RCIA for 1883:305).

The 1880–81 winter bison hunt was poor. Only $12,500 worth of robes and furs was sold, and meat was scarce. Both Agent Young and the commander of federal troops in Montana, Colonel Ruger, urged Congress to appropriate an additional $15,000 for provisions for the Blackfoot, because the $35,000 normally appropriated was insufficient to prevent starvation. Colonel Ruger explained that the nearest hunting ground was in the Musselshell River valley, 25 days' journey southeast of the Blackfeet Agency. With the intervening territory now taken by ranchers and other settlers determined to keep Indians out of their range, and whiskey sellers slipping into the camps at night, danger attended the traditional hunt. Young recounted how in July 1881 a picnic was held for the schoolchildren and their families, 130 people traveling in eight wagons ten miles upriver (Badger Creek) from the agency. Officers of a detachment of troops camped twelve miles away had been invited to join the picnic. When they appeared, the Blackfoot were thrown into panic, fearing that the excursion was a ruse to massacre the families.

With few bison even in the Judith and Musselshell valleys, successful root crops on reservation farms persuaded 48 families to farm. Their plots were small, totaling only 85 acres. Agent Young required them to build cabins, and he praised the families' housekeeping: neat and clean, many covered log walls with brown muslin and tacked-up pictures from illustrated newspapers. The agency had a herd of 600 cattle, denied the Indians in expectation that eventually its increase would supply the Piegan with beef. Indians owned 80 cattle, 10 mules, and 4,000 horses. The agency's Indian police returned stray horses to owners, and also a few stolen from other Indian nations. Agent Wood's restoration of authority to band leaders had eroded after his brief tenure, and the police force were engaged as employees rather than all-comrades societies, but the role had continued. Young was pleased, in 1881, that a sawmill had been built, saving the need to freight lumber 160 miles; at the last journey, a rumor claimed that the job was a trick to get the young Piegan men to Fort Shaw to be imprisoned. With their own mill, Piegan floated nearly 1,000 logs 20 miles downriver to it. Ranchers on the Teton wanted to buy some of the lumber, but a law pertaining to Indians would not permit trading their lumber for provisions (Price 1882:lxvi).

The winter of 1881–82 was the point of transition from an independent, if progressively compromised, Blackfoot economy to one subordinated to the United States. For the first time in Blackfoot history, the first time ever, the people did not go on a winter hunt. Deciding to remain around the agency, considering how poor the previous two years' hunts had been and knowing very few bison had been seen, the Piegan depended on Agent Young's disbursement of agency farm produce and annuity provisions. Since the latter were never more than enough for half a year, the difference to be made up from the hunt, Young proposed the Piegan should pay for additional food by selling milled lumber from their sawmill. Told that this could not be permitted under legislation regulating Indians, Young "asked permission, which was granted, to solicit contributions among his friends in the East, to prevent suffering among his Indians"! (Price 1882:lxvi). That desperate plea brought in enough to tide the Piegan over into 1882, but by the autumn of that year, starvation again threatened: appropriations were less than one ounce of beef and less than one and one-half ounce of floor per person per day (Price 1882:lxvi). Similar rations were given to the Blackfoot in Canada, resulting in people so pitifully starving that the North West Mounted Police felt compelled to issue them a few ounces each of flour and beef, enough, the police inspector said, for two days—but that ration had to somehow stretch over seven days. The Mounted Police's doctor, John Kittson, had written as early as 1880 that the Canadian rations—similar to those given by the United States to its Piegan—were absolutely inadequate. He had corresponded with prisons and asylums in Europe to determine that a minimum ration for a man is one pound meat, 0.2 pound bread, 0.25 pound fat. The Czarist regime in Russia fed its Siberian prisoners twice that amount. Mounted Police were issued 1.5 pounds meat, 1.25 pounds bread, plenty of beans and dried apples, and sugar, tea, and coffee. Dr. Kittson described Blackfoot, in July 1880:

> Gaunt men and women with hungry eyes were seen everywhere seeking or begging for a mouthful of food—little children . . . fight over the tid-bits. Morning and evening many of them would come to me and beg for the very bones left by the dogs in my

yard. . . . The only surprise is that they remain so patient. [quoted
in Lux 2001:38]

To make matters worse, without bison, the people's tipis wore out and
could not be replaced except with canvas, much thinner and difficult
to anchor firmly; they had too few robes left for blankets; and couldn't
make winter moccasins (Lux 2001:39). Canadian historian Maureen Lux
cites horrific memos from government authorities: an agent about to pay
treaty annuities at Fort Walsh said in November 1882, "I know they are
not getting enough flour but I like to punish them a little. I will have to
increase their rations, but not much" (quoted in Lux 2001:40).

Attempting to compensate for the hunt, the Montana Piegan cooperated with Agent Young to select locations for farms and build cabins
on them. Felling the timber in the mountains, floating logs downriver
or hauling them on wagons to the sawmill, Piegan built 130 cabins that
summer. The houses were described as "solid," with doors and windows
framed by the agency carpenter, but they were small, and during the winter, poorly ventilated. Infectious diseases, including tuberculosis, spread
very easily within cabins, susceptibility exacerbated by malnutrition and
inadequate clothing (Lux 2001:64). Another, more obvious (but related)
problem was that families refused to live in a dwelling where a death had
occurred. Agency draft horses, stronger than "Indian ponies," as well as
plows and harrows were lent to the new farmers, whose plots were between one-half and eight acres. "Ponies" hitched four to a wagon worked
well for hauling. Then, during the winter of 1881–82, mange hit the Piegan herds with high mortality, reducing them—the Piegans' wealth—
from 4,000 to 2,000. Twelve mules, 65 cattle, and (a new livestock) 150
"domestic fowl" were listed in the 1882 report. Population of Blackfeet
under the Montana agency was 6,000, reflecting that Kainai, Siksika, and
Aapaatohsi-piikani went to Canadian agencies; aggregate population
figures are not reliable because some families double-dipped, getting annuities at more than one agency, and others weren't counted. For what
they're worth, official counts were 3,164 Kainai in 1881, dropping to 2,270
in 1883, and 2,166 Siksika in 1884 (293 men, 599 women, 693 boys, 579
girls) (Lux 2002:59–61). Estimates by Agent Young in 1882 had 75 percent of Piegan subsistence coming from government rations, 15 percent
from "labor in civilized pursuits," and only 10 percent from hunting and
gathering native foods. One hundred five families were engaged in agriculture and 425 men performing 'manual labor in civilized pursuits."
In spite of ceasing the main winter hunt, $12,000 worth of robes and furs
were sold (Young 1882:98–100; RCIA for 1882:336–337, 356–357).

All the Indian nations assigned to the northeastern Montana and Canadian prairie reservations suffered appalling deprivation in 1883 and 1884. The 1883 annual Report of the Commissioner of Indian Affairs quotes an inspector:

> There can be no doubt but many of the young children died from lack of food during last winter and spring [1883]. Never before have I been called upon to listen in an Indian council to such tales of suffering. Three or four years ago this [Blackfeet] reservation abounded in game and these Indians were, practically, independent of the Government; now, nowhere else have I ever seen a country so destitute of it as this, and there is, practically, nothing for the people to live upon but what is furnished by the Government. . . . Last week [week of August 15, 1883], 3,200 persons presented themselves as actually in need of subsistence, to furnish which, in the established quantities (which are found to be merely sufficient to sustain life) for the balance of the fiscal year, would require at least four times the quantity of flour supplied, and although but half a ration is issued, it will all be exhausted about midwinter, and all the beef available will be gone about the same time, although but one-fifth the established ration is being issued. This reservation cannot be farmed without irrigation, no preparation for which has been made; therefore but little can be expected from Indian cultivation, and as illustrative of the seasons here, this morning, August 21, the ground around the agency is covered with snow. [quoted in Price 1883:lx]

For the Fort Peck agency (Assiniboin, Yanktonai, Santee, and Lakota), an inspector declared that one million pounds of beef (equivalent to about 2,500 bison) should be added to the regular appropriation. The Fort Belknap agent, writing for his Assiniboin and Gros Ventre, said that the year's supply of flour and beef, 100,000 pounds of flour and 180,000 pounds of beef, amounted to a ration of one pound of flour and two pounds of beef *per week* per person (he italicized "per week") (in Price 1882:lxi). Appropriations had actually been reduced by Congress, disregarding the consensus that Indians could no longer find bison and would starve. Agents and inspectors warned that unless substantial additional provisions were appropriated by Congress, the Indians would be forced to "commit depredations" upon agency and neighboring ranchers' cattle. On the Blackfeet Reservation, Cree and "half-breeds" (Métis?) said to be from Canada raided in the spring and summer, running off horses and fighting pursuers. Piegan who had settled along the Two Medicine River moved close to the agency on Badger Creek, occupying tipis in place of their cabins and neglecting their little farms. Neither agency Indian police nor U.S. soldiers sent several times to the reservation were able to apprehend these raiders. The agency herd of 182 cattle was kept corralled at night (and note that 182 animals could not feed the 4,500 Piegan for long). Piegan had lost half the horses that had survived the previous year's disease, having only 1,000 horses, 5 mules, and 20 Indian-owned cattle, and only 50 domestic fowl. Income from selling robes and furs dropped to $900 (RCIA for 1883:294–295).

Commissioner Hiram Price was outraged that the northern Plains people's suffering was laid to neglect by his office. On the contrary, he asserted, the fault lay with the Congress, for delaying passing the annual appropriations bill. Since the Board of Indian Commissioners had established a lengthy business procedure for asking for bids, letting contracts, executing bonds for contractors, many goods manufactured after contracts awarded, and long journeys of goods to remote reservations, delivery was often not possible within the year. What caused the famine of 1883–84? It

> was attributable *directly* and *entirely* first, to the fact that the appropriations for them were not made until three months after they should have been made [early in the session of Congress], and second, that when made, the amount allowed was less than was asked for by this office [Indian Affairs]. . . . The Blackfeet, Blood and Piegan Indians, and those at Fort Peck and Fort Belknap agencies, were driven to great straits to sustain life during the winter and spring of 1883 and 1884,being compelled to kill many of their horses and young stock cattle for food, and to resort to every possible expedient, such as eating bark, wild roots, &c., and there is little doubt that many deaths amongst them were the direct result of lack of food. [Price 1884:iv–v]

Major Young resigned in protest against the lack of provisions for his charges. Reuben Allen, appointed to the Blackfeet Agency in April, reiterated the commissioner's description of dire conditions. "All bore marks of suffering from lack of food," he wrote, "the little children . . . were so emaciated that it did not seem possible for them to live long, and many of them have since passed away. To feed these Indians, about 2,300 in number [note, only half the population previously reported], I had . . . only 1½ ounces bacon, 3½ ounces beef, and less than 5 ounces flour per day for each individual . . . no beans, rice, hominy" (Allen 1884:107). By May, he ran out of rations and issued bacon that had been condemned, finding it wasn't quite as bad as had been supposed. It was in *June and July* that the people ate the inner bark of trees—cottonwood inner bark had been a sweet spring snack, and winter feed for horses when snow was heavy, but in 1884, it was food for families. With the clamor from the Indian Commissioner, agents, and newspapers, money meant for later in the fiscal year was finally released for immediate purchase of provisions, and in January 1885, Congress allocated additional funds. About 500 Piegan starved to death during the 1883–84 winter and spring (Ewers 1958:294). Today the place near the Badger Creek agency where many were buried is called Ghost Ridge.

Inexorably, over two centuries the bison herds had retreated westward from expanding European colonization. They disappeared east of the Mississippi, then from the lush prairies east of the hundredth meridian. The Blackfeet Reservation and bordering Cypress Hills in Alberta were their last refuge. Pushing First Nations who had hunted over present North Dakota out of that territory into northeastern Montana obviously put too much pressure on these last herds, which were further stressed by loss of their pastures in southern Montana, so that droughts of the early 1880s could not be compensated for by moving out of the dry zone of eastern Montana. No one in Montana was blind to the threatening extinction of the herds. The fault, the blame for the tragic famine, lay in Washington (and north of the line, in Ottawa) where Congress (and Canadian policymakers) balked at giving Indians taxpayers' money. Compounding the burden to taxpayers were fiscal crises: in 1873, the United States, following European nations, ceased setting a price for silver as money, prices fell for agricultural products and government debt rose as revenue fell. Agricultural producers and a range of related businesses struggled for twenty years until the Panic of '93 spread collapse to banks and railroads (Morison and Commager 1942, II:244–251). The Office of Indian Affairs was niggardly to its Indian wards, but it was under intense pressure from Congress to reduce expenditures. Ultimately, the long drawn-out tragedy, spanning two generations of First Nations confined to reservations, resulted from Anglo ideology enshrining the "Protestant ethic" that bread is earned by sweat, that they who do not labor are defying God's will. At the same time, those who actually perform sweaty labor were seen as a lower class destined to be led by educated men, men whose literacy conferred the privilege of governing. The superior class, unhappily, could not ensure a revenue stream properly sustaining its benevolent obligations.

Tutelage was the principle through which United States and Canada, but, significantly, not Mexico, governed its interior colonies, the conquered First Nations. Through the 1860s and 1870s, Congress appropriated monies to pressure First Nations to learn an Anglo way of life. Annuity payments stipulated in treaties were preferentially paid in goods rather than cash, and the goods were selected by Eastern officials, not Indians (recall the Blackfeet agents explaining that Piegan had difficulty preparing coffee). Easterners assumed that tutelage could transform northwestern Plains hunters into subsistence farmers, a notion underlying the repeated requests and efforts for constructing irrigation on the Blackfeet Reservation, despite so much experience of killing frosts even in summer. Ranching eventually was established by default of any other agricultural pursuit in Blackfoot country, and agents continued to try to teach through control of Indians' herds, blind to their own ignorance and Blackfoot savvy in raising animals on the range. Leaders such as Little Dog and Running Rabbit who earnestly tried farming could not know, initially, how unsuited agents' plans were for Blackfoot country. Whether a generous program of issuing cattle during the 1870s would have been sufficient to build herds that could sustain the people in the 1880s, we do not know; we know only that while white emigrants built ranches in former Blackfoot lands, Congress and the Indian Affairs Office pushed a Jeffersonian image of English-style family farms. Pushed the image, but did not appropriate money to purchase ox teams or draft horses, plows, harrows, and root cellars to break the virgin sod and raise the only crop, potatoes, that generally survived on reservation farms. Famine might have been averted if large sums had been sent through the 1870s to develop ranches and potato fields. Something important is missing in this line of thought, though: famine *would* have been averted if the original Blackfeet Reservation covering most of eastern Montana between the Yellowstone and Canadian border, and Canadian lands in Treaty Seven, had been preserved from emigrant colonization. Then that large territory would have been a refugium for bison. If, further, Dakota Territory First Nations had not been packed into that Blackfeet Reservation, the refugium might have sustained the Blackfoot.

Respecting Blackfoot expectations that their treaties would protect their subsistence base (Treaty Seven Tribal Council 1996) would have conflicted with an even more basic principle of Anglo policy, the premise that educated Englishmen are the pinnacle of evolutionary progress (Carter 1999:79, Prucha 1986:206). The reason the Red Man needed tutelage was that he, and she, was ignorant and untrained. Literate Englishmen and their relatives in North America had God's revelations transmitted through the Bible, Greek and Roman science and political structures, and modern scientific agriculture and technology for the foundation of their prosperous life. American Indians lacked all these transmitted branches of knowledge; therefore they needed to be tutored if they were to achieve a decent life. Only ignorance let them be contented with a life of nomadic hunting. Many Anglos, and French-speaking Catholics, were also motivated by God's "Great Commission" to "go into the whole world and preach the gospel" (Mark 16:15), saving souls through Christian baptism. Blackfeet agents again and again reminded the Indian Affairs Office that the Methodist Church had been granted the Blackfeet Reservation for missionary work including schooling, but had not sent anyone. Agents Vaughan, Young, and Allen read Christian service on Sunday and tried to teach the religion. The principle of tutelage, built on the premise of ignorance, encompassed inaugurating both an Anglo way of life and Anglo beliefs.

Boarding schools were believed to be the best means of tutoring ignorant Red Men. As Blackfeet agents repeated annually, day schools were popular with children, the children were remarkably attentive and obedient to their two lady teachers (Young 1883:97), but parents' travels to the hunt carried away the children. In January 1883, a boarding school was opened on the Blackfeet Reservation near the agency, housing seventeen students, a matron, and her assistant. Agent Young noted that their progress in speaking English was accelerated, since using English "is much discouraged by Indians among themselves." By the end of June, when vacation was offered, many families had taken away their children, and the matron and assistant resigned because "they were tired of living a civilized life, and wished to return to their old habits," the school was closed (Young 1883:97). Agent Allen reopened the school in October 1885, enrolling twenty students, and sent other children to the Catholic schools at St. Ignatius in the Flathead Valley and St. Peter's Mission a hundred miles south of the reservation. A few years later, the Piegan claimed that most of their children sent to St. Ignatius died there (Baldwin 1888:151). All the boarding schools emphasized manual training rather than academics. Perpetually underfunded, the schools utilized the children's labor. More than that expediency, training boys in farming, livestock care, blacksmithing, and carpentry, and girls in sewing and housekeeping put them into "civilized pursuits," and according to Anglo philosophy, on the road to social progress. Said the Commissioner of Indian Affairs:

> The history of agriculture among all people and in all countries intimately connects it with the highest intellectual and moral development of man. . . . civilization as naturally follows the improved arts of agriculture as vegetation follows the genial sunshine and the shower, and . . . those races who are in ignorance of agriculture are also ignorant of almost everything else. The Indian constitutes no exception . . . .Steeped as his progenitors were

> . . . in blind ignorance, the devotees of abominable superstitions, and the victims of idleness and thriftlessness . . . suggests to a great Christian people like ours . . . how to . . . direct him . . . to the light and liberty of American citizenship. . . . Agriculture and education go hand in hand. [Atkins 1885:III, v]

Underlining this principle, the commissioner decreed that each school should grow most of its foods (Oberly 1885:cv).

At this time, mid-1880s, boarding schools were built on reservations and parents permitted to visit their children. In an interview in 1939, Agnes Chief All Over, a Piegan, reminisced about her local boarding school experiences about 1889:

> Mother would get after the grandmother because (father would tell mother) "It is good for Agnes to be educated and learn the white language."
>
> They had then moved to Willow Creek.
>
> "When we have any work, men come here and we don't understand them or they us, and they don't know our sign language. We must have someone to speak English."
>
> Day she went to school, grandmother came home, and found out. She got after her mother and told her that Agnes would be treated mean.
>
> Mother: "She isn't far away—you can go up and see her."
>
> Grandmother: "She'll die of lonesomeness. She'll get sick and die. Lonesomeness cannot be cured."
>
> Boarding school—went in last of October—stayed until June. About four or five miles from home. Grandmother came up every Friday. Mother came up every two or three weeks [Agnes lived with her grandmother]. I'd cry to go home with them. First part of the year [they] didn't come often till I got used to the school. Grandmother would bring dried prunes and Pimm crackers. Mother brought nuts, candies, oranges, cookies (recorded August 1939, by Sue Sommers [Dietrich], manuscript in Marquette University Archives). (Agnes' mother was Insima, English name Mrs. Cecile Sanderville Yellow Kidney, and her grandmother Mrs. Margaret Sanderville, daughter of Red Bird Tail and Twice Success.)

Officials in the Office of Indian Affairs believed that parents would be favorably impressed by seeing their children washed, dressed in uniforms, eating politely at table. "The adult savage is not susceptible to the influences of civilization" except through parental pride (Oberly 1885:cxiii). The Blackfeet Boarding and Day School in 1884–85, with twenty students boarding, employed Mr. and Mrs. Bartlett, superintendent and matron, age 43 and 40, 17-year-old Nora Allen (likely the agent's daughter) as principal teacher and 15-year-old Kate Graham as assistant teacher.

Intervention by the governor of Montana and the Helena Board of Trade, coupled with Agent Allen's letters, brought a Congressional appropriation for three months' additional rations for spring 1885, enabling Allen to increase winter rations. "As a consequence the death rate was much less than in the preceding year" (Allen 1885:117). Population of Blackfeet was given as 2,000 (900 males, 1,100 females), 18 being mixed-blood, plus 69 whites "unlawfully on reserve." Two hundred births were registered, 270 deaths, and 1,200 Indians received medical treatment by the agency physician, of which 698 were "taken sick or wounded": 463 treated for conjunctivitis (eyes), 58 for skin disease, 133 for constipation, 33 for acute diarrhea, 16 for hemorrhage from stomach, 39 for acute bronchitis, 9 for consumption, and 29 for scrofula (both tubercular diseases), no one for caries—and two persons for "starvation." Two hundred "full-bloods" were engaged in agriculture, none of the mixed-bloods, according to the agent. Eighty percent of Piegan subsistence came from Government rations, 8 percent from hunting and gathering, 12 percent from "Indian labor in civilized pursuits," in this case agriculture. Value of robes and furs sold fell to a mere $200. The agency cattle herd had increased, by purchase and calving, to 553 head, but no cattle were owned by Indians. What did the Piegan own? 1,100 horses and 4 mules, and 40 domestic fowl (RCIA for 1885:342–343, 362–363, 388–389, 398–403).

A Piegan perspective comes from Agnes Chief All Over's mother Insima, Mrs. Yellow Kidney in 1939: When the Piegan

> lived at Old Agency, people claimed they were being starved. That was when they first learned to make a garden. Potatoes, rutabagas and carrots—about 57 years ago [1882]. Men plowed and women put in seeds.
>
> When first issued, rations [were] flour, meat, bacon, rice, crackers, coffee, tobacco, a big long plug, salt, tapioca—[we] call it fish eggs.
>
> In fall when garden ready, [the agent] issued it [produce] to them like rations. Have a great big slab of bacon. Scared of the flour because they found bones in it. Claim it was ghost bones— bones from human skeleton. [Rodent bones may have occurred in the flour. Difficulties in shipping food the long distance without

refrigeration, government practice of accepting the lowest bids, and chicanery from suppliers all contributed to the likelihood of contamination in flour and other rations.]

Had to use it but would pick bones out. When we started to eat it two or three died every morning complaining of their stomachs.

White man there with Indian wife who talked English and acted as interpreter [Farr (1984:29) identifies Malenda Wren as interpreter at Old Agency]. Woman would tell them what husband dreamt last night, that he made two or three coffins and sure enough next morning he have to make that many coffins. Then buffalo all gone—no other way—not permitted to roam—had to stay right there. Think flour poisoned them. [Canadian Blackfoot similarly died, and believed chemicals put into food as preservative poisoned them (Lux 2001:60).]

Didn't like smell of cows and so didn't like to eat them and didn't like so many different colored animals.

At Old Agency women did all the work. Agent, Grey Beard, put out two saws and two axes and when he'd open up tool house all the women rush over.

Hand out saw and tallest would grab and same with rest. Pick out best friend to help her with the saw. Be 4 women and 2 axes. Usual to pay them paper money and white paper. The white paper was for sugar. Saw and axes would put up a cordwood and get $4 for one cordwood.

Green paper—a dollar.

Each get $4 and $1 for sugar.

Men would go up to mountains and haul timber for the agency. One with big load—get $7—way up to mountains. In those days wagons very scarce. Build little log houses. Wouldn't stand long and roofs broke in. Took them long time to guide a team and [learn] how to put harness on. [Sommers (Dietrich) interview, August 1939]

An issue that would fester for a century until it boiled over into a class-action lawsuit against the Bureau of Indian Affairs/Department of the Interior entered Commissioner Atkins's reports beginning in 1885. The following year, 1886, Atkins addressed it under "Indian Moneys" and "Cash Payments to Indians." Atkins recounted that in 1876, it was brought to the attention of the then Commissioner of Indian Affairs, that fees from a "tax" upon non-Indian users of reservation land, timber, and other resources was handled by reservation agents and used for those reservations generating the moneys. Then, in 1883, Congress added a paragraph to a bill addressing funding deficiencies, 22 Stat. 590, directing that the fees "shall be covered into the Treasury . . . and the Secretary [of the Interior] shall report his action [disbursing monies] in detail to Congress at its next session." Somehow, the Secretary of the Interior simply reported the monies without taking them out for the reservations. In his first annual report, Atkins had proposed a bill to clarify that the Secretary of the Interior would be authorized to convey the funds, then totaling $13,096.81, to the reservations without getting specific Congressional approval for each payment.

The matter came up in Agent Baldwin's report for 1887 (Baldwin replaced Allen the previous summer). Approximately $4,000 had been collected in fiscal year 1886–87 (July1-June 30) from ranchers grazing cattle on the reservation or driving herds through it to Canada, and Baldwin urged that the money be made available to the Piegan. With no recourse, Piegan fell to creating family farms. No communal farms were permitted, the individual families in each band assisted in selecting small farmsteads along the valleys, although the strung-out hamlets did maintain loose band structure: John Ewers's elderly informants in 1951 listed the bands' settlements in order along Badger and Birch Creeks (see below) (Ewers 1974:131–133, 1958:298–299). By Summer 1887, somewhat over one thousand acres of Indian allotments were fenced, 250 acres had been broken, 300 tons of hay put up, everyone wanted "citizens'" clothing—having no alternative—and, Baldwin proudly announced, "Many have quit painting their faces." (Agnes Chief All Over had explained, in 1939, "Grandmother would paint face red if she [Agnes] ran around all day, to prevent chapping or sunburn. In winter, painted it so it wouldn't get frostbitten. It keeps the face warm"; quoted in Sue Sommers [Dietrich] 1939.)

AMSKAPI PIKUNI BAND SETTLEMENTS, EARLY RESERVATION PERIOD

As recalled by Adam White Man and Louis Bear Child in 1951, accompanying John Ewers and Claude Schaeffer in the Badger Creek valley around Old Agency, these were the band settlements in order eastward from the westernmost Black Door band:

> Black Door band—Badger Creek from the crossing of the Browning–Heart Butte road eastward.
> Lone Eaters—from the site of the first Badger Creek Agency downstream to the end of Albert Mad Plume's property.
> Mixed bands group led by Big Plume—north side of Badger Creek opposite Mad Plume School.

Grease Melters (also called Fat Roasters or Fries)—led by Three
   Suns (Big Nose), they had settled on Two Medicine River in
   1881 but returned to Badger Creek in 1883 following Cree
   raids.
Black Patched Moccasins—led by Little Dog [son of the 1855
   Little Dog].
Mixed-bloods, the White men married to Piegan women and
   their families—around the crossing of the present Highway
   89.
Elderly people housed in cabins built at Old Agency.
Small Robes—near Old Agency.
Joe Kipp's trading post a mile east of Old Agency on the flat
   south of Badger Creek.
Buffalo Dung band—just east of Kipp's trading post.
Black Patched Moccasins group—mostly older people of this
   band. The first Okan in which cattle tongues substituted for
   bison tongues was held on the flat south of this community.
Buffalo Dung band—families led by Shorty White Grass.
Bugs [also called Worms]—a small band much reduced by the
   1883–84 Starvation Winter.

Along Birch Creek:

Blood band, led by Fast Buffalo Horse.
All Chiefs, led by Horn
Skunks, led by White Calf.

Mr. White Man [a Piegan] confirmed that Two Medicine Valley was not
settled by Piegan until 1888, following the 1887 treaty council (Ewers
1974:131–133).
   Further settlement information is in the censuses composed by Holy
Family Mission priests. For 1896, they list:

Two-Medicine—73 houses, 295 people
Willow Creek—47 houses, 164 people
White-Tail Creek—30 houses, 110 people, with an average of
   4 persons per family (Holy Family parish records, Little
   Flower Church, Browning).

The government herd of 500 cattle did well in spite of a very severe winter, the Piegan appreciated having brood mares available to improve their
breeding stock of horses, and Indians held 200 cattle. Stronger horses
were needed to pull plows capable of breaking the tough sod. The 1,927

Piegan still owned 1,200 horses, 5 mules, but now 300 domestic fowl. The sawmill had cut 60,000 feet of lumber, and Piegan had freighted 100,000 pounds using their own teams, by which they earned $1,250. Sale of robes and furs totaled $500. Mixed-bloods now numbered 119, 48 Piegan could read, and 67 had everyday fluency in English. The boarding/day school, strictly taught only in English, was operating at capacity, prompting Baldwin to request funds to enlarge to accommodate one hundred boarders; the children raised all the produce they consumed. Three boys were apprenticed, to the blacksmith and carpenters. The agency slaughterhouse was improved by constructing a flume from the irrigation ditch to bring in clean water, and each Friday cattle were slaughtered there, hung overnight, then butchered and doled out to the Piegan families on Saturdays, the hides given to the women for making moccasins and parfleches, only half a hide available per housewife. That year, 1887, was the first in which government provisions of beef and flour were considered sufficient to sustain the people. Medical statistics showed only 261 "taken sick or wounded," 11 deaths (5 under 5 years of age) and 61 births to Indians, one to a white and one half-breed infant. One death was that of Agent Baldwin's oldest child, an 11-year-old girl. Apparently the cause of her death was not clear, for her father urged the commissioner to provide medical reference works for remote agencies such as his, so that the physician need not depend entirely on memory (Baldwin 1887:130–132, RCIA for 1887:356–357, 386–387, 406–407).

Commissioner Atkins's 1887 annual report on Indian Affairs is a landmark. That year, 1887, Congress passed a bill introduced by Senator Henry Dawes in December 1885, to allot Indian lands in severalty, that is, break up tribal territory into individual allotments. Doing away with communal holdings and cooperative work had been a goal of the United States since Jefferson. Desire to acquire private household farms drove Anglo colonization. Giving war veterans the opportunity to acquire farms at subsidized rates, as compensation for their service to the nation, had been United States policy from the Revolutionary War. Commissioner Hayt in 1878 advocated legislation to allot Indian lands, claiming "an almost universal call for lands in severalty . . . come[s] from nearly every tribe. . . . The loss of the buffalo, which is looked upon by Indians as disastrous, has really been to them a blessing in disguise" (Hayt 1879:3). Senator Coke of Texas had brought in such a bill but failed to get it passed. The Dawes Act, as the successful bill is known, was promoted by evangelical officials in the belief that Christianity and civilization rest upon each man's willingness to labor as an individual—farmer, wage earner, or businessman—to support a wife and children. "The Indian . . . proud of his manhood . . . will cheerfully and proudly accept the responsibilities which belong to civilized manhood" (Atkins 1887:ix). What was poorly understood in the late 19th century was that capitalism's profits, and the prosperity attending them, depend on ever-expanding markets. The wealth of the United States did not come so much from proliferation of family farms as from proliferation of consumers, some of them home- stead farmers but more of them a hierarchy of workers, small and bigger business owners, and at the top, barons of railroads and industry. Plains First Nations had been an integral part of United States and British/ Canadian capitalist economies from the 18th century, as suppliers more than as consumers (because high transport costs to roadless outposts con- strained the market). Enabling Indians to be greater consumers would have been in line with capitalist development, and such a goal would have encouraged selling Blackfoot-milled lumber to Montana ranchers, instead of forbidding it. It didn't take those ranchers long to figure out that cattle were the best economic bet in what had been Blackfoot coun- try. Only Anglo ideology, the conviction that farming is the essential pre- cursor to civilization, upheld Indian Affairs' dogged insistence that First Nations must go through a generation of peasant farming on the road to American citizenship.[31] Allotting lands in severalty was, Commissioner Atkins asserted, "the dawn of their emancipation from the bonds of bar- barism, which for centuries have held their people in an iron grasp. . . . [O]pposition comes from or is instigated by squaw men and half-breeds" who the Commissioner was sure were only out to cheat ignorant red men (Atkins 1887:x).

Coupled with insistence that First Nations go through the societal stage of primitive agriculture was adamant insistence that their children speak only English:

> There is not an Indian pupil . . . who is permitted to study any other language than our own vernacular—the language of the greatest, most powerful, and enterprising nationalities beneath the sun. The English language as taught in America is good enough for all her people of all races. . . . Every nation is jealous of its own language, and no nation ought to be more so than ours, which approaches nearer than any other nationality to the perfect protection of its people. [Atkins 1887:xxi]

Interestingly, back in 1871 when the Peace Policy was inaugurated, the Indian Affairs Office conferred with representatives of church missionary organizations, and the Honorable William Welsh, speaking for the Epis- copal Society, said,

> I will refer to one point of great interest; that is the use of their

own language among the Indians. Some of us had the same idea that they should teach them nothing but English, but those who were the strongest advocates, now think it best to teach them their own language first, and they will afterward acquire the English much easier. . . . [W]e have found it far better to instruct them in their own language, and also to teach them English as fast as we can. [RCIA for 1871:177]

Allotment in severalty carried provision for limiting reservations to the total of the family farms, selling off "surplus" land. An Indian Commission traveled for a year to thirty reservations to discuss reductions. They spent the second week of February 1887 at the Blackfeet Agency, concluding with a treaty limiting Blackfoot to a rectangle between Birch Creek and the Canadian line, extending east from the mountains only forty miles, to Cut Bank Creek. Seventeen and a half million acres would then be made available "to the public"—excluding Indians.

In the opinion of the Commissioners, these Indians are not yet prepared to take lands in severalty, and even if they were so prepared, they declare positively that the country occupied by them is entirely unsuitable for that purpose. . . . It is in no sense a good agricultural country. . . . [I]f the Indians in northern Montana are ever to become self-supporting, they must follow the pursuits which the whites by long experience have found the country best adapted to—cattle, sheep, and horse-raising. . . . The promise of stock cattle was the principal inducement which led to the cession of the vast territory relinquished to the Government. [Atkins 1887:xxx]

A few years later, Commissioner Morgan remarked, "If the Indians are expected to thrive by agriculture they should not be thrust aside onto sterile plains" (Morgan 1891:5). The price to be paid the Blackfoot for being thrust aside was $150,000 annually for ten years, not in cash but, as usual, in stock, provisions, clothing, and tools. Eighty years later, the federal Indian Claims Commission found that the payment amounted to 29 cents per acre for land worth then 80 cents per acre (Indian Claims Commission 1967:287). Following the special commissioners' recommendation, it would be twenty years before allotment came to the reservation.

Commissioner Atkins was succeeded by John Oberly, previously Superintendent of Indian Schools. He concluded his first annual report with stirring words:

[T]he degrading communism of the tribal-reservation system
gives to the individual no incentive to labor. . . . The Indian . . .
must be imbued with the exalting egotism of American civilization, so that he will say "I" instead of "We," and "This is mine,"
instead of "This is ours." . . . The Government must . . . compel
the Indian . . . into assimilation with the masses of the Republic—
into the path of national duty. [Oberly 1888:lxxxix]

In May 1888, Congress approved the treaty negotiated the previous year,
signed by 222 Blackfoot "chiefs, head-men, and principal men," led by
Onesta-Poka (White Calf), Mokska-Atose (Big Nose, also called Three
Suns), and Em-ki-o-toss (Fast Buffalo Horse). The interpreters, who signed
their assurance that the Indians "thoroughly understood" the terms of
the treaty, were Will Russell, whose mother was the Piegan woman Glit-
tering In Front, father said to be a white man, and Joe Kipp, the trader
whose mother was Mandan, father white. Perhaps the only concession to
Piegan interests was in Article V, stipulating Indians engaged in "pastoral pursuits," not only "cultivation of the soil," would qualify for prefer-
ence in distribution of stock, goods, subsistence, and implements (Oberly
1888:302–304, 316–319).

Insima (Mrs. Yellow Kidney) described the early reservation settlement, about 1887, from Piegan experience:

Yellow Wolf [her husband then] told father that he was going to
Browning's Willow Creek to see if it was a good place to build a
home. Moved with another family, Black Bear [cousin of Insima's
brother Oliver Sanderville's wife Mary].

Moved. Camped right where Browning is now. Rode and
looked Willow Creek over and decided on a place on which they
can settle down and soon to get cattle and cut hay.

Next day moved to mountains to cut house logs . . . and poles
for corrals. When through hauled them down as far as Browning on wagons. Build house there. Finished. From there used to
go to Old Agency [on Badger Creek] for rations. Yellow Wolf got
mowing machine, rake, and grindstone from government. Bear
Paw joined them and asked, Why they didn't let them know they
were going to move. Yellow Wolf: Thought I wouldn't want to
move. After bought machinery a white man came—Mr. Stuart—
He married an Indian woman. Told Yellow Wolf, I heard about
this place and you're going to have a lot of hay. Come to put it up
for you so you can give me some. Agreed. First time they learned
how to cut hay and put it up. When through put up corral and
barn. Then heard some cattle was to be issued to them.

Black Bear said, They should winter cattle at Cut Bank because here there isn't much shelter. We'll take hay down there.

Yellow Wolf went to Old Agency. Each family got four cows
and four calves regardless of size of families. They told him about
milk and he knew how to milk and so did it right away but didn't
know how to make butter.

North of Browning they found a place [to winter cattle]—
thick trees for good shelter. All three—yet—Black Bear and Bear
Paw had hayracks and in no time had half the hay there. Sometimes made 3 trips a day. When enough hay there they moved
there. Made house there of cotton[wood] trees. [Sommers (Dietrich) 1939, interview 8/16/39]

Yellow Wolf at this time had three wives, one senior and one junior to
Insima.

There were, in 1888, according to Agent Baldwin, 2,268 Blackfoot, of
whom 130 could read, 260 able to converse in English, and 285 families
in houses, with 83 percent of the people's subsistence from government
rations, 12 percent from "civilized pursuits," and 5 percent from hunting
and gathering. Piegan now farmed 340 acres and had 2,300 acres fenced.
The agency's police force was praised, as usual in Blackfeet agents' reports, and in part due to their efforts, at last there was a year without
reported homicides or horse raiding; 34 Indians had been punished, most
for intoxication (there was now a little jail in the agency) by the agency
Court of Indian Offenses,[32] with three local Indian judges—not usually
actually convened, according to what Agent Steell heard in 1891 (Steell
1891:267). There was a church building, although not yet a missionary,
and 86 church members. Agent Baldwin claimed that in 1888 no Medicine Lodge had been held. He had forbidden the policemen to attend,
and demanded the previous autumn that anyone taking a government-
issued brood mare must promise not to take part. Baldwin displays his
ignorance of the ceremony he denounces by stating that "none of the females were permitted to participate" in the Sun Dance—a Blackfoot Okan
("Sun Dance") is led by a vowing woman, the Holy Woman (Baldwin
1888:150–153).

A new commissioner, Thomas Morgan, took charge of Indian Affairs
in 1889. Morgan fervently advocated off-reservation boarding schools
such as Carlisle and Hampton, already in operation, even though Indian
parents strongly objected to sending their children far away. It was true
that many children died from tuberculosis and other diseases flourishing in the crowded schools among poorly nourished children. The commissioner made the astonishing statement that, "Owing to the peculiar
surroundings of the mass of Indian children, they are homeless and are

ignorant of those simplest arts that make home possible." It followed, according to Morgan, that schools for Indians "must be a boarding and industrial school, where the students can be trained in the homely duties and become inured to that toil which is the basis of health, happiness, and prosperity." "Methodical regularity of daily routine" was significantly important, he added (Morgan 1889:99–100). Furthermore,

> It is of prime importance that a fervent patriotism should be awakened in [Indian children's] minds. . . . [They should] memorize choice maxims and literary gems, in which inspiring thoughts and noble sentiments are embodied. . . . [T]hey should be made familiar with the lives of great and good men and women in American history. . . . They should hear little or nothing of the "wrongs of the Indians," and of the injustice of the white race. If their unhappy history is alluded to it should be to contrast it with the better future that is within their grasp. . . . It is more profitable to instruct them as to their duties and obligations, than as to their wrongs. [Morgan 1889:101–102]

"Civilization" was progressing rapidly on the Blackfeet Reservation. A new agent, John Catlin, echoed his predecessors in praising the people's eagerness to take homesteads and put in crops, and their deep disappointment when, this time, drought ruined their potential harvest. The only reluctance Catlin noticed was that of older men with more than one wife to choose between them to satisfy the agent's demand to end polygyny. Baldwin had mentioned, in his report, that lacking a priest and with the nearest marriage registry 250 miles away (and no one there speaking Blackfoot), he could not expect couples to attain legal marriage; he asked for a simple form that he as agent could fill out to register marriages. Catlin observed that younger Piegan were in monogamous relationships. He reported a population of 2,263—953 males and 1,340 females—with 160 families in houses and 215 in farming "or other civilized pursuits." There were 78 Indians born, 21 half-breeds; 817 taken sick or wounded, 21 deaths, 53 Indians with conjunctivitis, 22 with otorrhea (ear infection), 23 tonsilitis, 36 cases mumps, 47 whooping cough, 9 remittent fever, 6 tubercular (4 scrofula). Catlin's figure of 150 church members must include those who came to the Catholic services occasionally held by priests visiting from St. Peter's Mission (Catlin 1889:222–223; RCIA for 1889:504–505, 522–523, 528–535). The next year, 1890, the Jesuits built a Catholic boarding school accommodating 100 children, Holy Family Mission (Fig. 6), on Two Medicine River, land for it donated by White Calf and money ($15,000) donated by Katherine Drexel, a wealthy Philadelphian who founded a religious order. Forty-five children were sent to the Carlisle Indian industrial school in Pennsylvania, including a son of Running Crane and Richard Sanderville (originally Sandoval), brother of Insima and later, John Ewers's esteemed interpreter and collaborator (Catlin 1890:114–115; Ewers 1978) (Fig. 7) [photo of Richard Sanderville].

By 1891, the 1,953 Piegan owned 4,149 horses and mules, 1,986 cattle, and 404 domestic fowl. Their wagons freighted 275,400 pounds, earning them $3,442. They occupied 533 houses, 444 could speak passable English, and 176 could read it. (If any wrote or read Blackfoot, it is not reported by the agent.) No families lived by hunting and gathering, 83 percent of Blackfoot subsistence through government rations, and 17 percent through "civilized pursuits" (stock raising, freighting, 19 men employed as police, a few others employed at the agency). The new agent, George Steell, determined to stamp out whiskey, for several years sold at a saloon in Robare just over Birch Creek (Fig. 8). He succeeded in getting three white men convicted, fined, and imprisoned. Steell, himself a cattleman from Texas, praised Commissioner Morgan for recognizing that the Blackfeet Reservation was fit only for stock raising—"their only salvation," is how he put it—and he said the Piegan competed for the best hay land. They had greatly appreciated receiving 800 heifers and 25

FIG. 6a. Holy Family Mission School for Blackfeet children boys' band during bishop's visit. Credit: Marquette University Archives, Bureau of Catholic Indian Mission Records.

Fɪɢ. 6b. Holy Family Mission school girls in school uniforms, 1923. Credit: Marquette University Archives, Bureau of Catholic Indian Mission Records.

bulls in August 1890, which gave them 550 calves. Enough rain and, as of August 26, no harmful frosts should have produced good crops, but only the manured school plot bore well, convincing Steell and the agency farm instructors that the reservation land lost its fertility quickly. Steell's predecessor had "loaned out" the sawmill to non-Indians for two years; Steell reclaimed and repaired it, moved it into mountain timber, and intended to use the milled lumber to build better homes than the Piegans' "very poorest of little log cabins, poles for roofing, covered with earth." (Steell may not have realized that a well-chinked log cabin with thick sod roof is warmer than an uninsulated frame house.) The agency buildings were dilapidated, bottom logs rotted, roofs leaking: he anticipated moving to a new agency before too long (Steell 1891:265–267; RCIA for 1891:78–79, 96–97). This was accomplished in 1895.

[Pl. 2 Chief Mountain, center of the Amskapi Pikuni landscape, seen from Duck Lake in northwestern sector of Reservation.]

The final location for the Blackfeet agency, on Willow Creek, was near the Great Northern Railroad line. This transcontinental major line was built through the reservation in 1891, without permission from Piegan since the president of the United States had reserved the right to put railroads through in Article 8 of the 1887 treaty. Sixty thousand ties were cut, for which the Blackfeet were to be compensated. With fast commercial transportation to and through the Rockies, the mountains forming the western sector of the reservation lured both gold prospectors and wealthy

FIG. 7. Richard Sanderville and Little Blaze, standing before a pile of bison bones to be shipped out to be ground into fertilizer. Credit: Blackfeet THPO.

FIG. 8. Crossing Birch Creek in wagon at Robare, early 20th century. Credit: Blackfeet THPO.

Eastern outdoors recreation enthusiasts. The 1887 treaty had forced the
Blackfoot to cede the Sweet Grass Hills, at that time overrun with gold
prospectors. Now the Rockies' Front Range beckoned. Like the Sweet
Grass Hills, the mountains held timber, elk, beaver, and berries. More than
these, a cosmic elk lived in a mountain lake, Walter McClintock was told,
and Thunder spent the summers in a lodge high on Chief Mountain (Mc-
Clintock 1910:61, 425–426). None of this mattered to the local entrepreneurs, including professional guide James Willard Schultz and his former
employer, trader Joe Kipp, nor to George Bird Grinnell, professed "friend
of the Indian" and real friend of Teddy Roosevelt and Gifford Pinchot.
Grinnell, editor of *Forest and Stream* magazine, prolific writer of ethnographies, in 1895 led negotiations with White Calf, Three Suns (Big Nose),
Little Dog (son of earlier chief), and councils attended by large numbers
of Piegan. The government concluded a formal agreement whereby the
Blackfeet ceded the mountain strip for $1,500,000—half what the Indians
considered a fair price. The agreement stipulated the Indians retained
rights to go onto the ceded land, hunt, fish, and cut timber for their own
use (not commercially). Beginning in 1901, Grinnell lobbied hard to make
the strip a national park. It was legally created in 1910 as Glacier National Park, with additional land on the west side of the Divide, in the
Salish and Kutenais' Flathead Valley. Hunting, fishing, and timber cutting
were banned in the Park, no exception made for Indians; white landhold-
ers along the western strip *were* permitted to continue their accustomed
hunting! Curly Bear, Wolf Plume, and Bird Rattler visited Washington
in 1915 to protest the way the park was renaming its landmarks, negat-
ing Blackfoot history connected to named places. For decades after the
initial creation of the park, the National Park Service tried to extend its
eastern border by taking over more of the reservation, from East Glacier
north to and including St. Mary's River to its crossing the Canadian border. This would wholly include Chief Mountain, too. These repeated attempts were adamantly opposed by the Piegan, who insist still that they
had ceded only mineral rights to the western reservation strip in 1895,
and had never made further concessions. In fact, neither Blackfoot nor
Salish and Kutenai were invited to the negotiations for Glacier Park, nor
to those permitting the Great Northern Railway to exploit it. Very few
Indians were ever hired as park staff or in the Great Northern hotels except as menial laborers. Picturesquely outfitted Blackfoot were engaged
to camp in tipis beside the hotel in East Glacier, perform dances, and greet
tourists at the train station, especially during the 1930s and 1940s, when
these poorly paid show jobs were about all older Piegan men and women
could get (Fig. 9). People said they enjoyed the admiration of tourists.
Pleasant summer days on the lawn of the big hotel never obliterated the
conviction that in 1895 the Nation had not, so far as they understood the

FIG. 9. "Glacier Park Indians." Amskapi Pikuni were taken to New York to advertise Great Northern Railroad and Hotels holidays in Glacier National Park. Credit: Blackfeet THPO.

negotiators and interpreters, given up their mountains, and therefore, subsequent deals made by the Park Service were without merit (Keller and Turek 1998; Burnham 2000:187–218).

Clark Wissler apparently felt that by 1890, the Aamsskaapi-piikani had moved from their independent indigenous cultural pattern to the encapsulated dependency he saw in the early 20th century. Or to put it succinctly as human ecology, they had shifted from bison procurement to stock raising. His sketchy 1933 outline for his "History of the Blackfoot Indians In Contact With White Culture" skips from 1889 to 1898–1901, 1905, 1907, 1911, 1916, then very briefly refers to 1921–23, 1925, 1926, 1927, 1929, 1930, and 1931.

Twentieth-Century Blackfoot

A pattern established by 1890 held through the 20th century. Stock raising was the only viable economy, but it was vulnerable to severe winters, droughts, national and world markets, and until the last quarter of the

century, Indian Agents' control. It requires extensive rangeland and relatively little labor, so limits the number of families that can be supported
on the reservation. Who shall be privileged?

From 1889 to 1919, the course of Piegan life ran along steadily increasing alignment with the dominant Anglo society. No one demurred
from the conclusion that cattle must be the basis of the economy. This had
several correlates. The superintendent of the boarding school, in 1898, explained why the school held a herd of a hundred: "Without exception,
all Piegan children who for any reason leave the reservation ultimately
return to it, and the cattle interest is practically the only business here to
which they can turn their hand for a living . . . this industry is essential to
an ample furnishing of these boys for their life work" (Matson 1898:186).
The irrigation engineer stated, "Irrigation alone is the method by which
the Indians on the Blackfeet Reservation can be made self-supporting"
because "[t]he wild grasses are becoming shorter every year on the at one
time natural hay meadows, and it is only a question of time till no hay
can be harvested without irrigation. The lack of hay and shelter were the
causes that led to the 40 per cent loss of cattle during the winter from January 1 to April 15, 1898" (Jenkins 1898:187). As early as 1884, Piegan were
irrigating hay meadows and watering cattle from ditches, and as Jenkins
mentioned in his 1898 report, the ditches they built and maintained considerably amplified those he and his crews constructed (Fig. 10). Irrigated
hay meadows were the foundation of Piegan self-sufficiency, reasonably
well achieved by 1900. White ranchers and wheat farmers in ceded Blackfoot territory east of the reservation were also irrigating, drawing from
the Milk River. Realizing how crucial water would be to agriculture along
the High Line (northernmost Montana, around present Highway 2 and
Great Northern [Burlington Northern] railroad), the United States wanted to divert the St. Mary's River so that Canada could not draw its water
in Alberta. The Milk, arcing through southern Alberta, also potentially
could be drained in Alberta, and Canada proposed in 1904 to divert the
Milk north into the St. Mary's. The two nations signed an agreement in
1909, after several years of negotiations—none of them involving Blackfoot—combining on paper the waters of the two river basins, St. Mary's
and Milk, disregarding that the St. Mary's ultimately flowed into Hudson's Bay and the Milk into the Missouri and so ultimately into the Gulf
of Mexico! Canada and the United States would divide the combined water equally. The previous year, 1908, the U.S. Supreme Court had ruled in
Winters v. United States that reservation waters are reserved for the reservation's Indians, restoring diverted Milk River water to the Fort Belknap
Reservation Indians in eastern Montana. The year after the International
Boundary Water Treaty, 1910, farmers in Montana's Havre area extended

FIG. 10. Irrigation canal, Two Medicine Valley, early 20th century. Credit: Blackfeet THPO

their irrigation projects to draw on the St. Mary's as well as the Milk, thus taking without acknowledgment, much less negotiation, substantial water rightfully belonging to the Blackfeet Reservation and necessary for its hay meadows (Clow 2003).

Piegan in 1898 numbered 2,022, according to the agent's "particular care and attention" to a census: 501 males over 18, 644 females over 14 (note difference in "age of maturity"), 236 boys between 6 and 16, 185 girls within those ages, and totals, 970 males and 1,052 females. In April 1898, the ceded western strip was opened and more than 500 non-Indian men rushed in to prospect. Agent Fuller dryly predicted that, no gold having appeared by late August, most would rush out by November. On the reservation, 1,000 acres were cultivated by Indians, 37,000 were fenced, 1,000 bushels of oats and barley raised, 9,060 bushels of "vegetables" (mainly potatoes), 6,000 tons of hay cut, 500 pounds of butter made, and of livestock owned by Indians, there were 20,000 horses and mules (nearly all horses), 10,002 cattle, and 500 domestic fowl. The freighting business had drastically declined once the railroad came in, earning only $737, while the "value of products of Indian labor disposed of to Government" was $33,994 and "otherwise disposed of," $50,000. Beef cattle were the principal products of Indian labor, they selling 800,000 pounds of beef to the government and shipping "several train loads of prime steers . . . to eastern markets." Although the Crow sold 14,000 horses ("Indian ponies") at five to twelve dollars per head in 1900–01 (Edwards 1902:258), the Black-feet agent makes no mention of selling horses. Agent Fuller said 800 Indi-ans could read, 1,000 speak passable English, about 620 families lived in houses, and subsistence was 50 percent by "labor in civilized pursuits," 50 percent by government rations. Approximately 155 Indians were counted as church members (whether to the new Methodist mission or to Catholic Holy Family is not specified); the next year, 1899, the number went up to 507 (RCIA for 1899:569). The Court of Indian Offenses, presided over by three "full blood men of intelligence and good repute," Shorty White Grass, Running Crane, and Wolf Tail (in 1901, Wolf Tail, Little Plume, and White Calf [RCIA for 1901:765]) (RCIA for 1898:675), "dealt with 160 'In-dian criminals' (Fuller 1898:182–186; RCIA for 1898:602–603, 618–619). Two doctors served the Piegan, one at the agency and one at the Wil-low Creek boarding school. They reported an epidemic of measles among the children, some cases progressing into fatal pneumonia. The agency doctor treated 790 cases, exclusive of office visits for minor ailments, re-corded 32 full-blood births and 18 "part bloods," and deaths of 14 per-sons over 5 years of age and 20 younger than 5 (Martin 1898:183–184). A census conducted in 1896 by the Holy Family Mission recorded for the Two Medicine valley, 73 houses and 295 people; for Whitetail Creek, 30 houses, 110 people; for Willow Creek 47 houses, 164 people; an average of four persons per family; and a total of 248 "Married Indians" (*legally* married, presumably).

The largest part of the 1898 Blackfeet Agency annual report was con-tributed by Dr. Z. T. Daniel, physician to the Willow Creek school and the hospital in Browning at the agency, on Willow Creek 2.5 miles east of the school. Dr. Daniel declared,

> The location of the Willow Creek School is probably the most des-olate, dreary, unfruitful, rocky, barren, cold, windy, and inhospi-table spot on this reserve. . . . [A] cellar at the school floods every spring. . . . The location of the new agency, also, was another fatal fall down . . . in a quagmire and alkali bed, where a tree won't grow and a vegetable can't be raised . . . where the wind howls in terrific blasts the year round, driving snow, dust, pebbles, and everything movable before it, rocking the hospital and dwellings like aspens. . . . The central part of the [hospital] structure is two story, and in high winds it don't rock like a cradle in the deep . . . the building shivers so in the wind. . . . The hospital building is a fraud . . . wholly inadapted for the purpose intended. There is not one feature of it that is acceptable. [Daniel 1898:184–185]

Within these miserable structures, Dr. Daniel attempted to deal with "tuberculosis in one form or another [which] affects nearly all Indian children." He surgically removed scrofulous (tubercular) ulcers, though the operation was only a remission offering temporary relief. "This disease is the worst foe I have to deal with. . . . If the Indian could be freed from this disease he would increase like ourselves, but it seems that the day is rapidly approaching when there will not be a pure or full-blooded Indian on the face of the earth, and the cause of his extinction will be tuberculosis" (Daniel 1898:185). The school superintendent in 1901 echoed Dr. Daniel in reporting that during the nine years he was at the Blackfeet School, 418 children were enrolled, of whom 46 died, 37 of them from tuberculosis ("consumption" or "scrofula") (Matson 1901:257). Not until 1905 was the agency boarding school moved to a sheltered, pleasant location in the Cut Bank valley north of Browning, and not until 1909 was the Willow Creek building closed. A day school opened in Browning in 1905, too (Farr 1984:53, 60).

William Jones, Commissioner of Indian Affairs, in 1901 announced a new policy ordering all "ration agencies" to discontinue issuing rations to able-bodied Indians, except "in return for labor performed, either for themselves or for the benefit of the tribe." Jones claimed that "in almost every instance the ration is a gratuity and not stipulated by any treaty, as in the case of the Sioux" under the Black Hills treaty of 1877 (Jones 1902:6). Insofar as Indian Affairs continued to help build Piegan herds, as it did in 1901 by issuing 3,500 fine two-year-old heifers, the policy could be reasonable, although whether rations were a gratuity not entailed in treaties seems questionable. The 1901 heifers were branded with the Piegans' own brands, by this time totaling some five hundred, and now the number of cattle, 18,000, equaled the number of horses and mules, 17,006. There were now 1,000 domestic fowl, too (RCIA for 1901:713). Jones's policy on rations dovetailed with his policy on Indian education, based on his idea that schools must transform the "wild Indian of the plain into a quiet everyday average citizen" (Jones 1898:10). He lauded the boarding and day schools where, he rhapsodized, "The child of the wigwam becomes a modern Aladdin, who has only to rub the Government lamp to gratify his wishes" as he enjoys the affluence of hot baths, electric lights, and similar luxuries (Jones 1901:2). By Indian Affairs' own statistics, the majority of Indian young people returned from the schools "is doing as well in his own environment as the same type of the American,' that is, working at earning a comparable living (Jones 1902:40–41). Among the 2,043 Piegan in 1901, 1,100 read and 1,200 spoke English, and every single person wore "citizen's dress." Bottom line, still, was that in 1901, half of

Piegan subsistence came from Government rations (RCIA for 1901:712). Four years later, 1905, the agent, Captain Dare, assured Commissoner Francis Leupp that "[t]he issue of rations to all able-bodied Indians has ceased." Yet, he admitted, opportunities for earning wages, three summer months on crews fencing the reservation or constructing the Cut Bank Irrigation Ditch, were "not sufficient to supply his wants during the year" (Dare 1906:237).

Comparison of Aamsskaapi-Piikani with Canadian Blackfoot Reserves

Wissler copied figures from the 1904 reports to Canada's Department of Indian Affairs, to assess whether Blackfoot under Canadian dominion differed significantly from those in Montana. From the Peigan [Canadian spelling for Northern Pikuni] report he compiled this list:

TABLE 1.15. Canadian Blackfoot Reserves, 1904

Churches	0	Mowers	37	Steers	167
Schools	1	Plows	35	Cows	680
Log houses	92	Horse rakes	21	Young cattle	1093
Frame houses	21	Wagons	113	Row boats	6
Horse stables	36	Buggies, etc.	39	Rifles	20
Cattle stables	25	Horses	300	Shotguns	35
Milk houses	2	Mares	440	Tents	97
Colts	300	Crops	0		

Population for the Peigan Reserve was 1196: 294 men, 408 women, 281 boys, 213 girls. Like their southern cousins, they occupied cabins in winter, tents in summer. Lucien and Jane Hanks noted, more than thirty years later, that the North Blackfoot "move in winter to small log shacks along the river where, though they are more cramped for space, they have warmth, easy access to firewood and water, and many neighbours. The houses provided by [the government] are usually lacking in these four respects" (Hanks and Hanks 1950:113). Canadian Blackfoot had, already by 1904, opportunity to earn money by mining coal on the North Blackfoot reserve, and harvesting sugar beets. Sugar beets remained an important crop relying on Indian labor in the white-owned fields.

The Board of Indian Commissioners advising the Indian Affairs Office in the United States decided in 1914 to compare Canadian and U.S. Indian policies. Its secretary, Frederick Abbott, traveled through Canada visiting reserves, including the Blackfoot in Alberta (Samek 1987:9–10).

Wissler consulted Abbott's report, published in 1915, and copied these figures:

TABLE 1.16. Blackfoot in Alberta, 1915

	Blood	Blackfoot	Piegan (Canada)	Piegan (U.S.)
[Area, in acres	354,086	175,580	93,141	1,503,450]
[Acres per capita	310.61	233.5	203.8	529*]
Population	1140	752	457	2842
Per capita income	$54.10	$76.59	$80.08	$117.74
Horses	2458	1871	1434	6100
Cattle	3279	1085	1060	12,106
Sheep	—	—	—	3,600
Hogs	—	—	5	510
Acres farmed	1737	36	1824	5,000
[acres per capita	1.5	0.04	4	1.76]
Administrative cost	$7,500	$6,400	$5,020	$25,302

*The Montana reservation had been allotted in severalty by 1914, allowing leasing of acreage to whites and non-enrolled mixed-bloods; Canadian Blackfoot could apply for "location tickets" to forty-acre parcels of farmland, basically usufruct rights (Abbott 1915:52, 82). A generation later, Lucien and Jane Hanks were told that "the South Piegans have the reputation of being modern and sporting, thus less true to Indian ways" (Hanks and Hanks 1950:151).

The original table breaks down income by sources; farm products and hay; beef; wages; fishing, hunting and trapping (only the Canadian Blackfoot); other industries (this would include coal mining in Alberta). "Administrative cost" is detailed, with all four reserves employing an agent and at least one clerk, physician, farmer, stockman, the Canadian reserves each an interpreter, the Blood a mail carrier, the Canadian Peigan a blacksmith, and the Montana Piegan four "mechanics," eight forest guards, eleven policemen, and five "miscellaneous" (Abbott 1915:83). Wissler made no comments on Abbott's table; it would seem to indicate the Montana Piegan were more "progressed" than their Canadian congeners, in terms of ratio of cattle to horses, diversity of livestock, and per capita income. Variations between the three Alberta reserves indicate, too, how local conditions and particular choices, of agents and of Indian people, affect human ecology.

Whether Wissler influenced her to develop this project, we have not been able to discover, but in 1939, Columbia University professor of anthropology Ruth Benedict set up an ethnographic field training "laboratory" straddling the 49th parallel, some of her graduate students on the Canadian reserves, others in Montana. She also induced the psychologist Abram Maslow to come out to evaluate whether his research on human psychological needs could be generalized to non-Western people. Maslow, a New Yorker throughout his life, was too uncomfortable in Blackfoot country to persevere, but the students completed their assignments, resulting in Esther Goldfrank's *Changing Configurations in the Social Organization of a Blackfoot Tribe during the Reserve Period: The Bloods of Alberta, Canada* (1966), Lucien and Jane Richardson Hanks's *Observations on Northern Blackfoot Kinship* (1945) and *Tribe Under Trust: A Study of the Blackfoot Reserve of Alberta* (1950), and Oscar Lewis's article, "Manly-Hearted Women Among the North Piegan," (1941) (his dissertation, published 1942 as *The Effects of White Contact upon Blackfoot Culture*, was drawn from library research). Another student, Sue Sommers (Dietrich), did not publish her Piegan interviews but we have included excerpts from her transcription of Insima's reminiscences (see also Kehoe 1996). Hana Samek followed the comparison idea in her 1987 book, *The Blackfoot Confederacy 1880–1920*.

In her autobiography, Esther Goldfrank gives a 1940 outline, written up by Lucien Hanks, of the projected comparative study of Blackfoot:

> The Psychological Effects of Certain Economic and Administrational Systems of the Blackfoot Reserves
> An Historical Introduction to Blackfoot Culture—to be written by Oscar Lewis
> The Economic and Administrational Influences on the Blood reserve—Goldfrank
> The Northern Blackfoot Reserve—Jane and Lucien Hanks
> The Blackfoot Reservation of the Southern Piegan—Rae Walowitz
> An analysis of the foregoing data—Ruth Benedict (Goldfrank 1977:148)

(Walowitz was married to a political writer, Max Geltman, and did not continue in anthropology.)

Goldfrank remembers the other couple with the Montana Piegan, Gitel and Robert Steed, and "a young woman" whose name she forgot, who would have been Sue Sommers (Goldfrank 1977:128). World War II deflected Benedict's plan for coordinated publication of the several ethnographic studies. She, as well as the students (including the women) turned to the war effort, and the students' experiences led to professional work in other regions. Benedict died in 1948, a year after Clark Wissler. It may be that she found it painful to contemplate further work with the

Piegan material, for she was deeply affected by the tragic death of the project's helpful interpreter, Jim Little Plume, riding in a car driven by Bob Steed that overturned on a gravel road. Surviving project members we have spoken with—Sue Sommers Dietrich, Jane Richardson Hanks, Ruth Maslow Lewis (Oscar's wife and collaborator, Abram Maslow's sister)—agreed that their experiences with Blackfoot people were important to them, and helped orient them to the larger global issues with which they engaged after the war.

Benedict felt her experience with Blackfoot revealed a better way of life, although her version of Blackfoot was, to put it mildly, uncommon; a Benedict biographer sums it up thus:

> The Blackfoot . . . are optimistic and *free from violence*. They operate according to an ethic of care: leaders identify with followers, the wealthy make certain that everyone is provided for, and leadership positions are open to talented individuals. [Banner 2003:426, summarizing a 1942 article Benedict published in the *Atlantic Monthly*; our italics]

Over the summers of 1938, 1939, and 1941, the Hankses listened to many North Blackfoot (Siksika) whose parents were young adults when Treaty 7 was signed in 1877. Their informants had themselves witnessed selling off Siksika land in 1911 and 1917, from which the government held for them a trust fund and, still in 1938–1941, annually provided from it, rations of beef (paying Indian ranchers for their own cattle which were then butchered for the rancher as his ration), flour and tea, funds for building and furnishing houses, and for newlyweds, a wagon and team of horses (Hanks and Hanks 1950:xiii). Siksika informants told the Hankses that after the 1885 Riel Rebellion and disappearance of the bison, their parents realized there would be no more battles in which men could gain glory. Nor would there be months of hunting, moving camp, processing and preserving bison and plant foods. There was now an abundance of leisure and relatively sedentary clustering around agencies handing out rations. From these circumstances, remarked upon also by Clark Wissler in 1916 ("at the time . . . there were few outlets for the interests of young men" [Wissler 1916:870]), all-comrades societies dances and bundle ceremonies were held more frequently, and people sought to be distinguished as ritual leaders and bundle owners. "Prices for membership in the Horn society soared from a gun and blanket before treaty to a horse, and from one horse to several horses," drawing from herds increasing from 540 on the reserve in 1885, to 1,085 in 1890 and nearly 3,000 about 1900, when sixty horses might be given for a medicine pipe (Hanks and Hanks 1950:25).

Cessation of horse raiding no doubt helped each community hold and increase its members' herds.

Siksika, like Piegan, were pressured to farm, and like their southern congeners, had agents who learned the hard way that ranching is the only viable enterprise on the high Plains. The Hankses were told that during the 1890s, what crops of oats and potatoes Siksika did harvest, they sold to whites, depending on rations for food. By the end of the 1890s, white ranchers around the Alberta reserves went through the agent to hire haying crews of band leader and men, paying the crews with butchered steers or, later, cash to the leader (Hanks and Hanks 1950:29). During this decade of the 1890s, initial Siksika resistance to raising cattle (rumors said that families with their own cattle would no longer be given rations) gave way to willingness to accept government issue stock. Parallel to Commissioner Jones's Indian policy in the United States, the Siksika agent in 1901 decreed that no rations would be issued to able-bodied men (Hanks and Hanks 1950:33). Paradoxically, the same agent, A. J. Markle, pushed selling half the Siksika reserve in order to use the money to pay for rations! His objection to rations, though couched in the customary moralistic rhetoric of inspiring manhood in the degraded savage, vanished when it was the Indians' own money buying their rations (Hanks and Hanks 1950:49). From 1920 through the 1940s, the Siksika enjoyed an agent who kindly hired white farm instructors and stockmen to manage the farms and herds of improvident Siksika while allowing capable members of the reserve to care for their own, the agent free to continue the little welfare state because the money came from the interest-bearing trust fund built from the land sales.

Esther Schiff Goldfrank was directed by Benedict to the Blood Reserve. Mrs. Goldfrank was then a 1918 Barnard College graduate who had taken courses from Franz Boas, the leading anthropologist of the time, and the next year became his secretary. As such, she had accompanied him to the Southwest to visit Pueblos. She married, in 1921, a man with three young sons, giving up graduate study to care for them and the daughter she bore, until in 1935 her husband suffered a fatal heart attack. Returning then to graduate work at Columbia University, she took courses with Benedict and in 1939 requested to be included in the "Ethnographic Laboratory" project comparing the four Blackfoot reserves. Benedict assigned her, along with a younger man and woman, to stay with a Blood family, where Benedict would visit them later in the summer—as it turned out, too depressed by Jim Little Plume's death to work. The following year, 1940, Goldfrank married a scholar specializing in Chinese studies, and did not return to Blackfoot country.

Goldfrank described the Kainai as "wealthy," meaning by their own standards, number of horses. She noted that to curb the focus on horses, the Canadian Indian Affairs department had offered them twenty cows in exchange for twenty horses, and through that deal, "rich Blood" with plenty of horses had also built up cattle herds, prospering until the drought and severe winter of 1919–20 that decimated all the Blackfoot herds, particularly cattle (Goldfrank 1977:145). Like the Hankses, Goldfrank carefully observed the material aspects of Blackfoot life, compiling (with the younger woman on her team) statistics on economic and political change. Clark Wissler, reviewing her 1945 monograph, praised her for "giv[ing] most of her space to well-chosen statistics and case histories," permitting readers to construct their own views of Kainai history (Goldfrank 1977:149). Her observations were that the "rich," families with cattle and wheat fields as well as horses in 1939, were generous in giveaways and presentations for transferring bundles, but that it was other well-to-do families who benefited, that is, that horses and valued goods circulated within the upper class, *ototamapsi* (Hanks and Hanks 1950:101) or *istuisanaps*, one who is given respect (Goldfrank 1945:18, 28). Probably because she had managed four children (her stepsons were by then grown, and daughter in a summer camp), Goldfrank was particularly interested in *minipoka*, favored children, and recorded how much was spent upon them; she also noted how prestations for bundles had inflated, then fallen with the 1930s Depression, for example the Long Time Pipe had several times been transferred for one hundred horses, but only for twenty horses, and goods, in 1939 (Goldfrank 1945:29, 42, 45). Asked by Benedict to collect kinship terms, Goldfrank did so, coming afoul of Benedict's expectation of how relationships "ought" to be figured (Goldfrank 1977:143). Concluding her monograph with her list of terms, Goldfrank discussed changes from usage in nomadic band times, particularly more persons termed "grandparent" (*naa'xs*[a]), and suggested that 20th-century elders may have been accorded more prestige because they had experienced the autonomy of the bison-hunting days (Goldfrank 1945:28). While Goldfrank used pseudonyms for the Kainai she lived among, her 1945 monograph is full of vivid descriptions of everyday life on the reserve, especially showing the differences between upper class and commoners.

Comparing the Montana Piegan with the Canadians brings out the effects of local differences, for example, the coal seam on the North Blackfoot Reserve that provided regular winter income for many of its men. Frederick Abbott, in 1915, believed the Canadian policy of issuing "location tickets" for usufruct, instead of allotting land in fee simple, had protected Indians' land, and he praised the policy in the prairie provinces of retaining band chiefs in reserve administrative structure (which Agent Wood had done in 1875 for Montana Piegan) (Abbott 1915:48–52). Samek, more than a half-century later, considered Abbott's a rosy view: her examination in detail of reserve land surrenders after 1908 showed similar takeovers geared to white economic interests, somewhat whitewashed in 1918 by claiming World War I made unilateral governmental actions necessary (Samek 1987;109–118). Samek concluded that Canadian policy and administration were less volatile than those of the United States because Indian affairs employees, including agents, enjoyed civil-service appointments relatively disjunct from the political arena, but both Anglo nations created and maintained disastrous "Indian problems" based on their ideology of Anglo superiority (Samek 1987:179–182).

Wissler's Informal Observations

As he was preparing to retire, at 70, from teaching in the Yale University Department of Anthropology and, at 72, from head Curator of the Department of Anthropology in the American Museum of Natural History, Clark Wissler indulged himself in writing informally about his experiences on reservations, 1902–05. He refrained from identifying either reservations or people, thus readers can only guess which experiences happened with Lakota or Gros Ventres, which with Piegan. In contrast to later ethnographers, Wissler felt it improper to vivify monographs with dramatic cases or personal feelings, so much that we would use today, he considered "unscientific"; these observations he placed in his popular-style *Indian Cavalcade*.

One topic was traders. Wissler declared that traders were the true missionaries, persuading Indians to produce more to reach a higher standard of living (metal knives, kettles, guns, brightly colored cloth and beads, sugar) and conveying such "civilized" ideals as "the notion that it was the man who should produce and dominate his woman" (Wissler 1971:87). Traders did "labor unceasingly to make [the Indian] an up-to-date fighter and a producer of goods . . . for some 200 years" (1971:89). Even after two centuries, Plains people were puzzled that traders seemed unwilling to earn high respect through unstinting generosity. "What is the good of having so much, if nothing can be given away," an elder asked Wissler (1971:91). During his visits to reservations, Wissler saw that most Indians, being illiterate, did not understand exactly how much money was written on the checks they were issued at annuity days. When, formerly, they had traded hides, furs, and pemmican to traders, they were shrewd and firm in getting their money's worth, and if they were given dollar coins, they would buy dollar by dollar, carefully, but with checks, they handed the paper to the traders and took what they were told was the amount of goods owed. When Wissler looked on, traders usually were honest, and overall, he thought they kept honest books; but agents and licensed traders at their agencies supported one another, resulting in Indians seemingly perpetually in debt as they bought on credit and their income was immediately known to the trader. There was also the question of fair profit: should a single sewing needle cost fifty cents because of the high cost of transportation via St. Louis and up the Missouri? (1971:81).

Describing Indian police, Wissler first pictures men in ill-fitting blue uniforms, of good cloth, he says, with plenty of gold buttons, but no one had taken the trouble of tailoring the suits to the individual men. Then, too, the policemen wore cowboy boots with the high, sloping heels meant for stirrups, unsteady enough for anyone walking in them but especially so for men accustomed all their lives to moccasins. To Wissler, the police walked like Chinese women with bound feet—but not to laugh; those men carried "oversized six-shooters" and rifles. Indian police forces, he argued, were the one real success story of the northern Plains reservations, and this was because the police were recruited (unknowingly, on the part of most agents, though not John Wood) from all-comrades soldiers' societies. Thus, effective indigenous law enforcement was continued, enhanced by Indian ritual and sanctified power (1971:110). Wissler observed one sitting Court of Indian Offenses, quite probably Montana Blackfeet, the three solemn dignified judges in properly tailored black suits, the odor of a pipe offering filling the air, the proceedings entirely in the native language except for translations given to the agent and his guest the ethnographer (1971:129–138; Farr 1984:46). Later, Wissler invited the three judges to dinner, and was surprised when the men appeared in formal dinner dress of Prince Albert coats, white tie, creased trousers, well-shined shoes, and with one, a gold-headed cane—Wissler, the host, embarrassed at his own everyday clothes until one of his guests graciously remarked that of course Wissler would not travel encumbered by luggage for such elegant clothes (Wissler 1971:139; see Farr 1984:154 for photograph). Wissler comments here on the barbarous decree by the government that all policemen, all judges, and all male prisoners must have their hair cut. Not only does he think the "fanaticism . . . against male long hair" stupid, he is worried that what is meant as punishment to offenders is also demanded of their police and judges! Indians, he remarks, "had become reconciled to such inconsistencies" (Wissler 1971:135).

Agency physicians, Wissler said, "usually knew vastly more of Indian life than any other official [because usually longer in service on a reservation], but possibly because of professional inhibitions said the least about the subject. Nevertheless . . . the one person in the situation with whom one could talk man to man" (Wissler 1971:115). Doctors and Indian police kept track of expectant births, illnesses, and problems, and neither would necessarily tell the agent if it seemed better that he not be informed (1971:18). Wissler traveled with one physician making rounds on the reservation, seeing the "small cabins built upon their allotments; in winter time made as tight as possible; heated to a degree almost unbearable by a white man. Here they gather, old and young, male and female, sick and well, breathing the vitiated air, further contaminated by the fumes of the red willow [smudge]; usually without floors, always without beds, they sleep on the ground, and as the fire dies, the death's-head grins on them in a form of quickly contracted pneumonia" (an agency doctor quoted by Wissler 1971:119). It was evident to Wissler, and as he points out, supported by the number of cases seen annually by reservation physicians, that Indian people tended to accept the white doctor as a welcome addition to their own practitioners, a doctor with powers unknown to theirs whose efforts were likely to complement the native healers (Wissler 1971:117). These "medicine men," Wissler discovered, were "the wise men [given to] reflective thought, the formation of explanations. . . . They were relatively speaking not men of action, their attitude being one of detachment . . . though when professionally engaged they could proceed swiftly and continuously . . . as a boy did not play about with other children but sat upon the hills or walked about alone. . . . Most of them went through a long period of training. Even as late as my days on the reservation, each medicine man had one or more understudies. . . . From time to time his teacher delivered long monologues or lectures on the mysteries and the technique of handling the sick." Wissler asked a Piegan medicine man he admired, to "define a medicine man": the reply was that such men are no different from other men "except that he might be able to do one or two things no one else could do." A straightforward answer, and one that indicates the humbleness proper to someone who seeks power beyond the ordinary in order to help his people (Wissler 1971:256, 261).

"I regret not having given more attention to the Christianized Indians," Wissler confessed, "being antiquarian by nature." Christian Indians, it seemed to him, "lived in better houses, had better wagons and finer horses, dressed well and in general gave one the impression that they lived on a higher economic level than the pagans. I am not sure that all this prosperity was due to their having joined church; perhaps it was the other way around, having become more like white men economically they became church goers as a matter of course." Then Wissler described the home of "a blanket wearing Indian . . . medicine man" who rented out his allotment, and with this money and fees given to him for healing, built "a modern house with up-to-date decorations and furnishings . . . in the parlor . . . a fine mahogany chair which stood on an oriental rug." The house had an upper floor quite the contrast to the parlor: a large tray with sand for smudging and pipe, an earth altar and fireplace, medicine bundle on the wall, drum and rattles laid ready beside folded blankets for sitting on (Wissler 1971:163).

"The squaw man" was unjustly maligned, Wissler felt. One such rancher entertained Wissler in a home fitted up, like the medicine man's, with oriental rugs and quality furniture; because married to an enrolled Indian, he ran large herds on the reservation, prospered and sent his children to a whites' boarding school in California. Eventually, Wissler learned, the agent forced him to reduce his herds and he left the reservation (1971:180–183). Such exploitation of reservation resources by the stratagem of marrying an Indian woman was not, Wissler comments, the principal reason "squaw men" were ostracized by other whites. The men would be friendly with their fathers- and brothers-in-law, would tell them their rights and confirm corruption and dishonesty at the agency and traders' businesses. "Need we say more?" Wissler asked.

This chapter relevant to the Piegan ends with memory of Dave Duvall, Wissler's exceptionally able collaborator on the Blackfeet Reservation (see the introduction to the 1995 reprint of Wissler and Duvall's *Mythology of the Blackfoot* [Kehoe 1995]). Duvall was not a "squaw man," since he was classed as Piegan, but his father was a French Canadian (or Métis?) employee of trading posts who married a Piegan woman, Yellow Bird. Charlie Duvall, the father, died when Dave was small, and Yellow Bird in time returned to the reservation, marrying Jappy Takes-Gun-On-Top and settling in Heart Butte. Dave Duvall confided to Wissler that he felt he was "just nothing," neither Indian nor White. A handsome as well as very intelligent man, he married twice, but each Piegan woman left him, and perhaps despondent when his second marriage failed, he shot himself, aged 31. By coincidence, Dutch linguist Professor and Mrs. C. C. Uhlenbeck were dining next door to the room in Joe Kipp's hotel where Duvall pulled the trigger, and Mrs. Uhlenbeck records that it was the final day of the Okan. Contemporary Piegan people think perhaps Duvall's despair was rooted in his taking down and sending to Wissler, for publication, every detail of the holy ceremonies, thus bringing on power he wasn't trained to handle. Duvall was an exception to the reasonably comfortable adjustment of the majority of mixed-bloods, who tended to be healthier and more prosperous than full-bloods. "In short, they have found a place in the world and deserve our respect," Wissler states (1971:195).

Visiting a boarding school, Wissler heard the superintendent expound on "food, clothing, beds and how often his charges tried to run away," not on academic expectations or work. Boys in the school were instructed in band instruments, and Wissler "could see that these lonely, homeless Indian boys enjoyed playing. I was glad for them, since that was about their only chance to be happy. A glance at them working under compulsion in the harness shop, feeding pigs, and washing dishes and scrubbing floors, revealed the saddest child faces I ever saw" (Wissler 1971:146). "Once only was I present on the day when all the children to enter school were delivered to the [agent] for transport to distant government boarding schools, but that was enough. . . . [M]others wept, some of the children screamed as the horse trotted off, and fathers preserved their dignity by looking another way. . . . I rarely visited a school room, partly because I was not interested, but chiefly because I found the place depressing. Even at play the Indian children seemed to lack spirit . . . these boys would not play the games provided, unless forced to do so. No wonder! I asked if [the teacher] had tried Indian games; with a blank look he said the government rules specified what games were to be played. . . . The girls were the greatest sufferers in a return to reservation life. . . . [At] seventeen they were turned back to the reservation, immediately forced to take husbands and begin life in tipis or shacks, without the equipment they had learned to use." Questioning women who had been to boarding schools, Wissler heard happy memories of a teacher whom the girl had "idolized" (Wissler 1971:146–151). Perhaps the schools seemed less onerous to girls because home in the camps, they would have been working, learning homemaking, whereas boys would have been more free to roam about, herding horses their only task. The same year he published *Indian Cavalcade,* Wissler wrote in the magazine *Natural History* that by bringing together large numbers of Indian youth in off-reservation boarding schools, "a groundwork of common ties and language was laid . . . for the development of a widespread [pan-Indian] youth movement that could never have been possible without the unwitting aid of white teachers and missionaries" (Wissler 1938:110).

Summing up his observations, Wissler said, "Regarding the good intentions of the Indian Service the cynicism of the Indians was boundless" (1971:27). "The few white people around . . . were lost amid open spaces and Indian tipis. The most trying phase of their existence was to stand up against the feeling that they were gradually and surely losing touch with their own kind . . . no one I ever met spoke of the reservation as home" (1971:30–31) (Fig. 11). "The Indian's habit of standing about, staring at white folks, was not something peculiar to reservation days, it is an old time habitual attitude, a quiet cold-blooded appraisal of persons and events" (1971:153). "It is not true that our civilization is one of deceit and falsification, but it was none the less a tragedy that these interesting aboriginals found it difficult to see it otherwise" (1971:156).

Wissler recapitulated, in stronger words, his unflattering impressions of reservation life in his 1940 book *Indians of the United States*. The final chapter begins,

> The reader knows how transient were all agreements with the various tribes, how . . . as soon as the white men had taken all the free lands, they wanted the Indian lands, actually invaded them, started another war or induced the government to revoke the agreement. . . . Two or three such reductions made a concentration camp out of a reservation. . . . When the Indians were rounded up and placed on reservations . . . the white people always seemed surprised that sickness and death threatened their extermination; but there should have been no surprise, for even when white people are put into such camps the death rate rises. . . . War took its toll, though as a rule white losses were greater. Even in such decisive white victories as Fallen Timbers and Tippecanoe, the Indians suffered fewer losses than the whites. Their great losses came

Fɪɢ. 11. Agent's house, Old Agency. Credit: Blackfeet THPO.

with concentration upon reservations. . . . When Indians were first placed upon such a reservation, it was put into the hands of a political favorite from the East who knew nothing about Indians or the handling of concentration camps. . . . The Agent . . . possessed and exercised the powers of a dictator. [This was written as Hitler launched World War II.] He could put Indians into prison, determine their sentences, break up families, take children from their parents, decide where an Indian should place his residence, and prescribe his daily routine. . . . With government money the Agent bought large stores of food, clothing, hardware, farm machinery, harness, hay, oats, etc., which he stored in warehouses for issue to the Indians as he thought best. . . . If the Agent was so inclined, he could collect large sums as rake-offs on these purchases. The records show that many Agents did. . . . Two or more white men would be given a license to trade or to open general stores at the Agency. . . . Any Indian who found work with the Agent took his pay check to one of the stores, where he was charged high prices. . . . Indians, the victims of white culture expansion, the prisoners of war, as it were. . . . The Agents' instructions were to get the Indians to live in wooden or log houses as soon as possible; to force them to give up their original forms of shelter. The other point upon which they were to be insistent was that the Indian wear what was called "citizen dress." . . . Upon many reservations today there are log cabins still, but many Indians live in good frame houses, well furnished. . . . Indians are, for the most part, civilized, but for all that they are not Americanized, any more than are a number of other ethnic groups living in the United States. The Indians know they are not white men, and most of them consider it fortunate that they are not. . . . The Indian's chief grievance is the government. . . . The original idea of the government was to allot farms . . . but rugged individualistic white men soon had their farms and demanded that the government take care of the Indian as before. . . . At no time has the government given enough aid to raise the Indian above the lowest level of poverty. [Wissler 1940:281–291]

Professor and Mrs. Uhlenbeck Visit in 1911

We have another firsthand description of Piegan early in the 20th century, to add to Insima's account recorded in 1939, and Wissler's reminiscences published in 1938. Cornelius Uhlenbeck, a Dutch professor of linguistics, spent the summers of 1910 and 1911 on the reservation, transcribing stories and conversation in Blackfoot. This was the first professional study of the language, and was particularly significant in that Uhlenbeck took down boys' accounts of their everyday life, to include everyday spoken Blackfoot as well as the formal speech of respected men (Kipp 2003:102–103). His first, 1910, season was assisted by a graduate student, Jan Josselin de Jong, and his second only by his wife Wilhelmina. "Willy" Uhlenbeck kept a diary of her experiences that illuminates both Piegan daily life just at allotment, and the circumstances under which her husband labored. There are many, many lines about how cold it was, how strong the wind—it was rather worse than usual that summer for storms and chill—and many more descriptions of individuals (Willy had an eye for good-looking men) (Fig. 12) and the Piegan way of life. The material in this section is taken, with permission, from the translation from the Dutch by Mary Eggermont-Molenaar (Eggermont-Molenaar 2005).

The Uhlenbecks were hosted by Joe and Annie Tatsey. Joseph Tatsey was son of a Kainai, who took the adult name Kataiataxsi (Not-really-good), also the adult name of his father, a brother of Mekyaisto (Red Crow) and Natoyist-Siksina'. Tatsey's mother, "Granny" to the family and friends in 1911, was Piegan, a member of the All Chiefs band led by Fast Buffalo Horse. Annie Tatsey's mother, A'skxsainix'ki (Always Singing), was a sister of Three Suns (Big Nose), leader of the Grease Melters band. Annie's father was white, as was Joe's mother's father. The couple provided a square canvas tent for their Dutch guests, and daily meals in the Tatsey tent nearby. Joe and Annie had a ranch on Birch Creek, but spent the summer camped in the more northern valleys. As Wissler noticed, "Each family claimed a log cabin, but was seldom found living there" (1971:55). Only on one day that summer, July 23, did Joe go to check his ranch, although he had a contract to furnish beef to the agency, and did sometimes send his teenage oldest son, John, to check. First the Tatseys and guests camped on the Two Medicine close to Whitetail Creek, then they moved to Badger Creek, in each valley joining large encampments with tipis and tents. Ten children, in age from 20 to one, made the Tatsey camp lively; the second oldest, daughter Hattie, had married and had a baby of her own. "Granny," Tatsey's mother, had her own tipi beside the family's, and her half-brother Pietaunesta (Eagle Calf, also called White Man) and his two wives lived close, in a tipi beside their log cabin.

Joe Tatsey and Dick Sanderville were "councilors." Willy states, "Time and again people drop by to talk to" Tatsey, whose tent is "en route" for many people (8/5/1911). The Uhlenbecks considered Tatsey the best interpreter, plus he could teach quite a bit about former days and could dictate tales in Blackfoot. He went often to Browning on business (Fig. 13),

Fɪɢ. 12. Morning Owl, in stand-up bonnet and regalia, c. 1900. Credit: Blackfeet THPO.

Fig. 13. Browning, early 20th century. Credit: Blackfeet THPO.

much to Professor Uhlenbeck's disappointment since it took away time to work on the linguistics. The Uhlenbecks were unusual for their generation in that they respectfully referred to the Blackfoot with whom the Professor worked as his "teachers"—which of course they were—rather than "informants.

Eagle Calf was a handsome man, in Willy's eyes. His adult sons Duck Head and Adam White Man had their own families, while the youngest, four-year-old Paul, delighted Willy as he danced to his father's drumming or singing. Visiting Eagle Calf in his tipi, Willy watched one of his wives sew cowskin moccasins with thread she pulled, with her teeth, from "dried intestine" (probably sinew) (8/6/1911). Eagle Calf and his wives kept items from the past in their log cabin: a bison hide with the "beautiful long curly" hair on, a petrified bison rib with a hole drilled though it, a gambling wheel (hoop, for hoop-and-pole game), a heavy stone maul (a "pemmican hammer") with a handle wrapped in hide and the maul bound to it with intestines, and a pair of handgame sticks. When the two wives gave Willy the handgame sticks, they taught her how to play (8/20/1911). A few days earlier, the Uhlenbecks had welcomed Eagle Calf into their tent as he listlessly rode his horse, mourning the death of his elder sister, "Granny." The Dutch couple held his hand as he wept, gave him candy and tobacco. To reciprocate, he gave Willy a small, perforated whetstone from his pocket. She then presented him with a tea cloth she had expected to use to cover suitcases they might use as a table, except as it turned out, everyone who visited them sat on the suitcases. Eagle Calf was pleased with the colorful cloth and tied it around his head as a headband, which Willy notes were frequently used by the men, often with a single feather stuck upright in them. Next, Willy thought to give him a black-lined handkerchief that he tied around his neck, and Uhlenbeck gave him a half-dollar coin. The ceremonial exchange continued with Eagle Calf riding back to get a bison-hair fan used in sweatlodges to present to Uhlenbeck, and then formally naming him Omaxksitsanik (Big Bull), one of Eagle Calf's earlier names. Willy he named Sakoo-aki, the name of his mother. In the evening, Willy heard

> a small Indian boy sing, he walks high up on the highest hills and his Indian song sounds wonderful. And time and again I hear the drum. It must be Pietaunesta in the distance in his tipi. He must be sitting with his otter bundle, rubbing the sacred otter pelt, muttering and praying, then drumming again, expressing his feelings on this day. [8/16/1911]

Willy herself put on the only black dress she had brought, a party dress, but the best she could do to show respect for Granny.

The Uhlenbecks observed sweatlodges in the big camp on July 24, and on August 5, in front of the tent of one of their neighbors and teachers, Jim Blood (Kainaikoan). That one was covered with cowhides and over them, blankets to more completely close the structure. A woman, her forehead painted red, brought in the heated stones but waited outside while the men in it sang and prayed. As she waited, she smoked a large wooden pipe (8/5/1911). Jim Blood is described as

> an orator, narrates beautifully, relives the years of his childhood, is very affected by the great disaster of the cold winters now there is no buffalo meat and no buffalo skins. Bacon is expensive, the square sail cloth tents cold to live in! [7/23/1911]

The populous camp on Whitetail Creek near its mouth into Badger Creek impressed Willy (Fig. 14):

> How beautiful these tents look pitched there. How beautiful the Rockies seen against the clear evening sky. Such high prairie mountains, such large plains, what herds of horses and everywhere children colorful dressed, women in colorful skirts. There

FIG. 14. Blackfeet Indians, Fourth of July 1909. Irene McKnight in the saddle, Edna Rutherford on the ground. Credit: Marquette University Archives, Bureau of Catholic Indian Mission Records.

are also children swimming in the creek. They swim and flounder about. An old Indian is washing himself. A very old woman takes off her moccasins and crosses the creek. We see lots of people, hear lots of voices. [7/24/1911]

It is interesting to read of the meals prepared by Mrs. Tatsey. Willy was pleased that her hostess kept a neat, clean camp and served her guests on a low square table—seldom seen in a tipi—covered with a white cloth and set with a gray enamel plate, cup and saucer, knife and fork for each. The Uhlenbecks sat on a box to eat bread with bacon and jelly, coffee and tea. Bread and bacon were frequent breakfasts and lunches, sometimes varied by hotcakes, canned peas and tomatoes, fried potatoes, or warm rice with syrup. One breakfast consisted of beans, peas, stewed prunes and raspberries (6/22/1911). The same day that they had rice in the morning, Mrs. Tatsey served bacon, bread, and sweet corn, with dried peaches and coffee, for dinner. Other times, they ate cow tongue, peas, and prunes, or trout freshly caught in the river. The Tatseys butchered one of their cattle, so had beef, but Willy Uhlenbeck remarks that they told her they preferred bacon even though it was expensive. Rice with raisins was a favorite dish. Surprisingly, on September 11 the dinner was "lots of vegetables" with rice and raisins.

The Uhlenbecks were welcomed by Mountain Chief and his son Walter into the Medicine Lodge (Okan) camp put up on July 2 (a Sunday), near Browning. Walter had worked with Uhlenbeck the previous year as interpreter. On Monday, July 3, he invited the couple into his parents' tipi, beautifully decorated, Willy observed, with "all kinds of Indian artifacts hanging about," and an inner liner sewn like a quilt with "all kinds of colored pieces of cotton fabric sewn with other colorful figures." Walter's bed in the tipi had a similar "beautiful blanket, with pretty figures and quilted from extremely small pieces of fabric." Dinner was served, meat in square pieces and thick slices of white bread, the custom being to hold the bread in one hand and eat it alternately with bites of meat. During the afternoon, the Uhlenbecks watched the medicine lodge being erected, and a Crow Dance held in a tipi crowded with onlookers. Willy saw one of the three women on the reservation whose nose had been cut off for adultery; this woman wore a cloth over her nose, "is now remarried and behaves modestly." Indians from several other nations danced in the Piegan camp, affording Willy an opportunity to see, and admire, a variety of fine regalia. Also visiting the Medicine Lodge camp were George Bird Grinnell and his wife, who were planning to ride in the mountains—the future Glacier Park—after the Okan was completed.

On July 4, in the afternoon, people rode in on horseback carrying green branches for the Lodge. They dismounted and a couple of hundred people gathered for distribution of beef, in chunks of five to ten pounds, half a bag of flour, crackers, and sugar. Then a parade formed, making a procession to Browning. Afterward, drumming began and more and more dancers entered the field by the Lodge. "The women dance in close rows. They slowly shuffle along with their sedate faces, which don't match their face-painting, their colorful clothes, their colorful hair bands. The men dance . . . sometimes slow with small, quiet movements, then wild and passionate in peculiar wriggles, twisting the upper body, bending the knees in a stalking movement. Most of the Indians dance alone, just like that, in the crowd, some . . . separate beside one another." The afternoon ended with another Crow Medicine Dance in a tipi. Willy and the Professor were staying at Joe Kipp's hotel in Browning during the time of the Okan, rather than put up their tent in the camp.

On July 5, the Uhlenbecks sat for part of the morning near the Holy Woman's tipi, where she was enduring her four-day fast. Piegan "pray around her and rattle incessantly," and whooped. "A walking dance starts. Men and women walk in a long row behind each other, or they form a circle." In the afternoon, wagons (to make seats for spectators) were placed in a large square and a Grass Dance held inside it. About fifty men and the same number of women danced, first the men for about an hour, then the women, finally men and women together, always forming a single circle. Some of the women held a baby on the arm as they danced, others danced only while their baby slept under a wagon, watched by a husband or another woman. The dancing ended, everyone moved toward the Medicine Lodge where the top of the center pole was being decorated with leafy branches, strips of cloth, rattles, "etc." The Holy Woman, "her head decorated with feathers, looking like a crown," and a priest wrapped in a black blanket waited. The all-comrades societies solemnly marched in, singing, each man holding two large branches tied together at the top, their wives following them. Next, the Holy Woman, supported by her entourage, came to the center pole and prayed "for quite a long time" over it. When she had finished, all the pole bearers approached the center pole and "amidst long, anxious screaming and much emotion the thick tree slides into the prepared hole. Now it suddenly becomes quieter. The great tension is over. . . . This moment is impressive and I will never forget it. Can you imagine that we don't sleep! I hear and see all the Indians in my head. When I am awake, I hear them sing."

On July 6, the afternoon held another Grass Dance, and the Crazy Dogs dance with twenty or twenty-five men and women and small drums, not the big drum used for the Grass Dance. For the Crazy Dogs, "the dancers walk forward, stand still, form a square and their dancing starts." On July 7, the Uhlenbecks went to the camp at noon and sat in the Medicine Lodge, at the back until Mountain Chief led them to sit in the front, to see well. "The mock fights are curious: one person shoots, another dies, a tipi is being trashed, a woman in the tipi abducted, etc., etc. Lots of blankets and pieces of fabric, in general new, are being given

away as presents by the women, who carefully spread out all the pieces.
. . . After the pieces have been displayed for a while, they are being piled
up in order to make place for others just brought in. At the very end of
the ceemony a give-away is being held. In this way the less fortunate receive from the fortunate ones. In the medicine lodge, the 'sun dancer' is
most important, a slim, beautiful figure about thirty years old. . . . The
entire face is painted in a bright yellow. The sharp beautiful figures on
the face are beautiful. He wears a leafy crown around his head. Around
his neck is a thin, long, white and wide yellow trimmed cloth draped
down his back. . . . In his right hand he holds up a small feather, from
which three tassels hang, in the left he holds a little green branch. . . . In
his mouth he has a wooden whistle which is attached to a ribbon around
his neck, just like we saw at the beaver dance. . . . He is seated in the altar
made of dense leafy branches and comes forward and dances a repetitive
movement right in front of the altar, spreading out his arms or crossing
them over his chest continuously. He turns around dancing, each time
alternatively turning his chest or his back to the onlookers. . . . Indians,
men and women, keep approaching the sun dancers; with deep respect
they approach the altar. The man presents a pipe. Very soon plumes of
smoke rise; the woman presents a piece of fabric, tied to a branch with
a sheaf of green: an offering to the sun. First they pray standing upright.
Then the Sun dancer dances a long time for them. Finally they follow the
sun dancer. They also enter the leafy altar and pray there for quite some
time." Another Grass Dance was held later in the afternoon.

Saturday, July 8, "cold and bleak," discouraged the Uhlenbecks.
Nothing seemed to be happening in the camp, so they returned to their
plain and none-too-clean room at Joe Kipp's hotel to nurse the colds they
had developed. Sunday, July 9, was nice, but no dancing could be performed, it was forbidden on Sundays by the agent and the Catholic priest.
"It is too windy to walk a lot back and forth," Willy notes, "and Browning
is always boring, let alone on a Sunday." Monday, July 10, the Uhlenbecks planned to leave Browning for camp on Badger Creek, to resume
the taking down of Blackfoot texts. Willy noticed at noon, as they went
down to eat dinner in the hotel, "it strikes us that many Indians from the
camps are gathered in front of Joe Kipp's house. We don't know why and
don't think about it. We are still having dinner when nasty screams reach
us and they inform us that David Duvall, the well-known interpreter of
Wissler's, just shot himself in the inn. Today the case for the dissolution of
his marriage would have appeared in court. They say that his wife wanted it. . . . The screaming, sobbing and lamenting of a few Indian wom-
en sound very eerie. Duvall's mother, loudly wailing, sits in Joe Kipp's
doorway. . . . We learn that, due to the death of Duvall, there will be no

more dancing. The agent prohibits it. . . . A lonely Indian rides through the camp, he sings songs of lament. Walter [Mountain Chief] says that "It makes me sick. . . . I am mad at my people and I don't feel good, that my people kicked about that boy" (quotations from Willy Uhlenbeck's journal, 7/2/1911-7/10/1911).

Duvall's mother, Yellow Bird, and her husband Jappy Takes Gun On Top lived at Heart Butte, settled by Mountain Chief's Blood band, but just what Walter meant about "kicked about that boy," we do not know. Perhaps it was making him feel he did not belong, as he confided to Clark Wissler over the campfire. Perhaps it was his work for Wissler, collecting medicine bundles for the American Museum (but without the transfer ceremonies) and writing down rituals, word for word; still, Tom Kyaiyo, ritual priest and medicine bundle owner, collaborated with him on this, and people today don't speak ill of him.

Tragedy struck the Tatsey family, too. On July 31, 12-year-old Lizzy Tatsey and her little brother "Chubby" came to the Uhlenbecks' tent to ask whether they could give medicine for Josephine, the Tatseys' 20-year-old oldest child. The quiet, lovely, conscientious young woman felt ill and was coughing badly. Willy Uhlenbeck sent the children back with cough lozenges and Doveri tablets, brought from Holland. By August 8, Josephine had a high fever, tossing on her bedding in "Granny's" tipi—Josephine slept in the old lady's tipi and assisted her, as well as her mother, in daily tasks. The agency doctor had visited Josephine, declared her illness was tuberculosis and prescribed cod liver oil and cough medicine. He stopped by again, driving from Browning in his carriage, on August 8. Willy says the weather was damp and foggy, and exclaims of the sick girl, "She longs so much for the sun and heat." Mrs. Tatsey's mother died of tuberculosis; so did "many family members" (8/8/1911). In the middle of the night, Tatsey awakened the Uhlenbecks, begging for some whiskey or rum to revive his daughter. Willy handed him their half-empty bottle of rum, thinking, "How dreadful a situation for this sick girl! Her care—however good as it may be—is so very primitive. The camp bed [suggested to raise the girl above the damp ground] has not come. Now she lies in grandmother's tent and old Granny is weak, too, and worries about her granddaughter." The next day, Josephine seems very confused, although a teaspoon of rum with water and sugar relieved her a little. The agency doctor came, stood at the opening of the tipi, looked from there at Josephine, and told her mother, "It must be tuberculosis. I will give her some medicine." He had no time to look upon Granny; Willy Uhlenbeck wrote, "If all his visits to the poor, sick Indians go like this, he is a bad doctor." What the doctor gave them seemed to make Josephine sicker, so Willy opened the little medicine chest she had prepared, with a doctor's assistance, in Holland and sent Lizzy over with "potassium chloride for gargling and Doveri tablets for coughing and also our last Enzer pastilles and also half a box of cough drops from Sherburne [Sherburne Mercantile in Browning]." The potassium chloride and Doveri eased her sore throat and coughing a bit. "Granny" could not eat, she was pining away, and when the Catholic priest came from the mission to give her the last rites, she could not receive them for vomiting—nor would she want them, Willy Uhlenbeck said, for her spirit would go, she believed, to the Sand Hills and await her granddaughter there. On the 13th, the agency doctor came once more, after Tatsey complained to the agent about him, still declared the illness tuberculosis, and Tatsey spoke of getting a second opinion, perhaps taking his daughter to a hospital (there was one in Conrad). "Granny" died the evening of the 14th. Tatsey went to the Government Reclamation Project store on Badger Creek, near their camp, "to send a message to Browning for a coffin." The tipis and tent were taken down and the Tatseys' camp moved farther down the Badger valley. Two days later, on the 16th, the Uhlenbecks watched a funeral procession of buggies and people on horseback following Granny's coffin on a wagon, over the hills to the Holy Family Mission cemetery on the Two Medicine. Rambling over the hills on evening walks, the Dutch couple had several times come upon aboveground box coffins with household goods for the deceased, the wooden boxes decaying and wrapped skeletons visible.

The night of Granny's burial, the 16th, Josephine died. Hurrying to the Tatseys' camp when they get the news, the Uhlenbecks saw Mrs. Tatsey curled in a corner of her tipi, hugging her six-year-old Chubby. "I shall never forget her," the bereaved mother told her guests, clasping Willy's hand. Joe Tatsey they saw lying under a wagon, silent, away from the people come to help wrap the corpse. Once again, on the 18th, the Professor and his wife watched a funeral procession winding through the hills to the cemetery. Willy Uhlenbeck wrote, "Tuberculosis with rapid onset occurs often and grandmother was very old and tired and perhaps died of exhaustion." (7/31/11-8/18/11). We asked a couple of medical friends about Josephine's symptoms and they suggested diphtheria as a likely diagnosis.

Piegan after Allotment

The Uhlenbecks were on the reservation just before allotment was carried out. Nineteen twelve was the year this designated watershed in Indian life was implemented for the Piegan, following a very detailed census, 1907–08, listing every resident, their parentage, spouses, and children

(DeMarce 1980). Each verified Indian was entitled to 320 acres, either all in grazing land or 280 grazing, 40 acres irrigable. There were 46 miles of irrigation canals and lateral ditches completed at that time, estimated to permit irrigating 900,000 acres, but Piegan seemed uninterested in ensuring their allotments included access to irrigation, an oversight the agent was instructed to rectify by "adjusting" his charges' choices.

Even before allotment, in 1911, Piegan were grounded in 20th-century economy. That year, 1911, the 2,555 Piegan owned only 5,120 horses and mules, contrasted to 14,270 cattle (RCIA for 1911:225). They had been selling horses to the white settlers homesteading on former Blackfoot land (Farr 1984:100). The Office of Indian Affairs classified the entire reservation, 1,523,000 acres worth $15,250,000, as "grazing land," and listed the total value of Indian-owned stock at $1,050,000 of which $525,00 was owned by the tribe in common (RCIA for 1911:119, 262). For the calendar year 1911, Piegan sold 6,598 head of cattle for $292,160.96, and 1,044 horses for $49,949. Most of the stock grazed on open range, freeing their owners to camp together during the summer as described by Willy Uhlenbeck; in other words, the difference between hunting bison and raising cattle, for this generation making the transition, lay in the necessity of cultivating, reaping, and putting up hay and fodder to bring the animals over the winter. They chose their homesteads—if we may use this term for the allotments that were, by law, in lieu of homesteading, from which Indians were barred—for their capacity to provide winter shelter and sustenance for stock. This is clear from Insima's account of the settling of the Yellow Wolf family and their friends.

In 1911, 576 Piegan lived in houses with floors, 540 in houses without floors, and 164 in tipis or tents. Their houses and outbuildings (barns, etc.) were valued at $83,000, their furniture at $3,000, tools and implements at $1,500, and wagons and other vehicles at $8,500. Individual Indians also had funds in banks totaling $3,198, and "other property" worth a total of $5,000 (RCIA for 1911:149, 265). Other than stock, with which 37 Piegan made their principal living and 473 a partial living, the only other income-producing industry on the reservation was woodcutting, which supported 20 men (RCIA for 1911:132, 138). Wages to Piegan in 1911 totaled $68,704, contrasted with only $13,076 worth of rations issued; there were also per-capita and trust fund payments totaling $56,608, and "miscellaneous, proceeds from Indian labor, and Indian moneys" totaling $23,927 (RCIA for 1911:119). Twenty-five years after the last bison hunts, everyone by necessity wore "citizen's dress," now called "modern dress" by the Office of Indian Affairs. Their diet had changed; making allowance for their hostesses, Mrs. Tatsey and Rosie Mountain Chief (Mrs. Louis) Marceau, wishing to please them with "white" foods, the meals

with Indian participants described by Willy Uhlenbeck regularly included bread or rice, and she makes no mention of prairie turnips or camas.
Yet her accounts of "the camps," colorful with tipis, on Two Medicine and
Badger, and the frequent drumming she heard for bundle openings and
dances testify to the persistence of a Piegan way of life.

A quarter-century after the catastrophe of the disappearance of their
staff of life, Piegan had managed a reasonable adaptation to a substitute
economy. Two powerful factors challenged that: the fragility of any imported industry in the harsh climate of the northwestern Plains, and the
implacable Anglo policy determined to exterminate American cultures
alien to its own. Allotment in 1912 set the stage for decades of dramatic
struggles against both the perhaps insurmountable rigors of climate and
more predictable controversies over what might maintain the people in
the remnant of their homeland.

It is easier to chart the onslaughts of nature against Piegan. Two terrible events stand out in the 20th century, the collapse of the cattle economy in 1920 and the flood of 1964. Neither was simply a natural disaster.
Piegan stock did well up to drought in 1918 and 1919. Range grazing was
drastically reduced by the drought, and a severe winter, 1919–20, killed
large numbers of already-weakened animals. Starvation again loomed.
With money from earlier sale of land already expended, two-thirds of the
Nation had to depend upon government rations. Now that each Piegan
family had its allotment, there were 156,000 acres of "surplus" land on
the reservation (no account was taken of the next generation's needs until
1919, when children born after mid-1911 were recognized and additional
eighty-acre allotments made [Rosier 2001:27]). Selling the "surplus" land
would bring in money that could be spent for relief or invested either
in interest-bearing accounts, as with the Alberta Siksika, or in stock and
agricultural machinery. In 1911, "Indian moneys" from labor, set up as a
$10,000 reimbursable revolving fund, had been used, by decision of Pie-
gan leaders, to purchase a steam traction plow to break up "low land"
for cultivation (Valentine 1912b:37). After their experience of the drought
years, Piegan had no confidence in agriculture or herds to support them.
It was also troubling that the "surplus" lay in the eastern, Seville, sector
where water rights as well as land would be lost; irrigation systems built
by and for Blackfoot would go with the land (Rosier 2001:16).

Part of the irrigation system was a pair of dams at the edge of the
mountains, impounding headwaters of Two Medicine River and Birch
Creek. They collapsed in June 1964, unable to hold back unusually heavy
rains and snowmelt. Avalanches of water surged down the valleys, carrying away homes, stock, and human beings, wiping out families and possessions. New homes were built on higher ground, particularly by the

tribe in gridded clusters as little towns, or people moved into Browning (McFee 1972:27). The 1964 Flood powerfully reminded the people that the natural world remains almighty: the torrents had burst men's efforts to own the waters. Anglo notions of dominating life could not overwhelm Piegan country.

Vision of Anglo-style self-sufficiency, Thomas Jefferson's nuclear-family small farm ideal, continued to guide Indian Service agents decade after decade. At the same time, demographics were shifting, leading to a majority of enrolled Blackfeet having some non-Indian ancestry. Nearly all the "mixed-bloods' had white fathers or grandfathers; Willy Uhlen-beck said there were two African American men who had married Piegan women, and Clark Wissler in his informal memoirs described a Chi-nese immigrant who with his Indian wife ran a small log "hotel," but this was probably not in Blackfoot country. It must be remembered that the heavy toll of Piegan men taken by endemic wars left many women with poor prospects for marriage except as a junior wife, and also that as a matter of course, traders and their employees cohabited with indig-enous women. Aristocratic Natoyist-Siksina' with her Chief Trader hus-band Alexander Culbertson was a very positive role model for Piegan girls. Insima's daughter Agnes spoke approvingly of how Joe Kipp had formally arranged marriage of his good young employee, James Wil-lard Schultz, with her father Yellow Wolf's daughter by Potato, the se-nior wife, and how helpful Schultz was to his Piegan in-laws (Sommers [Dietrich] 1939:8/11/39). Because the United States thinks "one drop of blood," one forebear out of any number, will mark a person "racially," the number of "mixed-bloods" grew exponentially on the reservation as generations descended from 19th-century trading post employees and "squaw men." For example, both Joe Tatsey and his wife had white male forebears although Uhlenbeck found Joe both highly fluent in Blackfoot and knowledgeable on traditional culture, and his uncle Eagle Calf, stub-bornly clinging to his two wives, his tipi, his holy bundle, and teaching his little son to dance traditionally, was also called Whiteman because he had a white father, Charles Marcereau (Marceau) (DeMarce 1980:275).

Following allotment, that is, the act meant to be the decisive blow to a tribal economy, "full-bloods" were frequently contrasted with "mixed-bloods": supposedly, full-bloods spoke no English, could not and/or would not try to make a living American-style, were picturesque and na-ive, while mixed-bloods were said to be avaricious, ambitious ranchers likely to be in unholy alliance with similar men outside the reservation. The example of Eagle Calf/Whiteman shows how poorly the stereotypes fit. Another example challenging the stereotypes is that of Robert Ham-ilton (Fig. 15), son (whether biological or adopted is unclear) of trader

Fig. 15. Robert Hamilton. Credit: Marquette University Archives,
Bureau of Catholic Indian Mission Records.

Alfred B. Hamilton and a Piegan woman he said had died in childbirth.
Robert was brought up by his father and sent to Carlisle Indian School.
When he returned to the reservation in 1896, he married Rose Henault,
whose father Stephen Henault was white, her mother Maggie the

daughter of Aleck Guardipee, a Cree, and the Piegan No Charge. Hamilton first worked as a store clerk and interpreter, getting into trouble with agents Fuller and then Monteath, first for organizing a meeting room for young men to learn English and also Blackfoot heritage, from older men, second for arranging for an elected Blackfoot Council to take over from the agent-appointed council. Monteath went so far as to arrest Hamilton and hold him in jail on the charge of stealing horses—Hamilton had taken his father's herd when A. B. Hamilton died. (Others disputed Robert's right to the herd.) Once released after the case was dropped, Hamilton worked off-reservation for two years in a law office, until the beginning of allotment for the reservation excited his concern. Once more clamoring for a democratically elected council in place of the powerless agent-appointed consultant council, once more Hamilton was jailed, in 1910, and once more released without indictment. The new agent, Arthur McFatridge, allowed election of a Business Committee to advise on leasing and enrollment questions. Hamilton of course got elected to it and, with his law office experience, doggedly opposed selling off "surplus" unallotted land. He fought for compensation for Blackfoot territory removed from the reservation in 1874, for reservation subsoil mineral rights to accrue to the tribe rather than individuals, and to simplify cattle-raising programs on the reservation. Hamilton was perceived as a "mixed-blood," not listed on the 1907–08 Allotment census, he raised cattle, yet his politics aimed to respect "full-bloods'" desire to continue as much of Piegan culture as could outlive extinction of bison (Wessel 1982).

Mixed up in the "full-blood"/"mixed-blood" stereotypes is Anglo paternalism and a hidden contradiction in Office of Indian Affairs policy. "The Indian" is a *ward* of the Anglo government subject to unilateral decisions of a hierarchy of officials, on the model of a paterfamilias[33] deciding and dictating what is good for his dependent women, children, and servants. A paterfamilias maintained his status by being the only person in the household exercising political rights in their community; he alone had opportunity to participate in public affairs, learn about issues and opportunities, and risk, or conserve, the family's resources and labor. Supposedly, the paterfamilias was wiser than his dependents. Bluntly, he had power over them, they worked for him, and they had little or no recourse at law. So long as Indians were legally wards, they legally required a paterfamilias—an Office, or Bureau, or Department, of Indian Affairs—to administer them. If the Anglo governments recognized Indians as adults, competent to administer their own affairs in the same degree as other residents, then there would be no need to maintain a bureaucracy of several thousand employees. All the evangelism about "progress" toward citizenship masked a threat to those employees' jobs and whatever status and satisfaction they gained as overlords over Indian people. We do not know whether some, or any, of the visions and recommendations published by the Commissioners of Indian Affairs and their agents were consciously hypocrisy, but the conflict between avowed aims and perpetuating jobs is obvious. "Mixed-bloods" assertively competent to manage their own business threatened the bureaucrats, while keeping "full-bloods" isolated, poorly educated, and without capital kept the bureaucrats employed. On the Blackfeet Reservation, human ecology played into Anglo paternalism as Piegan more committed to their own way of life chose allotments nearer the mountains, the better to collect a diversity of traditional resources, while couples persuaded to American capitalist values took the eastern and northern sectors best for large-scale ranching. Ecology, bureaucracy, and politics together buttressed contrasts and conflicts ascribed to "full-bloods" versus "mixed-bloods," the labels in turn stereotyping and helping perpetuate "two cultures" vying for the Piegan homeland.

Agent Fred Campbell, appointed in 1921 after two disastrous years decimated herds, decided that cattle raising was too risky, especially under the heavy restraints imposed on Indians. Campbell had worked on the reservation as stockman, so knew the contrasts between the relatively few "mixed-bloods" ranching on the northern and eastern sectors of the reservation and the "full-bloods" preferring a simpler life closer to the mountains in the beautiful stream valleys. He believed the allotments would sustain families at a subsistence level if they kept a vegetable garden, sheep, and limited planting of wheat and oats. Horses, the "full-bloods'" preferred livestock, didn't figure in the equations. Campbell's Five Year Industrial Program was to be realized through a Piegan Farming and Livestock Association divided into 29 local chapters able to purchase machinery, seed, and stock cooperatively. Members of a chapter were elected president, vice president, and secretary, to lead and manage the chapter. Community halls and women's auxiliaries broadened some chapters' reach. Because the chapters were based on local communities, they coincided to some extent with pre-reservation band communities settled into these localities (Farr 1984:101–102; Rosier 2001:34–40; Wessel 1982:67–69). Campbell further reinforced older settlement divisions by working out an agreement that instead of one weeks-long Medicine Lodge for the whole reservation, three Medicine Lodges would be held, one in each major population area, and only lasting one week each (Ewers 1958:321). Some of the contrast claimed between "mixed-bloods" and "full-bloods" lay in the persistence of these bands in the hamlets they had formed, compared with ambitious "mixed-blood" ranchers moving onto open lands away from the main river valleys traditionally chosen for winter camps and then hamlets. Campbell's organization provoked stronger division. It did not help that Campbell publicized his innovation as the salvation of Indians, convincing the Office of Indian Affairs to pros-elytize it throughout the Indian Service—it was instituted on the Navajo Reservation in 1927, and local chapters are still the basic political units on that reservation (Shepardson 1983:626).

Politics got complicated in 1924. The United States unilaterally made all its Indian people U.S. citizens. By no means all wanted citizenship, which had been available previously to several classes of Indians (such as armed forces veterans) and was linked in many minds, white and Indian, with termination of treaty status (Prucha 1986:226). Robert Hamilton did see an advantage. The ten years of money earned from ceding the west-ern strip had ended, so that when rations were issued, they were bought out of the tribe's reimbursable funds. Hamilton argued that because all Piegan were now citizens, they, or representatives they elected, should govern the Blackfeet Tribe. Agents, he insisted, should be answerable to the Piegan elected council. He and his political party (usually called a "faction," as if First Nations don't have politics) called in 1926 for Camp-bell to be removed, on the grounds that he neglected the Blackfeet as he promoted his Five Year Industrial Program plan to other reservations. Not a problem for Campbell; he declared the Blackfeet Tribal Business Council, an elected body led by Hamilton, to have no standing. The Office of Indian Affairs supported Campbell's disregard of any elected council (Rosier 2001:34–41). Only Hamilton seemed to entertain the notion that being a U.S. citizen entailed a right to democratically elected governance.

Anglo colonial policy paternalistically manipulating its Indians—wards and citizens—toward assimilation as the lowest sector of the work-ing class, continued until Franklin Roosevelt's New Deal. That Anglo capitalism was the culmination of social evolution and/or God's gift to the most intelligent men could no longer be taken for granted in the Great Depression's global economic collapse. Taking the presidency from engi-neer Herbert Hoover in 1933, Roosevelt boldly ordered massive govern-ment spending to create employment, particularly programs that would give wages to local people to work on public projects. One of those projects we see today at the junction of highways 2 and 89 in Browning, the Mu-seum of the Plains Indian. Indian Affairs needed more than local building projects to sustain its domestic dependent nations. Roosevelt appointed an agitator for social-work reform, John Collier, in 1934 to be Commis-sioner of Indian Affairs. Collier was enamored of the romantic "tribal" Indian living communally close to nature, shown him by eccentric heiress Mabel Dodge Luhan at Taos, New Mexico. Her final marriage was to a member of Taos Pueblo, and she invited intellectuals, writers, and artists to the large adobe home she and handsome Tony Luhan built near the pueblo. Collier wanted to save tribal homelands, encourage "traditional" arts, let Indian languages be used in schools, and find viable economic enterprises for reservations. His 1934 Indian Reorganization Act seemed sensitive and respectful, until one got to the paragraphs explaining Collier's version of "Indian Self-Government," the core of his policy: reservations made into chartered legal corporations with constitutions and elected tribal councils to administer them. For all his admiration of old ways, Collier would not recognize chiefs selected in a traditional manner from pre-conquest leading families. Apparently he never realized he was jamming a foreign mode of governance upon First Nations. He didn't see it, but thousands of Indian people did, and opposed his reorganization.

Collier held a series of nine regional congresses to present his plans and the Wheeler-Howard Indian Rights congressional bill to his Indian constituents. (Burton Wheeler, senator from Montana, vacationed in Glacier National Park.) The Plains meeting was in Rapid City in March 1934, with eighteen Blackfeet attending. The audience deeply appreciated the unprecedented step of the Office of Indian Affairs consulting with its wards, and Collier's willingness to modify his plan so that pooling allotments into tribal communal land would be voluntary rather than imposed. Blackfoot delegates were prepared to listen critically to Collier because a month earlier, the Blackfeet Tribal Business Council had met with close to seven hundred Piegan to examine his proposals. In April 1934, in Washington, Wheeler's Congressional Committee on Indian Affairs listened to four members of the Blackfeet Tribal Business Council testify that their Nation wanted real self-government. Senator Wheeler, untouched by John Collier's romantic image of aborigines, suggested to the delegates that they simply run for offices in the state legislature and Glacier County, a cynical suggestion given that Wheeler could not have been ignorant of prejudice against Indians in the white communities of his state. Following many meetings on the reservation, 994 Piegan voted on a snowy October 27, 1934 (out of 1,785 eligible to vote), and 83 percent favored adopting Indian Reorganization Act (IRA). A factor strongly in its favor among Piegan was the opportunity to get some capital through the revolving loan fund promised by Congress (Rosier 2001:78–95).

Ironically, as soon as the Blackfeet Tribe adopted the IRA, the Office of Indian Affairs moved Forrest Stone, agent since 1929 and respected by Piegan, to another reservation. Stone was seen to have been unusually successful in working with (the OIA would have said "guided") the nation to favor the IRA, so he was transferred to guide a recalcitrant tribe. Arbitrarily changing administrators without consulting tribal councils was supposed to be against IRA policy. Topping this betrayal, the Office of Indian Affairs let the National Park Service propose to take over a strip of reservation land bordering Glacier Park; the tribe's consent was requested, and denied, in a meeting between OIA and Park Service representatives and Joe Brown, chairman of the Blackfeet Tribal Business Council. Although the OIA accepted the tribe's rejection of any sale, Piegan resented being invited in only after the two government agencies had drafted the sale agreement. Brown, son of a white man and his full-Piegan wife (DeMarce 1980:46), came out of this year of political activism a hero when he declared, "I am ready to defend my position. This might cost me my job, but I would rather be a respected citizen among my people than to be a dog in the Indian Service" (Rosier 2001:107–110, quotation p. 109).

When the IRA-mandated constitution was passed, in November 1936, and elections to the Blackfeet Tribal Business Council the following January, the fact that "full-bloods" were by then a minority in the Nation was very apparent. The constitution fixed tribal membership at the census list of January 1, 1935, plus children born to blood members legally resident on the reservation when the child was born (Ewers 1958:324). (This latter clause indicates how few Piegan were living off reservation at that time, compared with the population during and after World War II.) Voting districts roughly followed older clusters that, as mentioned, roughly comprised band settlements, but Jim White Calf, son of one of the treaty-period principal chiefs, and Rides At The Door, an active member of the pre-IRA Council, lived at Starr School which was listed in the Browning district. Browning, home to many "mixed-bloods" employed there, voted for "mixed-blood' candidates and, being more populous than Starr School, these candidates won over the two "full-bloods."

Revitalization of cattle-raising came with the New Deal. More than 5,000 head, including several hundred purebred Hereford bulls and cows, were taken to the reservation from drought-stricken southern Montana in 1934; nearly one-quarter of the weakened animals died over the severe and prolonged following winter. This encouraged extension agents to advocate sheep, especially for "full-bloods" who supposedly couldn't stick with the longer-term management needed for cattle (Rosier 2001:138–142). None of the officials seem to have noticed that "full-bloods" did well with horses, or recognize that "worthless Indian ponies" had been bred by Blackfoot for two centuries to survive the harsh conditions of the northwestern Plains. Nor did they realize, as John Ewers did, that horses had been more than an absolute necessity for 19th-century life and symbol of wealth and upper-class status; they had given healing power to Piegan through the horse medicine dance and its medicinal knowledge (Ewers 1955:257–279). The 1936 extension agent saw that Campbell's farm chapters program was foundering, and tried to substitute 4-H chapters

Fig. 16. Young Pikuni women in sewing club, 1930s. Nora Spanish is in center
beside matron. (See Plate 8) Credit: Blackfeet THPO.

instead, yet another instance of the Anglo assumption that "progress"
would come by indoctrinating the young. It didn't take long for the extension agent to see that 4-H, developed for mixed farming in the East
and Midwest, wasn't going to succeed quickly on the reservation. Interviewing a number of people who had begun ranching before and after
World War II, anthropologist Malcolm McFee could see that those who
succeeded in developing a cattle herd relied on family cooperation, some
tending the stock while others got wage jobs to bring in necessary cash
(McFee 1972:59). This pattern, rational as dictated by weather and price
fluctuations and by the need for large holdings to provide necessities for
cattle, was a continuation of the extended family cooperative unit basic
to pre-reservation economy as well as later, as John Ewers noted (Ewers 1955:321–322). The Blackfeet Tribal Business Council at this time hired
game wardens and a range rider to enforce its fish, game, and grazing
regulations, recognizing the tribal responsibility for guarding its economy and ecology (Rosier 2001:140–143).

Money from the Revolving Credit Fund was made available also to women to create a cooperative for making and selling Blackfoot crafts. Under the Works Progress Administration (W.P.A.), sewing clubs had been organized: seven women in the Two Medicine sewing club are pictured in Farr's 1984 book, page 134. Significantly, the woman in the center is Nora Spanish, and flanking her are her cousin Mae Williamson and Louise Pepion, who would support her in leading the cooperative for decades (Fig. 16, Plate 8). Mae Coburn Williamson was a founder in 1932 of the Blackfeet Indian Welfare Association, served on the Blackfeet Tribal Business Council 1938–39 as its first woman member, and remained prominent, unusual among women in being publicly recognized as a political leader. Initially, in 1937, the Blackfeet Arts and Crafts Association was a council of representatives from eight local chapters, and engaged two Piegan women to interview elders on traditional techniques and forms, in turn teaching these to the nearly two hundred women in the clubs (Rosier 2001:308–309, n. 65). In line with Collier's romantic goal of preserving the past, craftsworkers in the co-op were told not to copy from popular crafts books or use "white" designs such as the American flag (Ewers 1945:63; Kehoe fieldnotes). Operating their own workroom in the Museum of the Plains Indian and its shop there and at St. Mary's, and selling also through Glacier Park shops, the Crafts Association provided income for reservation women and influenced retention of heritage skills and designs.

The Indian Arts and Crafts Board, under which the Museum of the Plains Indian operated, was a U.S. Department of the Interior unit but not part of the Office of Indian Affairs. Collier saw it as an instrument to keep inviolate "traditional" First Nations cultures, materially encouraging manufactures, merchandising them, and guaranteeing them with its tags. A Mohegan woman from Connecticut, Gladys Tantaquidgeon, was employed by the new Indian Arts and Crafts Board to promote its work on Northern Plains reservations. Tantaquidgeon had assisted noted University of Pennsylvania anthropologist Frank Speck in ethnographic recording among East Coast Indian communities, and had studied anthropology at the university. She had been a community outreach worker with Yankton Lakota in South Dakota, people suffering Dust Bowl conditions heaped upon Depression economics. Some parents hesitated to send their children to new reservation day schools because, having grown up in boarding schools, they had to ask the social worker, "What would we do about food and clothing?" (Fawcett 2000:114). Changing to the Indian Arts and Crafts Board gave Tantaquidgeon pleasanter duties, focusing on facilitating production by Indian artists and providing opportunities for them to teach on other reservations and participate in national fairs and

expositions. Thanks to Collier's high-society friends, he obtained internationally known art specialist René d'Harnoncourt to head the Indian
Arts and Crafts Board, and patronage by Franklin Roosevelt's activist
wife Eleanor. (Tantaquidgeon told her grandniece how, at a formal lun-
cheon for the large staff of the 1939 San Francisco Exposition, popular
ventriloquist Edgar Bergen put aside his famous dummy Charlie Mc-
Carthy and picked up the baby of a Navajo artisan couple, placing the
tiny child on his knee and startling the parents by making it appear to be
talking [Fawcett 2000:119]). With approval from d'Harnoncourt and Collier, Tantaquidgeon urged agents to cease interfering with Sun Dances,
for which Chewing Black Bone gave her a whistle he used in the Medicine Lodge (Fawcett 2000:120; the whistle was displayed in the Mohegan
Museum built by the Tantaquidgeon family). Tantaquidgeon attended an
Okan "at the fairgrounds not far from the museum where we worked.
There was food passed around . . . I felt a little concerned about accepting
food because we were on salary, and here were some destitute families,
but Nellie [Nellie Star Boy Buffalo Chief, her co-worker] said, 'accept the
food,' since she knew a family with several children and she would pass
the food on" (Fawcett 2000:121; Fawcett misidentifies the reservation as
Crow).

Touring the reservation in late 1937, Office of Indian Affairs officers
recommended that the Blackfeet Tribal Business Council use Revolving
Credit Fund with tribal and federal monies to rehabilitate the Two Medicine irrigation system, on the lower reaches of the river in the eastern
sector of the reservation. Livestock—cattle—would be the only viable
economic enterprise for the reservation, a cattle industry would be viable
only if Piegan raised winter feed for the stock, and winter feed would
be reliable only with functioning irrigation. Using reservation water
would also safeguard Blackfeet water rights, against efforts by ranchers
outside the reservation to draw down those waters. Families were to relocate from Browning's "shacktown" to irrigated hay meadows (Rosier
2001:148–156). The real alternative was exploitation of oil and gas, something going on from the 1920s and affording royalties to the tribe that
could be distributed as per capita payments, as well as income to owners
of allotments containing wells (Fig. 17). Profiting from oil had one serious
drawback: oil extraction offered very little employment to Piegan. Population had nearly doubled over a generation, so dividing tribal oil income
into per capita would not do more than ameliorate poverty. Historian
Paul Rosier notes that in 1940, Wright Hagerty served on the Blackfeet
Tribal Business Council although his father was white and mother only
one-eighth Indian. Hagerty's parents ranched on the Milk River, and he

Fɪɢ. 17. Mrs. Morning Gun christening new oil drill. Credit: Blackfeet THPO.

ran sheep and held oil and grazing leases, bringing his net worth to close to half a million dollars in 1942 (Rosier 2001:177). Potential for wealth was there for a few, but that potential in oil and stock raising rested in controlling large acreages.

World War II galvanized the Blackfeet Reservation. Two hundred and fifty members went into the armed forces, more than 300 moved to cities to work in defense industries, a similar number left seasonally to pick hops and other fruits, and "victory garden" committees promoted subsistence gardens in twelve districts of the reservation. John Ewers wrote,

> Blackfoot Indians served with distinction . . . in every major theater of the war. They flew bombing missions over Germany, they helped man destroyers and battlewagons, they fought with our ground forces in North Africa and on the European continent, and they took part in amphibious operations in the Pacific. [Ewers 1958:324–325]

To safeguard their soldiers, Piegan prayed for them in the Medicine Lodge and at bundle openings and pipe ceremonies. Whether in combat zones or defense labors, Piegan encountered relatively little negative racism in the wartime spirit of standing shoulder to shoulder against ruthless common enemies. Demobilized veterans and defense workers knew they could hold their own in America. They could see, too, that the reservation economy could not support everyone. Another factor reinforced the idea of remaining Piegan but living off-reservation: by mid-20th century, half of the enrolled population was only one-half or less Piegan, and "full-bloods" were, disproportionately, older people. The Blackfeet Tribal Business Council kindly sent many of the elders over the mountains to relieve their rheumatism in hot springs in the Flathead Valley, but this failed to mollify some politically active "full-bloods" demanding a larger share of the Nation's income. Yellow Kidney, husband to Insima, argued that Piegan who had sold their allotments no longer should claim shares in the Nation's territory or income from it; he and his conservative friends had resisted selling out even though it meant continued impoverishment (Rosier 2001:189–192). Anthropologist John Ewers observed at this time, "Along with that traditional custom of sharing, the traditional ideal of generosity survives to inhibit the adaptation of the white man's ideals of budgeted expenditures and saving for a rainy day" (Ewers 1955:322). An honorary council of elders existed, and to defuse the Yellow Kidney party's complaints, the Blackfeet Tribal Business Council let the honorary council send two members to sit as nonvoting discussants at Tribal Council meetings. In 1945, the "full-blood" elders advised the tribe to set criteria for tribal membership at one-sixteenth or more Blackfoot ancestry ("blood"), plus residence on the reservation, at least nominally (Rosier 2001:202–203).

Nineteen forty-five was an interesting year. Besides fixing enrollment criteria, a convention of a range of representatives from reservation constituencies recommended a $5,000 fund to aid Blackfoot students to attend college. This reflected the looming problem of returned veterans not finding jobs, while at the same time wartime experiences had raised confidence and understanding of potential advantages within the greater American society. The National Congress of American Indians, founded in 1944, met that year in Browning for its second annual convention. D'Arcy McNickle, Salish/Cree from the Flathead Reservation, had been one of the organizers of the NCAI, and his reservation co-hosted the 1945 meeting.[34] Issues that affected Piegan and Indian people nationwide were brought home, entangling new U.S. president Harry Truman's push for civil rights protection, veterans' economic and employment expectations, calls for termination of wardship and the Bureau of Indian Affairs, and final legal settlement of First Nations' claims on land and just compensation (Cowger 1999:49–50). Earl Old Person would become executive director of the NCAI, 1969–71, before beginning in 1978 his long tenure as Chairman of the Blackfeet Tribal Business Council.

Nationally, reaction against years of Depression and wartime restrictions fed conservative politics. Franklin Roosevelt died in 1945 and his New Deal was then denounced as socialist, a particularly dangerous epithet as the cold war against the Soviet Union escalated. So many Indian people had shown themselves to be capable citizens, why should the government call them wards and run their affairs? Senator Wheeler of Montana opposed John Collier's policies in spite of having co-sponsored the Indian Reorganization Act (Wheeler-Howard Bill). In 1947, the Senate Civil Service Committee asked the Office of Indian Affairs for a list of economically viable tribes that might be terminated from Federal wardship. Land and compensation claims would be settled once and for all time, reservations turned into municipalities under state jurisdictions, and individual Indian people "freed" to be fully assimilated into the national society. This, of course, could be done unilaterally by Congress, on the precedents so frequently set in the past. What about treaty rights and obligations? Popular sentiment said treaties were ancient history, 19th-century, frontier, quaint documents with no place in modern America. Not only should reservations be terminated, most of their residents should be assisted to move out to cities, to relocate. The 1950 Commissioner of Indian Affairs was Dillon Myer, whose previous appointment was director of the War Relocation Authority, responsible for incarcerating Japanese Americans in desert concentration camps. (German Americans were not disturbed, even though Germany was as much America's enemy as Japan was.) An observer at the time remarked, "Myer was the first man in history to end a federal bureau—the War Relocation Authority. That is why they made him commissioner of Indian affairs" (Tax 1995:133). Myer knew he knew best and best knew how to accomplish Indian "self-determination": get Indians out of Indian Country so individuals could determine their own lives (Cowger 1999:100–125, Philp 1999).

Nineteen fifty saw the formation of a Governors' Interstate Indian Council pushing for the federal government to turn Indian populations and lands over to state jurisdictions. Montana's state constitution specifies that "all lands owned or held by any Indian or Indian tribes shall remain under the absolute jurisdiction and control of the congress of the United States . . . until revoked by the consent of the United States and the people of Montana" (quoted in Wilkins and Lomawaima 2001:194). Notice that the language does not demand consent of Indian tribes! Mid-century policy pushed assimilation of Indians as individuals by relocating them to cities where they would be small minorities, and by extinguishing special status under law for tribes (i.e., First Nations) and their enrolled members. Myer's push to assimilation did benefit Indian people by permitting them to take their money from agency control and put it into private bank accounts, to mortgage or sell their property (but not tribal property), and to benefit from Veterans and Farmers Home Administration loan programs. The New Deal (1934) Johnson-O'Malley Act, authorizing contracting with states for education and health on Indian reservations, was utilized by Myer to turn over Indian schools, including boarding schools, to state administrations. He also encouraged placement of Indian children into white foster homes (Philp 1999:93–99).

At this time, 1950, Piegan were demanding termination of Indian Affairs supervision. Hundreds of high school graduates and more than one hundred college graduates comprised a pool of members qualified to deal with contemporary economics and politics. Blackfeet Tribal Business Council chairman Henry Magee and, after a June election, his successor George Pambrun criticized Indian Affairs' high-handed actions with Blackfeet monies, which operated contrary to the council's 1947 formal resolution to end Interior Department control, in line with the Senate Civil Service Committee's discussions on federal termination earlier that year. The Bureau of Indian Affairs[35] could not let go—effective termination would terminate itself—and countered with detailed charges of gross fiscal mismanagement by the Blackfeet Tribal Business Council, citing incomplete records, unsecured risky loans, and tribal government expenses that exceeded income. Council members admitted sloppy accounting and unconventional business actions, but would not apologize for lending a total of $209,000 to 900 destitute Piegan during the killing 1950 winter. When push came to shove, the Blackfeet Tribe wanted hands off its money but continued treaty status with the federal government, while Congress and the Commissioner of Indian Affairs wanted to wipe out special status for Indians. It was hardly a new thing for the United States to unilaterally abrogate treaties, but now Indians were citizens, a high percentage had off-reservation experience in American society, and the New Deal had given them an exceptional lawyer, Felix Cohen, to argue their cases. Cohen had drafted the Wheeler-Howard Bill and remained on the Indian Affairs staff until the administration changed in 1947; he then maintained a private practice representing First Nations on issues with government. His *Handbook of Federal Indian Law*, first issued in 1942, is an indispensable reference work. The Blackfeet Tribal Business Council retained Cohen as its legal counsel in 1949 (Philp 1999:125–130; Rosier 2001:322). Commissioner Myer's Billings Area Director wrote to him in April 1951 that "Mr. Cohen will be at Fort Belknap this weekend and at Blackfeet next week.

. . . [A]pparently Felix is working for the tribe for nothing" (quoted in Drinnon 1987:217; in fact, the Blackfeet Tribal Business Council offered him $5,000 per year retainer but Cohen would accept only $3,600 [Rosier 2001:324, notes 95, 97]).

Felix Cohen recognized First Nations sovereignties under their treaties. He believed the Wheeler-Howard Act would allow considerable freedom to the nations to rebuild their societies, conserving traditions of respect and generosity to the poor. What Cohen favored was old-fashioned social democracy. George Pambrun accused the Bureau of Indian Affairs of running "a communist dictatorship" that Stalin could have studied (Philp 1999:130). In 1951, the governor of Montana convened an Indian Affairs Conference, and Cohen addressed the meeting. Later that year, the Montana Inter-Tribal Policy Board adopted an "Indian Declaration of Independence" patterned after Thomas Jefferson's 1776 Declaration. Using the Montana Declaration, written by Tom Main from Fort Belknap, Pambrun testified in 1952 before the U.S. Senate Committee on Interior and Insular Affairs (taking over Indian Affairs from a previous committee). Behind Pambrun was a volatile conflict on the reservation between the Tribal Business Council and Guy Robertson, BIA superintendent, once an assistant to Myer in the administration of the Japanese-American camps. Each planned an election, each claimed the other's election would be illegal. The BIA supported a party supposedly representing "full-bloods," led by Louis Plenty Treaty and Charley Reevis (whose father was white, but Charley was raised by Big Nose [Three Suns]). This party abjured participating in commercial stock raising and white business practices. They felt tribal income from oil and grazing leases should be distributed per capita rather than invested by the tribe. "The Indian way" of personalized generosity was an important aspect of their heritage in their opinion (Rosier 2001:240–241). This was hardly the way the BIA wanted tribal accounts handled; the BIA and the "full-bloods" agreed that the Tribal Business Council too readily lent money to its members and friends, but the "full-bloods" certainly didn't want the slow wheels of bureaucracy insisted on by the BIA. Two elections were held the same day, neither one obtained the Blackfeet Constitution minimum number of 30 percent of the 2,800 eligible voters (Philp 1999:134–139). Commissioner Myer could disregard both elections.

In April 1951, George Pambrun, on Felix Cohen's advice and with the lawyer beside him, took over a vacant Blackfeet Agency house to demonstrate Blackfeet Tribe ownership. The tribe had won a major land claims case it had filed in 1935, but before the sum was paid them four million dollars was deducted for buildings and other capital improvements the BIA had made. Cohen stated that "by all ordinary standards of law, equity, and morality," these improvements then became the property of the tribe that had paid for them. Cohen told Robertson that he would take responsibility for the takeover act—the BIA would have to deal with him directly (Drinnon 1987:217–221; Philp 1999:125). Commissioner Myer went on to write a bill, which he persuaded the Senate and House judiciary committees to introduce in January 1952, to "Authorize the Indian Bureau to Make Arrests Without Warrant." Already, Myer's BIA employees carried weapons. Felix Cohen, general counsel to the Association on American Indian Affairs as well as to the Blackfeet Tribe, Oglala, San Carlos Apache, and Laguna Pueblo, led the fight against such gross disregard of American citizens' rights. Myer vilified Cohen, insinuating that he was a communist (this was the era of Senator Joe McCarthy's witch hunt), that there was a communist conspiracy that included men in "black sedans" driving around Plains reservations, and further, that Cohen stood to gain millions of dollars as fees in Indian claims cases. J. Edgar Hoover's FBI investigated; he had to tell Myer that none of the charges had any truth (Drinnon 1987:222–224).

After achieving national notoriety in 1951, Piegan lost the spotlight, for the happy reason that they resisted headline-making termination. Myer's staff made a list of actions to be carried out to terminate the Blackfeet Tribe's relationship with the federal government:

> Close the Rolls. Sell the heirship land. Issue certificates of ownership to each individual for their proportionate share of tribal assets. Help to prepare necessary legislation. Insist that such legislation be mandatory and not subject to approval of local and state authorities or of Indian council and Tribes [quoted in Rosier 2001:275].

Without creating issues over control, Montana and Glacier County extension services were welcomed to the reservation, welfare payments were conducted jointly with Glacier and Pondera counties, and the state took responsibility for reservation day schools. Only law and order activities were more or less left to Federal supervision, in spite of the Blackfeet having adopted a code of laws under IRA (Rosier 2001:277–279). Felix Cohen had informed Commissioner Myer in 1950 that his clients, the Blackfeet Tribe, were already "the largest tax-payer in Glacier County, and that the members of this tribe pay in Federal taxes a sum very much larger than the Federal Government spends on the Blackfeet Reservation" (quoted in Drinnon 1987:216). When Commissioner Myer listed the tribes he intended to terminate (without consultation or consent), Blackfeet were not on the list. Nor were the other First Nations that retained Felix Cohen as general counsel. Grateful Piegan bestowed the honored name Double Runner upon Cohen (Drinnon 1987:214).

Earl Old Person began his political career on the Blackfeet Tribal Business Council in 1954, age 25 (Rosier 2001:275). Termination was still in the air, with transfer of health and medical services from the BIA to the Public Health Service that year. It was clearly stated that health would improve only as economic conditions improved (Prucha 1986:353–354). Toward that end, the BIA launched its Branch of Relocation to merge Indians into the urban work force. Relocation operated from 1952 to 1961, when a newly elected Democratic regime in Washington, led by President Kennedy, ostensibly changed direction. Termination was no longer openly urged, and the Kennedy administration's Commissioner of Indian Affairs, anthropologist Philleo Nash, stressed economic development on and near reservations. Kennedy's assassination in 1963 did not affect this direction, as his successor Lyndon Johnson oversaw the creation of the Economic Opportunity Act, authorized by Congress in 1964, that included Indians in its War on Poverty (Prucha 1986:350–359). Assiniboin activist Hank Adams charged that there was not, in fact, as great policy change between the Republican Eisenhower administration of the 1950s and the Democrats under Kennedy and Johnson in the 1960s, that they simply renamed Relocation "Employment Assistance" (Adams 1995:240).

Bill Fredricks, with a Piegan mother and white father, grew up on the Blackfeet Reservation. From 1977 to 1990, he was executive director of the Los Angeles City-County Native American Indian Commission, an umbrella organization bringing together sources of funding and social services programs, and acting as advocate for Los Angeles Indian groups and people. In his youth, he admitted, he had acted as "the supermacho Indian man," drinking and brawling; his grandparents spoke Blackfoot in the home but used English with their grandchildren. Fredricks accepted BIA relocation to Los Angeles, finding his social life in Indian baseball, basketball, and bowling leagues and in bars known as meeting places for Indians. Even with these friendly groups, Fredricks felt uncomfortable in the big city and returned to the reservation after a few months. Life on the rez wasn't satisfying, either, so back Fredricks went to Los Angeles. A few more tries, and he settled down in the city, marrying a woman who was part-Sioux and studying public administration at University of California-Los Angeles. Except for his high-status public-sector position in Los Angeles, Fredricks typified the reservation person relocated to a city during the 1950s (Weibel-Orlando 1999:184, 202, 234–238). A minority of Relocation Program participants settled permanently, while the majority decided menial jobs, ghetto housing, and battling racism in daily life were more negative than unemployment and frustration back home.

The Relocation Program got a lot of publicity, obscuring the greater number going into cities on their own, using relatives and friends already there to help them adjust. The Economic Opportunity Act benefited both people in cities and those on reservations, through Head Start, Neighborhood Youth Corps, Job Corps centers, and numerous grants for community programs (Prucha 1986:359). Nineteen-sixties agitation over civil rights, enshrined in the 1964 federal Civil Rights Act, extended specifically to First Nations people in 1968 as the Indian Civil Rights Act. This spelled out how constitutional guarantees should apply to American Indian citizens, immediately raising issues of tribal sovereignty, which came to a head in 1978 in the case of *Santa Clara Pueblo v. Martinez*, in which a Pueblo woman contested her nation's rule that only children of male members could be enrolled. Mrs. Martinez's husband, father of her children, was Navajo; ironically, the Navajo Nation favored children of Navajo women, thus doubly penalizing the Martinez family. The United States Supreme Court ruled that the Pueblo had sovereignty over enrollment, overriding an individual's constitutional rights against discrimination based on a citizen's sex. While that issue didn't affect Piegan, the ruling made clear the Supreme Court's willingness to recognize First Nations sovereignties (Prucha 1986:363–364).

The watershed shift in United States Indian policies came in 1975 with President Richard Nixon's Indian Self-Determination and Educational Assistance Act, Public Law 93-638. The fundamental right guarded by this legislation was First Nations' power to contract directly for services, instead of being forced to obey BIA decisions. Earl Old Person spoke about the act in 1983, explaining,

> The Blackfeet Tribe has been very careful. We have not contracted for very many federal programs. . . . We asked whether those programs would continue to be funded once the tribe took over. The federal government refused to guarantee funding in the future to back up the tribe. There is more to tribal self-sufficiency than merely declaring that you are self-sufficient. . . . We were not given the opportunity to actually get into policy making. . . . Two years ago [1981], we were told that we could take over our child welfare programs. This sounded awfully good to us. We started a tribal child welfare program last fall [1982]. Six months later we were told that it would not be refunded, because the tribe supposedly failed to comply with federal requirements. . . . The government offered to give the Blackfeet boarding school back to the tribal council. . . . We agreed [but] they only promised to help [fund it] a year at a time. Contracting was used as a way of

getting rid of that boarding school. . . . It is no wonder that my people are very skeptical about so-called self-determination. [Old Person 1986:252–253]

Three years after the Indian Self-Determination Act, two more important bills passed Congress, the Child Welfare Act of 1978 and the Tribally Controlled Community College Act (Prucha 1986:377–380). The first was critically significant in stemming the movement to take Indian children from their homes; frequently, children living in their grandparents' home, as was common by Indian custom, were being declared "neglected" and put into white foster homes.

The second act provided federal funds to tribal colleges, recognizing the success of the first tribal college, Diné, on the Navajo reservation, founded in 1969. Tribal colleges including Blackfeet Community College got organized in the early 1980s, going through a decade or so of struggle to construct curriculum and services, not to mention classroom buildings. Meanwhile, Head Start could continue, as First Nations insisted on its worth. For Piegan under Dorothy Still Smoking's leadership it offered the opportunity for young children to hear their native language just when English was replacing Blackfoot as the language usually heard in Browning and among young people.

A third federal law passed in 1978 has been less well upheld. Public Law 95-341, American Indian Freedom of Religion Act, established "American Indian, Eskimo, Aleut, and Native Hawaiian . . . inherent right" to free exercise of their religions, then failed to protect this right in two major cases, when the Supreme Court ruled in 1988 that the Forest Service could cut a road through a mountain area holy to the Indian peoples of northern California, and in 1990 upheld the State of Oregon's prohibition against any use of peyote, even as sacrament in Native American Church ceremonies. Neither of these issues directly affected Piegan, but the rulings warned us that Public Law 95-341 could not be relied upon should similar challenges come up—such as when Piegan wish to protect Chief Mountain.

A 1990 law, the Native American Graves Protection and Repatriation Act, Public Law 101-601, does directly apply to Piegan. Soon after it was passed, Buster (John) Yellow Kidney and Curley (Clarence) Wagner went to the Field Museum of Chicago to bring back Piegan objects held there, although they had not been formally authorized to do so by the tribe. The museum cooperated; the newness of the legislation had not yet clarified just how authority for repatriation should be obtained. Since then, representatives of the Blackfeet Nation have visited a number of museums to identify Piegan holdings and research the nation's history.

On the economic development side, a former treasurer of the Black-feet Tribal Council, Elouise Pepion Cobell, in 1996 filed a lawsuit against the United States Department of the Interior concerning failure to man-age trust monies collected by the Bureau of Indian Affairs on behalf of Indians holding trust properties. Mrs. Cobell was lead plaintiff in a class action lawsuit.

Tragically, Mrs. Cobell did not live to see any personal benefit from her years of fearless litigation. She died of cancer at age sixty-five, Octo-ber 16, 2011, less than four months after federal judge Thomas Hogan an-nounced final approval of the 2010 settlement. Pikuni have from ancient times recognized outstanding women leaders, women who are exemplary wives and mothers while actively working economically and politically for their people. Elouise Pepion Cobell, great-granddaughter of Mountain Chief, was truly an *inawa'sioskitsipaki*, a "leader-hearted woman."

In 1999, the federal judge hearing the lawsuit had ruled in favor of the plaintiffs, ordering the Department of Interior to organize its records and pay monies due for leasing and royalties, to individuals and to tribes. Interior Department officials declared that the records were so confused or missing that it would be impossible to comply with the order, where-upon the judge held the Secretary of the Interior in contempt of court. Nothing happened, the next Secretary of the Interior was likewise held in contempt of court, Interior continued stonewalling and asserting it was in compliance (trying) even though nothing seemed to be happening with records. The lawsuit dragged on, plaintiffs refusing to give up what would amount to billions of dollars owed Indian people and nations, con-sidering accrued interest on top of failure to pay out monies collected. After fourteen years, in 2010 the plaintiffs reluctantly agreed to settle for $3.4 billion, of which $1.5 billion would be distributed to hundreds of thousands of individuals with trust accounts and the remainder used for buying up and consolidating allotments, by this time divided up among several generations of family heirs. Some of the money would go to fund scholarships for higher education for Indian and Alaskan Native youth.

Without waiting to achieve her goal in the Indian Trust Monies case, Elouise Cobell had, with the tribe, taken over the defunct Blackfeet Na-tional Bank in Browning and made it into a thriving asset to the commu-nity. She expanded it into the Native American Bancorporation, assisting other reservations to develop their own banking, and founded the Na-tive American Community Development Corporation to facilitate other financial investments such as new businesses and agricultural enterprises on reservations, including the Blackfeet Reservation (Plate 10). She also persuaded the Nature Conservancy to broaden its program to include threats to First Nations lands, helping the conservancy cooperate with the

Blackfeet Tribe to purchase the Flatiron Ranch west of Browning, preserving it for ecological study and education outreach.

The 2000 Federal Census enumerated 27,104 United States Blackfeet, plus 85,750 Americans claiming part-Blackfoot ancestry. The number of Piegan speaking Blackfoot was 1,356 (in Alberta, 2,740 of the members of the three Blackfoot reserves spoke Blackfoot). Blackfoot is taught in Browning public schools, Blackfeet Community College, and the private Cuts Wood language immersion school. The tribal government maintains a Tribal Historic Preservation Office, and the independent Piegan Institute, as well as the college, studies and archives Amskapi Pikuni history. This First Nation, with internationally known leaders such as Earl Old Person and Elouise Cobell, tenaciously sustains its magnificently beautiful homeland and people (see Plates 2, 5, 6, 9, 10, 11, 12, 13, 14, 15).

Elouise Pepion Cobell, 1945–
2011, renowned Amskapi
Pikuni economic leader.
Credit: Turk Cobell.

Plate 1. Amskapi Pikuni homeland, the Montana Blackfeet Reservation.
Credit: Alice B. Kehoe.

Plate 2. Chief Mountain (center) and Duck Lake, Blackfeet Reservation.
Credit: Alice B. Kehoe.

PLATE 3. Blackfoot Council, 1855 (Lame Bull Treaty), drawn by Gustavus Sohon.

PLATE 4. Rural Reservation homes, typical of earlier twentieth century. Credit: Alice B. Kehoe.

PLATE 5. Contemporary rural reservation allotment, homes of extended family. Credit: Alice B. Kehoe.

PLATE 6. Contemporary subdivision homes, Browning. Credit: Alice B. Kehoe.

PLATE 7. North American Indian Days (Blackfeet Powwow) parade, 1950s.
Credit: Thomas Kehoe.

PLATE 8. Memorial giveaway for William Spanish, tribal councilman, 1972, during North American Indian Days. Mrs. Nora Spanish is at left in wheelchair, her grandson Thomas Whitford beside her wearing his grandfather's regalia, their daughters and daughter-in-law on right. Nora Spanish led Blackfeet Craftsworkers Guild for many years. Credit: Thomas Kehoe.

PLATE 9. Browning, Montana, Blackfeet Reservation headquarters town.
Credit: Alice B. Kehoe.

PLATE 10. Downtown Browning, Native American National Bank at right.
Credit: Alice B. Kehoe.

PLATE 11. Blackfeet Housing Office, Browning. Credit: Alice B. Kehoe.

PLATE 12. Indian Health Service hospital, Browning. In foreground, sculpture by Jay Labre.
Credit: Alice B. Kehoe.

PLATE 13. Blackfeet Community College, Browning, administration building and library. Credit: Alice B. Kehoe.

PLATE 14. St. Michael's Cemetery, Browning, maintained by the community. Credit: Alice B. Kehoe.

PLATE 15. Cross at accident death site beside highway, Blackfeet Reservation. Credit: Alice B. Kehoe.

PLATE 16. Chief Earl Old Person. Credit: Earl Old Person.

TWO

The Amskapi Pikuni
from the 1950s to 2010

*By Earl Old Person, Member,
Blackfeet Tribal Business Council 1954–2008,
Chairman of the Council 1964–2008*

For the Blackfeet people, the 1950s brought about many changes. The changes didn't seem major, but their effects would be lasting. Gone were the roaming days, a new era was well underway.

Young Blackfeet men were being drafted to the army or attending college. The young women of the reservation were being taught home economics. The United States Government began a revised relocation policy for young people. Under the relocation policy the Bureau of Indian Affairs provided transportation, job placement, vocational training, and counseling to Indians who wanted to leave reservations. The majority of young Blackfeet men took full advantage of the program.

For those who were left home on the reservation, the traditional ways were quickly becoming a thing of the past. The practice of traditional social gatherings and dances was gone. The first commercialized "pow-wow" on the Blackfeet reservation was held in 1952. It was started by a local man who had attended a gathering in Wyoming known as the All American Indian Days. The reason for All American Indian Days in Sheridan, Wyoming, was to promote improved relations between the Indians and non-Indians. During this time it was not uncommon to see signs in shops and cafe windows in Sheridan: "No Indians or Dogs Allowed," and "No Indians Served Here." The Blackfeet Reservation was no different.

Picking up on the idea, the businessman remembered by Chief Old Person only as "Pat" approached the Tribal Business Council with the idea of replicating the All American Indians Days here in Browning. The idea was embraced by both the city businesses and the Tribal Council.

177

The result was the first North American Indian Days, held in July 1953 (Plate 7). From that time on, Indian Days was held on the second Thursday of every July. Added to this newfound celebration the following year was the addition of legalized liquor sales on the reservation.

According to Chief Old Person, there were two elder women, Maud and Annie Cobell, who often attended the monthly Tribal Council meetings, who requested open liquor sales on the reservation. He remembers them telling the council members, "If our young men can fight in the war, they can make their own decisions about drinking liquor." The tribal council agreed and liquor sales on the reservation were legalized. Chief Old Person also remembers that after about a year of legalized alcohol, the same two elderly ladies came back to the council requesting that alcohol sales be banned from the reservation. By May 1954, the first bar opened its doors on the reservation. Today there are still severe struggles with alcohol abuse that tears families apart.

In 1962, the Blackfeet Tribal Business Council discontinued the practice of open enrollment. The blood degree requirement was increased to one-quarter or more Blackfeet blood in order to be enrolled in the Blackfeet Tribe. The blood degree requirement for enrollment continues to be a hot topic among enrolled members, most often the full-bloods.

In the 1960s, the reservation was seeing its first high school graduates attend college. The BIA had again reorganized its educational programs, this time allowing for equal opportunities to go to college or vocational school. It was during this time that the young people who chose to attend colleges or vocational schools became active in the Red Power and the American Indian Movement, also known as AIM.

At that time, Indian life expectancy was just 44 years, one-third less than that of the typical American. Deaths caused by pneumonia, hepatitis, dysentery, strep throat, diabetes, tuberculosis, alcoholism, suicide, and homicide were two to sixty times higher than among the whole United States population (US Digital History 2006). Many Blackfeet families lived in unsanitary, dilapidated dwellings, many in tents. The young Blackfeet became more aware of their reservation surroundings by going off to college.

They began to realize that conditions on their own reservation were not unlike those found in underdeveloped countries. Many of the homes they left had no running water, some had no electricity, they used outdoor toilets, and woodburning stoves for heat (Plate 4). Some of the poorest homes were located on the south side of Browning, called "Moccasin Flat." It was during the late 1960s that young Blackfeet who left the reservation began to revolt against such conditions. It was the same group of young Blackfeet that continued their education and graduated from such prestigious colleges as Berkeley, Harvard, and others.

On the home front, Chief Old Person and other tribal leaders were mounting their own rebellion against conditions that Native Americans faced. In 1969, Chief Old Person was elected president of the National Congress of American Indians. During his tenure as NCAI president the United States Government continued to discuss termination of reservations. In a speech given to members of the National Congress of American Indians, Chief Old Person spoke of termination in these terms:

> Again, I say, "Let's forget termination and try a policy that has never been tried before—development of the Indian reservations for Indians and development of Indians as human beings with a personality and a soul and dreams for a bright future." Why is it so important that Indians be brought into the "mainstream of American life?" What is the "mainstream of American life?" I would not know how to interpret the phrase to my people in our language. The closest I would be able to come to "mainstream" would be to say, in Indian, "a big wide river." Am I then going to tell my people that they will be "thrown into the Big, Wide River of the United States"? [Earl Old Person 1969]

Chief Old Person sat on the Indian Self Determination Task Force from 1968 to 1970 and continued to help the federal government see the true plight of Native Americans. On July 8, 1970, President Nixon announced a new policy of "self-determination without termination" for Native Americans. In passing the new policy President Nixon said, "It is long past time that the Indian policies of the federal government began to recognize and build upon the capacities of the Indian people" (Nixon 1970). For the Blackfeet it meant new opportunities to control their own destiny.

The Blackfeet Tribe was always one of prominence, one whom every other tribe looked to for direction. In keeping up their legacy during these modern times, the Blackfeet Tribe, under the direction of Chief Earl Old Person, began the pursuit of economic self-sufficiency. The Blackfeet built a sawmill in order to create jobs and make use of their natural resources. The Bureau of Indian Affairs was strongly resistant to the tribe building their own businesses without their consent. The sawmill was the first of many businesses to be created by the tribe without the help of BIA. From that time on, the Blackfeet realized that they were in charge of their own destiny. In 1972, they opened the first pencil factory to be built west of the

Mississippi. This enterprise employed more than 250 people working on three different shifts. This success prompted the tribe to establish many more business enterprises throughout the years. Some were successful and some were not.

During the early 1970s, the young college graduates of the Blackfeet Reservation, still restless from the 1960s, participated in the Trail of Broken Treaties occupation of the Washington, D.C., BIA building. By this time the reservation was looking more promising and the young people settled down and began to participate in development activities.

One such project was the Blackfeet Community College (Plate 13). In 1972, Chief Old Person and his wife brought executives from the Arizona State University to visit the Blackfeet Reservation to begin the process of opening a community college. Soon the idea took off and the young Blackfeet fresh from the Trail of Broken Treaties assisted the Chief in offering college courses through Flathead Valley Community College. By 1981, Blackfeet Community College had its first graduates.

The Blackfeet continued moving forward on the national level as well. In 1975, the Sweet Grass hills claim was paid out to Blackfeet enrolled members. Each living enrolled member of the Blackfeet Tribe received $500. Two years later, Forest Gerard, a Blackfeet Indian, was confirmed as the first Indian Assistant Secretary of Interior for the BIA. Also in 1977, the National Tribal Employment Rights Organization (TERO) was established by the Blackfeet Tribe and made a national organization. TERO was established to access more employment and training opportunities for Native Americans and their families and to provide more business and economic opportunities for businesses owned by Native Americans. Currently, the majority of federally recognized tribes participate in the TERO Program.

Somewhere in the midst of the rush to take control of the reservation and create economic development, elders sat and quietly watched. It was in 1978 when the family of the last hereditary Chief, Chief White Calf, decided it was time to name a new chief for the Piegan Band of Blackfeet Indians. Old man White Calf chose Earl Old Person to accept the honors (Plate 16). Earl was 49 at the time and had been on the Blackfeet Tribal Business Council for 24 years. Today (2011), at 81, he still holds the title of chief. Many members of the Blackfeet Tribe still seek out his advice on family matters, business matters, and more importantly, traditional matters. Chief Old Person is one of a handful who remember songs, traditions, customs, and proper protocol for ceremonies, societies, and social gatherings.

1982—Oil boom on reservation—650 producing oil wells.

1982—Accounting Claim paid out to enrolled individuals.

1983—Ground broken for new hospital after 10 years of U.S. Senate testimony by Earl Old Person (Plate 12).

1987—Piegan Institute creates a language school.

1990—NAGPRA Law passes—its effects on Blackfeet Traditional customs.

1993—Blackfeet repatriate Scriver bundles.[1] Locals begin to revive traditions.

1993—State begins positive relations with Montana. Earl Old Person delivers first State of the Indian Nations Address at the State Capitol.

2008—Earl Old Person completes his 50th year as tribal councilman. Retires from public service.

2009—Charging Home Historical Society founded by Chief Old Person.

Reference

Nixon, Richard M. July 8, 1970. Congressional "Message from the President of the United States Transmitting Recommendations for Indian Policy."

THREE

Bungling

No doubt we shall go on bungling Indian affairs for the simple reason
that the problems presented are of no particular economic and social
importance to the nation at large.

–Clark Wissler, *Indian Cavalcade*

Clark Wissler's concept of human ecology means more than the interac-
tions of people with their landscape and natural resources: it covers political factors, too. The history of the Blackfeet Reservation is a chronicle
of inept administrators pushing misguided policies. Graft and conniving
flourished as agent after agent seemed unable to keep accounts straight,
or even to keep accounts at all. Without question, the United States failed
in—as lawyers put it—its fiduciary responsibility under its treaties with
the Piegan. The Blackfeet Agency despoiled the reservation to benefit
white stockmen. The politics were simple: white men voted, Indians, for
the most part, could not until 1924. Montana's congressmen, many of
whom had mercantile and ranching businesses, favored staunch members of their own political party, while federal government bureaucrats
were guided by idealistic programs meant to transform Indian people
into working-class Americans. Ironically, Piegan who pursued the American ethic of hard work and capital investment earned distrust from agents
as well as from "full-bloods" choosing a more traditional Blackfoot way.
The natural ecology of the reservation probably could have sustained a
tribal cattle industry providing a modest but decent life for the Amskapi
Pikuni; politics in Montana and Washington bungled range management,
beggaring the people. Two programs stand out for their disastrous effects:
agents' failure to protect Blackfeet range for Piegan use, and the million
dollar irrigation project.

    Under the Indian Claims Commission Act of 1946, the Blackfeet
Tribe filed a claim in 1951. Michael Foley compiled the record supporting their case. A component of a case in court, Foley's report is necessarily biased toward the claimant tribe, but it is meticulously documented,
and parallels more recent, scholarly historical studies (Carter 1990; Lux

2001; Shewell 2004; Tough 1996). Foley's descriptions of the tribe's agents agrees with Clark Wissler's memoir, picturing "the Major" as a petty tyrant, arrogant and dictatorial. Wissler said the Indian agent was always called "the Major," for "locally he was Major" (Wissler 1971[1938]:13). Summing up his observations, Wissler wrote,

> I suppose that most of my readers have by this time wondered if there ever was a good agent, especially since for a century or more, both official and social Washington have made him the scape-goat. Yes, there have been courageous, honest and lovable men in that office; also there have been rascals and innocent incompetents. . . . On every reservation I visited I heard Indian traditions of one or more great agents, though I doubt if any of these were rated high in Washington. The agent who took a realistic sensible view of the situation and called a spade by its right name, stood a good chance for a place in tribal tradition, but for this very reason would arouse the ire of the idealists in the East. . . . Every realistically minded agent saw himself the imposed head of a tribe of Indians, fenced into a reserve like predatory animals, more for the protection of the white people without, than for the well being of the Indians within. His duty was to keep these Indians from alarming settlers by wandering abroad, and to feed, clothe, and house them upon an inadequate budget. [Wissler 1972[1938]:23]

Michael Foley's report begins with the 1855 treaty and its promises. He quotes one of the first "Majors," Alfred Vaughn, whose wife was Indian:

> The gintiuella or sky blue blanket is high-priced, inferior & not desired; fancy list cloths are too fine & too flimsy; worsted yarn supplies no want in the lodge or field; calicoes of all kinds & descriptions are badly adapted for use or comfort on the prairie; Calico shirts are far inferior in durability to the common hickory; the N. W. guns are literally worthless . . . the powder horns are fine and unsubstantial, easily cracked and injured; butcher knives and half axes inferior in material and unreliable in temper. . . . The fire steels furnished are worse than useless, being no more than common iron [quoted in Foley 1974:9].

Throughout the 1860s, treaty annuities were paid in goods that not only were cheap and "worse than useless," but usually were delayed, sometimes for more than a year, if and when delivered lacked bills of lading and records of to whom distributed, and were likely to be purloined and traded to Indians for buffalo robes. Pierre Choteau Jr. held the transport contract and was believed to be responsible for diverting many boxes of goods to his own company's trade. Frontier storage facilities were so poor that in November 1869, 169,000 lbs. of "partially damaged corn . . . being damp, is likely to spoil if kept, and cannot be fed to animals, [therefore] it be issued friendly Indians in that vicinity" (Foley 1974:25)— as Vaughn had remarked, some of the annuity goods were "worse than useless."

Money was as slippery as annuity goods. Agent George Wright discovered in 1868 that Montana governor Smith had taken money issued in 1867–68 for the Blackfeet Agency to pay a personal loan, and Wright had to wait in Virginia City until Smith won $500 at faro, which he then handed to Wright for agency expenses. In 1897, Agent Steell had to request that the Office of Indian Affairs forego $7,000 from Blackfeet Agency accounts because its bank, in Helena, failed; fortunately, the bank was able to reopen the next month (Foley 1974:220).

Foley considered the merchants originally at Fort Benton, Isaac Baker, William and Charles Conrad, Thomas C. and John Power, and Charles A. Broadwater, the worst aggressors against the Piegan. Baker had written to the Secretary of the Interior that *"necessity has made the law inoperative . . . if the Hon. Secy. of the Interior believed [p. 24] it [i.e., that the law was operative], he has been derelict in duty, in not driving the thirty thousand settlers of Montana from the homes they are unlawfully holding on Indian lands"* (Foley 1974:23–24). In 1874, Baker complained to Montana's territorial delegate to Congress, fellow merchant Martin Maginnis, that Blackfeet Agent Richard May was trying to impose regulations on transport contracts; May was removed from his post, presumably through Maginnis's lobbying, and John Wood—the agent Clark Wissler most admired—was appointed, only to be removed when he also attempted to enforce honest business practices with the merchants. Foley suggested (1974:56) that profits from cartage enabled the merchants to build their immense cattle operations: in 1884, a Montana newspaper stated it took $100,000 to start a ranch. William Conrad was accused in 1882 of illegally running 12,000 head of cattle on the Blackfeet Reservation, and he and other big stockmen drove herds leisurely, grazing as they moved, across the reservation from south to north to sell in Alberta. During the winter of 1882–83, when the bison herds had disappeared, Agent Young tried to buy beef cattle to feed the Piegan, but the cattlemen refused to round up animals in winter. Then, in Spring 1883, Young contracted for 120,000 lbs. of beef on the hoof to T. C. Power, who later claimed he had subcontracted to a man who insisted he had not been told to deliver. When Young per-severed, Power said August was too late to deliver cattle. The result was starvation for the Piegan in 1883–84, when an estimated 10,000 head of cattle had moved through their territory en route to markets in Canada. By 1886, a Montana newspaper estimated 75,000 head of white ranchers' cattle were grazing on the reservation, some legally through fees paid to Agent Baldwin—ten cents to drive an animal through to Canada, $3.00 to $3.50 to graze through a winter. The severe winter of 1886–87 killed many open range cattle, compelling the big ranchers toward some closer management, but trespassing on the reservation grasslands never ceased, and those ranchers who paid fees for using Piegan forage continued to overstock, careless of overgrazing.

Some agents were denounced as "'a thief and a 'Squaw Master'" (Fol-ey 1974:37). Agent Young was seventy-two, but was accused of keeping a "harem of Indian girls." At the same time, 1883, Young closed down a "brothel" he saw operating in the agency trading store; he further chas-tised the trader for price gouging. Young was a temperance advocate, in contrast to several other agents notorious for drunkenness, and in George Steell's case, as a morphine addict. Steell, or his wife, in whose name an initial 80 head were registered, ran his own cattle on the reservation while serving as agent; he sometimes paid grazing fees, but by 1893 shipped $9,500 worth of cattle, and by 1897 was said to own $35,000 worth of cat-tle using the reservation range (Foley 1974:219). That year, 1897, an in-spector from the Office of Indian Affairs reported that Steell had provided a house for the agency butcher and that the butcher's wife was "a pro-curess" inducing local girls to live there for "assignations." Worse, George Steell himself moved into the house after he was terminated as agent that summer, while Mrs. Steell was in Spokane for medical treatment (Foley 1974:229–230, 267). Horace Wilson, Superintendent 1919–20, was arrested for bigamy after he left the agency (Foley 1974: 446). Agent Mark Bald-win's "mismanagement" of funds, 1886–89, earned him denunciation in the *New York Times*; notwithstanding this, in 1907 he proposed to the tribe that he represent it as attorney in its claims case. Agent McFatridge, dis-missed for malfeasance in 1915, took the check for $1,200 from reservation grazing permits to Canada and cashed it; agency records were so poor that it took two years for this theft to be discovered, and there seems no evidence that McFatridge repaid the tribe.

Coincident with the severe winter of 1886–87 discouraging white agri-business-scale ranchers, reports of valuable minerals in the Sweet Grass Hills prompted the federal government to buy the hills from the Black-feet. The tribe, only two years past its Starvation Winter, reluctantly pro-posed to sell for three million dollars. Treaty commissioners hammered that down to half, $1,500,000, *to be paid out over ten years, without accruing interest* and not paid directly but in goods, "livestock, agricultural implements, clothes, subsistence, education, new Agency buildings, medical care, mechanics shops" (Foley 1974:93). In other words, the tribe could not purchase its needs from suppliers of its choice. As with earlier annuity goods, short weights, shoddy quality, and sometimes failure to deliver robbed the Indian people of full value from their agreements; in this case, Agent Catlin, Baldwin's successor, had the gall to ask his superiors in the Office of Indian Affairs whether those goods should be used to pay Indians for labor for the agency—it was customary to recompense Indians for labor with tickets to be exchanged for rations or goods stored at the Agency (Foley 1974:113–114). Little Plume, White Calf, Bear Chief, and others, on an 1891 trip to Washington to discuss Blackfeet conditions with the Office of Indian Affairs, protested they did not want the Sweet Grass Hills money to be used to pay labor, nor did they want outside ranchers using their range.

Neither the Sweet Grass Hills nor, slightly later, the foothills that would be ceded and then made Glacier National Park contained the mineral wealth anticipated from first discoveries. What would substantially change the regional economy was the Great Northern Railroad, running just south of the Sweet Grass Hills and through the reservation into Marias Pass. Construction began in 1890, with crews cutting reservation timber and hay for their stock but not hiring Indians. A couple years later, the railroad paid for some of these resources. In 1892, the chief clerk of the Blackfeet Agency, E. C. Garrett, secretly wrote to Great Northern's "empire builder" James J. Hill asking him to work with Montanans plotting to take over the western strip of the reservation for miners. Hill replied that the Piegan could be removed to Dakota, a suggestion that Garrett thought unlikely to work (Foley 1974:141). A year later, Garrett and Agent Cooke and his son who was Agency Issue Clerk, registered 27 mineral claims along the mountains adjacent to the reservation. When the Piegan leaders were brought in to sell the western strip, in 1895, they—White Calf, Three Suns, Little Dog, Four Horns, and Little Bear Chief—tried to insist they would sell only the northern half of the strip, from the Canadian border to the head of Cut Bank Creek, and asked two million dollars (Little Dog asked three million). The government commissioners, who included writer George Bird Grinnell, supposedly a friend to the Piegan, demanded a strip running the entire western length of the reservation, for payment of $1,500,000 over ten years *to begin when the Sweet Grass Hills annual payments were completed*. Little Dog opposed what was in effect a continuation of traditional annuities, and Horace Clarke, son of murdered Malcolm Clarke and his Piegan wife, asked whether the federal government would assist the Piegan in developing the expected mineral resources rather than sell them to whites. Both these efforts to improve Piegan economy were ignored. It transpired that when the demanded land cession was pushed through, the commissioners *estimated* that they had taken 800,000 acres: their maps were inadequate to actually delimit the cession (Foley 1974:197).

Neither the agencies nor schools ever were constructed to properly meet local conditions and functional needs. A visitor from the Office of Indian Affairs in August 1895 described the new Willow Creek Agency as, "A more dreary, bleak, desolate spot would be hard to find. The buildings stand in the prairie, in a valley, where the wind sweeps with great power to and from the mountains about 9 [sic] days in the week. There is no grass, no shade, 'no nothing'" (quoted in Foley 1974:204). Much of the cost of the new agency came out of the 1887 treaty payment. In 1897, the boys' dormitory burned down, no fire protection having been considered, and in 1898, sewage contaminated the school water supply.

Running through all the reports by agents and Office of Indian Affairs inspectors are two related topics: the cattle industry and irrigation. Both reveal remarkable bungling and boondoggling. The irrigation projects ran over a million dollars, seldom were supervised by qualified engineers, and failed to attract Indians to irrigated farming. Only the Jesuits at Holy Family Mission successfully irrigated gardens, and they were not required to pay fees for the project (Foley 1974:464). Again and again, seepage from poorly constructed irrigation canals called for more thousands of dollars for repair, on top of the initial project costs. Construction of irrigation canals did provide cash wages for men, boys, and horse teams, for which reason many of the agents, Piegan, and Cree wanted construction to continue. The principal crop for the irrigated "forties" (40-acre portions of individual allotments located on irrigable land) was hay, but inept or reluctant agents seemed to leave the Piegan always short of mowers and rakes to harvest their hay. After allotment of the reservation, around 1910, the cost of the boondoggle irrigation was attached as liens on Piegan patents, and allottees with land within the irrigation projects (not necessarily receiving any water) were required to pay for irrigation. Once the St. Mary's-Milk River irrigation system for off-reservation ranchers was built, water that formerly maintained fine hay meadows in the northern part of the reservation was diverted downstream from the Blackfeet, crippling hay production on the Blackfeet ranches.

Beyond the practical problems lay Anglo dedication to mixed farming as not only ideal for supporting families, but somehow the essence of moral Christian living: unless and until the Piegan lived as private families on farms with wheat, oats, vegetables, milk cows, and chickens, they would not be civilized—and without far more water than falls as rain on the high northwestern Plains, there could not be such family farms. Therefore, policymakers in Washington and agents and missionaries on the reservation literally moved heaven and earth to irrigate the forties, often 20 to 40 miles from allottees' cabins, and persuade Piegan to live on them. Here is a good lesson on human ecology; the politics of Anglo domination, and incompetent or dishonest agents and Reclamation employees, assaulted the Piegan nation that knew, from centuries of visits to the irrigated fields of Mandan, Hidatsa, and Arikara down the Missouri, that Blackfoot territory is not amenable to irrigated agriculture.

The other side of the coin from irrigation farming is cattle ranching. This is what the reservation could support, *if* the land were reserved for Piegan cattle *and* Indian ranchers could manage their herds without interference from crooked or ignorant agents. Piegan learned quickly how to raise and market cattle. They quickly learned to harvest hay to carry stock over the winter, and to select sheltered wintering locations, as Insima and her husband Yellow Wolf did soon after the bison disappeared. What the Piegan could not do was prevent outsiders' cattle from overgrazing reservation range, nor get the capital and political connections to work advantageous deals in stocking and selling herds. Most of the Piegan had little choice but to sell their cattle either to local traders such as Sherburne to obtain credit for purchases in their stores, or let the agent handle sales or obstruct selling if he thought the Indian rancher should build a bigger herd or wait for better prices (even if that meant overwintering stock). Money from sale of Indian beef, as well as land sales, was deposited into "Miscellaneous Receipts" in the U.S. Treasury rather than into Indian Affairs accounts, until in 1908 the Department of the Interior succeeded in changing the practice, although that did not result in funds going into designated tribal accounts such as that of the Blackfeet. Bungling the livestock industry on the reservation was often actually criminal, Agents failing to control numbers of animals permitted and favoring, or at best unable to prevent, exploitation by big operators such as Dan Floweree, who in 1908 bought permits for 7,000 cattle but had twice that number, plus 650 horses, on the Piegan range. William Conrad, another big operator, settled on Birch Creek in 1904 and without any permission, built his own dam to divert much of the stream to his meadows. Around 1898, Piegan such as Bear Chief formally petitioned the Department of Interior to fence the entire reservation, using tribal money, to keep Piegan cattle in (some were said to have wandered as far as the Little Rockies and the Missouri) and outsiders' out. Others at this time urged hiring range riders to police the herds, since cowboys were known to carry wirecutters to open passageways in fences. When a fence was constructed, by 1904, it

did not rectify the problem because, aside from illegal entries, big cattlemen obtained permits. Meanwhile, Piegan at this time were required to
pay a grazing tax on their own animals on reservation range! Then, after
allotment was completed in 1912, the fence was to be destroyed, with the
tribe to hire range riders.

Exacerbating outside cattlemens' overgrazing, during the first half of
the 20th century some outside ranchers and some agents, such as Fred
Campbell, ran sheep on the reservation. As early as 1905, sage was replacing good grass forage on overgrazed land, prompting this resort to
sheep, which could eat such poor vegetation. In 1899, Agent Logan, who
had experience ranching in Texas, estimated the reservation carried 8,500
Blackfeet cattle and 21,000 horses. Three years later, Agent Monteath
claimed 19,709 Indian cattle. An Indian Office inspector in 1914 reported
12,000 Blackfeet cattle and 9,000 horses, yet people in Heart Butte district were said to be destitute and some families subsisting on wild berries. Piegan owed more than $115,000 for purchases of food and goods
from traders, allowing Sherburne Mercantile, for example, allegedly to
own forty thousand acres collected as debt payment (Foley 1974:435, 447).
White Antelope and two hundred other Piegan petitioned the Indian Office in 1914 to remove Agent McFatridge; their petition was dismissed on
the grounds that the Indians were ignorant, and spokesman Robert Hamilton, who certainly wasn't ignorant, was rejected because he had been
convicted of horse theft and forgery. The Indian Office did send its chief
inspector to the reservation, and when his investigation revealed McFatridge apparently kept no records—at least none were produced nor could
be discovered—and had swindled families, McFatridge was dismissed.

McFatridge's successor, C. E. Ellis, bought, from a reimbursable fund,
1,800 head to form a tribal cattle herd. At the same time, Ellis favored Piegan privately leasing allotments to outside ranchers, rather than keeping
leasing a tribal enterprise. World War I in 1917 escalated the price of beef,
increasing demand for reservation grazing and even benefiting poor full-
bloods selling their one market product, hay. Superintendent Ellis in 1917
claimed Blackfeet owned 35,000 cattle, not counting the agency-managed
tribal herd, and the next year, at least 74,000 cattle and horses—both Indian-owned and outsiders'—plus 5,000 sheep were grazing the reservation
range (another estimate gave 65,000 cattle, 25,000 horses, and 5,000 sheep).
Of 35,000 Blackfeet cattle, approximately five-sixths were owned by only
30 reservation families, or put another way, 3 percent of Blackfeet owned
95 percent of Indian cattle (Foley 1974:442, 450). Unhappily, the wartime
boom for cattle coincided, in 1917–18, with drought in Montana, reducing
forage just when incentive for expanding herds was greatest. Then, 1919
brought blizzards in November hitting undernourished cattle that, due

to Indian Office delay in approving beef sales, were still on the range. Expected winter feed had not arrived, nor had rations ordered for humans. Finally, in 1920, what was left of the tribal herd was sold with a reported loss to the tribe of $54,000—estimated at actually $150,000–$200,000 in a 1929 investigation (Foley 1974: 460, 490). Fred Campbell, taking over as agency superintendent in 1921, told the Indian Office that the Blackfeet Tribe was bankrupt (Foley 1974:467). So, too, were many Montana whites suffering winter loss of cattle and the postwar drop in beef prices. The American Red Cross sent a representative with emergency funds to the Blackfeet Reservation in 1921, but the money was deposited in a local bank that failed, losing the funds.

Fred Campbell had been livestock supervisor for the Blackfeet Agency, and in 1925 was named Supervisor of Livestock at Large[1] for reservations in five states, a position to be held simultaneously with running the Blackfeet Agency. The lesson he took from the disaster of drought plus harsh winter, in 1918–20, was that cattle were not a viable option for the Piegan. Instead of ranching, he advocated self-sustaining small family farms on fenced allotments, raising wheat and oats, a vegetable garden, chickens, pigs, a milk cow, and a few goats and sheep. Outside operators were encouraged to run sheep on leased land, against strong opposition by Piegan anticipating ruination of the range. Where previous agents had relied on agency staff farmers (non-Indian) to demonstrate family-scale farming, Campbell in 1921 corralled the agency farmer, matron, and other employees to travel with him systematically along the reservation valleys to personally visit every Piegan home, recording its condition and holdings and talking up with residents the advantages of Campbell's five-year plan to improve their lot. Only the southern districts of the reservation were thoroughly visited. For 1922, Campbell requested $75,000 for the farming plan, including $10,000 to exterminate gophers that he believed were destroying the land (Foley 1974:474). Most of the Piegan small farms he encouraged were heavily damaged by grasshoppers in 1924 (Foley 1974:483). To deal with the need for agricultural machinery for plowing and threshing, Campbell recruited people into district cooperatives to purchase machines. This decentralized administration and stimulated support for Campbell's policies. Ah, opportunity again for bungling! Appointing Campbell to be supervisor at large, the Indian Office required him to travel most of the year to other reservations, depriving the Piegan of a full-time superintendent and giving incompetence and corruption much latitude. Grazing was leased by the acre without specifying number or type of animals to be permitted, and in 1923, the Indian Office forgave 60 percent, $45,000, owed since 1918 by half-breed and white lessees to Piegan (Foley 1974:479).

Five years after the touted five-year plan was initiated, the average
Piegan farm was seven and one-half acres. Campbell chose to label his
plan an "unsuccess," not a failure (Foley 1974:487, 488). He still promoted sheep grazing, continuously opposed by Piegan whose unhappiness
was amplified by Campbell applying profits from wool to Indians' reimbursable loans (Foley 1974:484). Those thousands of horses on the range,
for many of the most conservative and impoverished Piegan their only
livestock, Campbell considered worthless, and took action by ordering
a great roundup in 1926. Chappel Brothers enterprise was let the contract to carry out the roundup, dip all Piegan horses against mange (said
by the Piegan to be common on outsider lessees' animals), and purchase
"excess" horses, the cost of roundup and dipping paid out of tribal funds
although ordered by Superintendent Campbell and his assistant Forrest
Stone. When a rival firm in Butte bid higher per head to purchase horses, its buyer was arrested (Foley 1974:488). This scandal, and other complaints, led the United States Senate to send its own investigator, Walter
Liggett, to the reservation in 1928. Liggett's conclusion was that Campbell
was not criminally corrupt but a poor and too-often-absent manager; that
far too much was drawn from tribal monies to pay for agency equipment
including automobiles, to pay, for example, $7,000 to the Jesuits for Holy
Family Mission, and to pay for that immense boondoggle, irrigation (Foley 1974:490). As so consistently appeared during investigations, the Blackfeet Agency could not produce records to cover transactions or account
for Indian leases, and lack of records for disputed actions pitted Piegan
against the word of agency staff or white traders (Foley 1974:495). In a follow-up under President Hoover, Campbell denied running his own sheep
on the reservation in spite of his brand being seen on animals. Campbell
was relieved of his office in 1929 and his sidekick, Forrest Stone, made
superintendent (Foley 1974:498). The Great Depression and Dustbowl
drought of the 1930s ensured hard times on the reservation as elsewhere,
only 138 families self-supporting in 1934 and 747 families depending on
relief (Foley 1974:530). Because northern Montana was relatively greener
than the Plains farther south, 5,500 starving cattle were shipped in 1936
to the reservation. Several hundred died during the following difficult
winter. In 1943, in a prime example of bungling, the Blackfeet Tribe was
ordered to pay for the "drought cattle," worth $12 each when shipped,
at 1943 inflated wartime beef prices, $70 per head. White cattlemen in
Montana who accepted "drought cattle" were not asked to pay for the
animals (Foley 1974:543–44). Dispute over payment continued until, in
1952, a Congressional hearing was held on the issue (Foley 1974:565).

The Great Northern Railroad looms behind the reservation for a century. Louis Hill, son and successor to "empire builder" James J. Hill, cut

a deal with agency superintendent Horace Wilson to push through the Tribal Council a ten-year lease for exploratory oil drilling. Tribal council-men recalled discussion of the number of wells that needed to be drilled and time limits, but somehow none of these details appeared in the legal document. Hill drilled only one well, to less than required depth, plugged and covered it, then tried to retain leased land to rent out (Foley 1974:502–504). The Great Northern bought gravel from reservation quarries for as little as $50 for 25,000 yards, an amount worth about $2,000. In a more complicated scheme, the Indian Office transferred reservation land to the Reclamation Bureau, which in turn leased it to the (Glacier) Park Saddle Horse Company, a subsidiary of the Great Northern running a monop-oly on furnishing horses to tourists in the Park (Foley 1974:493). Walter Liggett's investigation charged that the Great Northern toured Blackfeet through the East to advertise its Glacier Park hotels (Fig. 9) and arranged for families to set up tipis, wear costumes, and dance by the East Glacier hotel, but did not pay them and supplied only food scraps from the hotel restaurant for their support; families were obliged to pass the hat among the tourists for payment. The real bungling was Blackfeet agents' bland acceptance of Great Northern and Glacier Park policies of not hiring In-dians except for menial work out of sight of tourists. Not until the end of the 20th century did the park begin to employ Indian people, or give in to allowing Piegan entrepreneurs to enter the park.

Franklin Roosevelt's New Deal for Indians, through his 1933 ap-pointment of John Collier as Commissioner of Indian Affairs, brought anthropologists to the reservation to assess and recommend policy. Da-vid Rodnick, there for three months in 1936, described the seemingly profound differences between "full-bloods" and "mixed-bloods," the lat-ter obtaining, he said, a disproportionate amount of reservation funds. Confirming that petitions by full-bloods were often ignored, not passed on to Washington officials, Rodnick urged reform of election districts so that small conservative communities such as Starr School would not be minorities in larger districts such as Browning (Foley 1974: 535). Eight years later, John C. Ewers, living in Browning as curator of the Museum of the Plains Indian, reviewed Superintendent McBride's proposed ten-year program. Ewers agreed with fellow anthropologist Rodnick's con-cern with disparities between the conservatives ("full-bloods") and fewer, prosperous "mixed-bloods" (Foley 1974:551). Commissioner Collier's le-gal counsel Felix S. Cohen suggested in 1945 that full-bloods form their own tribal organization to better pursue their interests (Foley 1974:552). Cohen told the Tribal Council in 1950, after he had resigned at the end of 1947 to open a private law practice advising Indians, that "we have a hard job ahead of us, trying to combine Blackfeet generosity and white man's business practices" (quoted in Foley 1947:563). The Piegan custom of generosity to relatives, friends, and people in need constantly raised accusations of impropriety in council payments and loans, which were again and again found to lack adequate records and reimbursements. It could be debated whether outspoken successful ranchers on the council such as Brian Connolly and George Pambrun should be considered corrupt for their many personal deals with tribal money. However we judge these mid-20th-century council leaders, we can't accuse them of bungling. The second half of the 20th century was fractious and frequently discouraging on the Blackfeet Reservation as Piegan struggled to resolve Cohen's "hard job." It was nonetheless a movement out of "the Major's" control. The Amskapi Pikuni survived a long century of remarkable bungling, and so did their thousands of horses on the range.

FOUR

Schooling

Formal schooling has been a divisive issue on the Blackfeet Reservation. "Education," meaning schooling, was the instrument grasped by Anglo missionaries and their associates the United States and Canadian bureaus of Indian Affairs. Amskapi Pikuni attended U.S. Bureau of Indian Affairs schools on Cut Bank Creek near Browning; at Fort Shaw, near Cascade, Montana, Chemawa in Oregon, Genoa in Nebraska, Haskell in Lawrence, Kansas, and Carlisle in Pennsylvania; Catholic Holy Family Mission on the reservation and at St. Ignatius to the west and St. Peter's Missions and Robare south of it; and public schools in communities near the reservation such as Valier and Cut Bank. John Collier's New Deal policy reforms promoted day schools on the reservations with some curriculum materials in the Indian language, developed for Navajo and Lakota children but not yet implemented elsewhere before cut short by World War II priorities. After the war, integration of Indian children into public schools neighboring reservations was pushed, both in the United States and Canada, as means to assimilate them into Anglo society—a goal no different than the 19th-century aim, but less expensive than boarding schools. Finally, the mid-1970s Indian Self-Determination legislation began a shift to Indian control of Indian education.

In 1939, Agnes Chief All Over described entering boarding school on the reservation; it must have been the B.I.A. Willow Creek school, opened 1892, and she would have been about twelve:

> *School*. First time sat at table with utensils. Didn't know how to dish out or eat. Watched others and followed them and imitated them. Scared of everything, even the school building. Window high up and [I] asked how they go out—told that one climbed a ladder (steps). Dinner was meat, gravy and potatoes. Through, got up to walk out. One of the white waitresses came over and

pulled out my chair and told me, "Sit down." [I] Didn't know English. Didn't understand. Other child explained—not to walk out until the others did.

Bell rang—[I] imitated others—pushed chairs under table. Bell rang again—[we] walked out of doors.

[I] Told friend '"Want to go to toilet." There's little house— we'll go to the back of it. Done several times before matron found out. Asked all the children who did it. [I] told—Matron took us to privies. Pick up dress, unbutton pants (first I had ever worn), sit on hole. Afraid to sit on hole. Afraid I'll go through and told other girl to hold my hands tight. Girl buttoned my pants, and I did same for other girl. Matron stood and laughed at us. Kept talking, but we didn't understand her English. Matron talked to older girls to tell them not to go outside again and not to be scared of holes—they can't break.

Every few minutes—I wanted to go. Everyone acted strange and felt guilty.

Boarding school—we went in last of October, stayed until June. About four or five miles from home. [Agnes' family, Yellow Wolf and his three wives including Agnes' mother Insima, English name Cecile Sanderville, settled on Willow Creek three miles from Browning.] Grandmother came up every Friday. Mother came up every two or three weeks. Didn't like to come [because] I'd cry to go home with them. First part of the year [they] didn't come often till I got used to the school. Grandmother would bring dried prunes and Pimm crackers. Mother brought nuts, candies, oranges, cookies.

[In school, the students] All lined up and marched into hall, at about eight o'clock. Few stood back afraid of ladder (steps). Looks high and dangerous. Don't want to go up. Light up there and next place dark—ghosts up there.

Two of the oldest girls carried them pick-back.

First time [I] slept on spring bed—every time [I] moved, bed would rock. [I was] Scared something [was] under bed. First time ever [I] had slept alone. Other girl scared and crying. Finally [we] got in bed together.

Next morning [we] got up about six o'clock. Someone woke me up—[I] didn't remember where I was. Woke other up. Walked around easy—afraid floor would break through. Every time we stepped on floor, it creaked, and we got scared. Walk out to hall— backed up—scared. Rest of girls tell us to walk down. [We] Refused. Finally [we] sat on step, feet on next step, and both got down that way, hanging on to banisters. Every time the stairs squeaked, we cried.

Older girl took us to place to wash. [I] Didn't know how to comb and braid hair. Each girl had towel of her own. Given towels and told to hang them up when through. Never used soap before and wouldn't use it—remembered what my grandmother had told me. So did the other girl—only used soap on hands. [A] Girl braided [my] hair with one braid. [I] Protested. [She] Said all must have only one braid. [I] Said if grandmother sees it she won't like it.

Washed three times a day and combed hair twice—morning and evening. Second night, [we were] carried up picky back again. Next morning, [we] walked down. Third night—walked up ourselves. Told girls someone moved beds all night and was told it was the spring and not a person. Not afraid anymore.

Ages of girls five to some twenty and over and boys the same. Eat and have classes together. Long tables—one side boys and one side girls. Big girls and big boys at head of table. Saw boy and girl write notes to one another, didn't know what was in it. Imitated—wrote "Did you see a dog?' etc.—and gave it to a boy.

Used to cook when eight—wash dishes. Learned how in school. Learned how to keep clean. When grandmother saw my one braid, said I'd never have long hair. Braided it in two then, instead of four.

[I] Told grandmother of the steps and where we sleep. [She] Said my feet will be very big from climbing steps so often and [I'll] have bunions. [Grandmother] Don't let me wear underwear—if I wore it all the time, it will smell.

Did dishes in school, with another girl (never allowed to talk one word of Indian after the fifth month.) If we talked Indian, we were made to stand in a corner one hour till 9 o'clock and then go to bed. When roll taken—one of the girls [assigned] to tell matron if we had talked Indian. I had done it once. [We were] Locked in waiting room. In a few minutes, [we] sneaked out of window 6 ft. high—jumped out and went to pantry. Each took a loaf of bread and chunk of meat. Had a hard time getting in. One stood on other's shoulder. Where to put meat? Put in underwear legs. Both did this (foolish–we got enough to eat). Big flannel legs in underwear. Put bread in one and meat in other. Stood in corner and unlocked door. "Go up and go to bed." [We were] Hardly able to walk because of bread and meat. Got in front of her. Going very slowly. Wore big loose hickory aprons. Got upstairs and told the [other] kids. Divided it with others, and ate it. Never were found out.

[We] Bathed every Friday afternoon. Friend and I working in bath room. Had about four baskets of dirty clothes to take to laundry. Boys bathe there. Friend: "Let's take the clothes over now."

We might get punished. We knew boys were bathing. [We] Took hold of one basket, out the back door and quickly walked to the laundry. Opened door—big box there for dirty clothes. Three big boys were standing on it naked. About thirty boys there—rest ran in every direction, but those three stood there. One in middle: "I'm German because I twist my mustaches." But he didn't care. We ran in and threw in the clothes. We ran out but we saw everything. Agnes said, "Why did he say that? Gosh, he looked funny." [interview transcribed, August 1939, by Sue Sommers (Dietrich)]

Mrs. Chief All Over remembered the school's demands that she give up her language and habits. Apparently the memories were not bitter, perhaps because she did see her grandmother and mother fairly frequently, perhaps because she did retain fluency in Blackfoot—she was translating for her mother, Insima—and left school for a traditional marriage in her middle teens. Contemporary Indian people are angry at Anglo policies denigrating their heritages, forbidding their forebears to speak their languages or practice their religions, and imparting trade skills rather than college-preparatory education. Often, researchers interviewing people like Mrs. Chief All Over have been surprised that they like to tell amusing anecdotes and talk about the friendships they made, rather than recall grief. Effects of the policy for assimilation to Anglo culture were delayed a generation: it was the mid-20th-century generation of parents who gave up speaking their language, and they did so to help *their* children do well in school. Throughout America in this period, children whose grandparents—immigrant or American Indian—habitually spoke another language were taught by their parents to speak only English. It was the effect of Anglo schools, but indirectly as parents from non-English-speaking homes tried to spare their children the struggles they remembered.

Carlisle Indian Industrial School

Around 1900, Piegan children had limited opportunities for schooling. Few lived close enough to attend a day school (at the agency), and the two reservation boarding schools could not accommodate more than a

TABLE 4.1. Students at Carlisle Indian School Listed as Piegan or Blackfeet

Abbott: Maggie, Nellie	Ell: Charles, (Murphy)	Many Hides, Philip
Allison: Lafe, Wendell	George	Marceau, Charles
Anderson: Lee, Rupert,	Ellis: Martha	Martinez, Joseph
Wilbur	Evans: Irene, James, Joseph	McClure, Frank
Arrowtop: Philip, Silas	FlatTail, John	Morgan, Claudie
Aubrey: Alice, Rose	Frost, John	No Chief, Mary
Austin, Anthony	Gagnan, Joseph	Oscar, Peter
Bailey, Mary	Gilham: Anthony C.,	Pablo, Eva
Bear Chief, Joseph	William	Pambrun, Francis
Bear Child: Ben, James	Gobert, Irvin Leo	Alexander (Piegan,
Bear Leggings, Peter	Gohr, Henry	Shoshone)
Big Top, Fred	Grant: Carl, Dick, James,	Pepion, Aloysius
Bogy, Thomas	Richard	Perrine: Florence, Julia,
Boyd, Oscar	Ground, John Grover	Minnie, William
Buck, Charles	Guardipee: Francis, Maggie,	Racine: Joseph, Henry
Burd: Charles, Henry, Ira,	Thomas	Robinson, George C.
James, Nancy, Phoebe,	Hall: Thomas, William	Rose: Irene, Isabel
Sampson (he may be Nez	Hamilton: Joseph, Robert	Running Crane, Eddie
Percé)	Harleth, George	Running Wolf, John
Carson: Alphonso, Charles,	Harwood: Paul, William	Russell, John
Muriel (?) (she may be	Hazlett: George, Stewart,	Saint Goddard, Archie
Menominee)	William M.	Samples, Jess J.
Cecil: Leon, Leona, Sallie	Heavy Runner: Joe, John,	Sanderville: Agnes, Brigette,
Choate, Mary	Vinnie	Nellie, Richard, William
Choquette, Eliza	Henrault [Henault?], Clara	Sheldt, Joseph
Clark, Malcolm	Horn, George	Schildt, Carl
Cobell: George, Joseph,	Houck, Eleanor	Sellew, Philip M.
Julia	Houk, Presly	Sherman, Mary
Comes-at-Night, Maggie	Howard: Agnes, Annie,	Shoots, Irene
Connelly, Brian [later,	Henry	Shoots-First: Maggie, Celia
Connolly]	Jackson: Julia, Thomas	Shorty, Launy
Corson, Charles	Jamerson: Abbie, Mary	Smith, William (Smallboy)
Crawford, James	Juneau, Dennis	Spaniard, Joseph
Crownin, Alphones	Kennedy: Esther, John, Leo,	Spanish, Joe
Culbertson, Josephine	William	Spearson, Albert
Curly Bear, Charles	Kennerly: Agnes, Bertrand,	Steele, William
Davis, Bryan	Harriet, Jerome, Lea,	Tatsey, Lizzie
Delaney: Fred, George	Leo, Perry, Sallie Wright,	Thomas, George
Devereaux, Spyina	Wright	Trombley, Cecilia
Douglass, Grace	King, Charles	Vielle: Jack, James, Peter
Dubray, Gordon	Kipp, Helen	White Dog, Henry
Dunbar: Andrew, Carrie,	Lahr, Henry	Winsborough, Walter M.
Esther Booth, Frances,	Langley, Josephine	Wolf, Herbet R.
James	Lillard, Nellie E. [Kainai]	Wolf Plume, Wesley
Duscharm, Cecelia (also	Little Plume: Martha,	Wren: Ella, Lizzie, Mary
Pend d'Oreille, Kutenai)	Mollie	Jane
Edwards, Rose	Mad Plume, Mary	Yellow Kidney, Mike

(Source: Compiled by Barb Landis, Cumberland County Historical Society, Carlisle PA)

couple of hundred children. As late as 1915, two-thirds of Piegan children were not being schooled. Government policy favored off-reservation
boarding schools because these would cut off the children from Indian
life, force them to speak English, drill them in white culture, and promote
marriages between men and women from different Indian nations, with
the school experience in common rather than tribal culture. Anglo paternalism sought to make the children identify with their white teachers and
wish to be their servants.

From its beginning in 1879 to closing in 1918, Carlisle Indian Industrial School, deliberately built in Pennsylvania far from most Indian communities, was the elite educational establishment for Indians. Best known
today for its star athlete Jim Thorpe, the school enrolled many children of
aristocratic families. Piegans there included both sons and daughters of
mixed couples such as the Aubreys, Burds, Cobells, Connellys, Marceau,
and Pambrun, those of chiefs Curley Bear, Heavy Runner, and Little
Plume, of some leaders such as Yellow Kidney and Mad Plume, and those
from longer mixed lineages, Culbertson and Sandoval/Sanderville.

Carlisle Indian Industrial School was the brainchild of Captain Richard Henry Pratt (1840–1924). His father left his family in southern Indiana
to pan for gold in California and was murdered when Pratt was thirteen, forcing him to leave school to help support his mother and younger
brothers. Like the youthful Abraham Lincoln in the same frontier region,
Pratt split rails to earn a few additional dollars. Outbreak of the Civil War
took Pratt, then working as a tinsmith, into the Union Army. Fighting
throughout the war and earning a lieutenant's commission, Pratt decided
in 1867 to enlist in the regular army, which posted him to a garrison in
Indian Territory (Oklahoma). Although in eight years of active service on
the frontier he never rose above first lieutenant, he had been awarded
brevet captain rank in recognition of his Civil War service, and for the rest
of his life he preferred to be known as Captain Pratt.

Pratt commanded a regiment of African American soldiers in Indian
Territory. At that time, and in fact until after World War II, black soldiers
were segregated into exclusively black regiments, with exclusively white
officers. Leading these African American men and the Indian men acting
as scouts, followed by three years, 1875–78, guarding Indian war prisoners in Fort Marion, Florida, convinced Pratt that "the colored races" were
innately as intelligent, capable, and moral as whites. All that was needed
to bring "the backward races" to the height of civilization attained by
whites was comparable education—not simply formal academic education, but socialization among Anglos. In 1879, with the encouragement
of liberal, German-born Secretary of the Interior Carl Schurz, Pratt left

his station at Hampton Institute in Virginia to open a school for Indian children in former cavalry barracks in the southern Pennsylvania town of Carlisle. Hampton was a vocational school for African Americans that took in Indians beginning in 1877; Pratt believed lumping black and Indian students was unjustified, because, he stated, "the negro may need race pride to sustain him in his forced separation; the Indian does not need it, since he is not forever set apart as a peculiar people" (Pratt 1899, quoted in Lindsey 1995:180). Technically, Pratt remained in the U.S. Army while administering the school.

Army discipline pervaded Carlisle Indian Industrial School. Strict clock schedules regulated activities, children constantly lined up to march, they executed parade drills, and they wore uniforms, for the boys modeled on army uniforms. Such external discipline supposedly molded an inner self-discipline that would propel the Indian along the straight and narrow path to responsible American citizenship. To prevent the Devil from finding improper pastimes for idle hands, the students were kept busy under constant supervision. What today seems remarkable is that only one-half the students' day was spent in academic classroom learning; the other half was employed in chores and manual training. Carlisle was, as its name says, an Indian *Industrial* School, its program following that created at Hampton for recently freed blacks. Boys were taught blacksmithing, harness making, metalworking, carpentry, tailoring, and farming, girls were taught to clean, sew, launder (no washing machines!), and cook. The Commissioner of Indian Affairs in 1884 circulated an order: "I want to impress on your mind that if you must neglect either, it should be [the Indian's] literary studies and not his manual labor exercises" (quoted by Rogel 1990:29). During summer vacations, the students were sent out to work on farms. Pratt believed his "outing system" was his greatest contribution to Indian welfare, immersing the children in white rural family life held up to them as ideal for their own adult life. Because Pratt was convinced that only immersion throughout childhood in white society would enable Indians to leave ward status and become economically comfortable citizens, Carlisle students usually did not see their parents for years.

Carlisle was a model school, and Pratt did not favor harsh punishment. Compared to young English aristocrats in the famous "public" schools such as Eton, Carlisle students were better cared for. The great difference was that the English boys received rigorous academic training while the American Indian children were shortchanged, their academic level at graduation only equivalent to eighth grade. One Carlisle graduate, for example, was given an appointment to West Point but first needed to attend a white high school for the college preparatory courses not given at Carlisle. Pratt himself complained to officials, and the public, that the government ordained only three years of schooling for Indians—as he put it, "three-eighths of what the white child must receive to reach the beginning of the high school" (Pratt 1964:282). In spite of the low academic level, Carlisle staff set up formal debates and literary productions, exhibiting students' prowess at "civilized" pursuits before invited audiences of government and charitable visitors. The children did not mix with white children during the school year, and in summer had limited opportunity to socialize, Pratt being concerned to protect them from dissolute whites such as he had seen during his army service on the frontier: just as he, as a father, shielded his own children from bad company, so he sought to guard the Indian children under his protection.

When challenged by politicians, which was often, Captain Pratt doggedly contended that he had never been funded to fully carry out his strategy to save America's Indians: "to civilize the Indians, get them into civilization; to keep them civilized, let them stay" (Pratt 1964:285). He meant to use three years at Carlisle to teach English, literacy, basic arithmetic, geography, and history, *sufficient to prepare students to enter public schools distant from the reservations,* there to earn high school diplomas and, for some, be admitted to college. Public schools adjacent to reservations wouldn't do, because their communities, including most teachers, were prejudiced against Indians; it was critical to give Indians a fair chance by placing them in communities unfamiliar with the degradations of reservation life. This was what Pratt meant by "immersing" the students in Anglo society, not the few years of segregation and vocational training at Carlisle but a dozen or so years living with white families, earning room and board by working before and after daily attendance at a white public school. Once they had earned a real high school diploma and fully adjusted to Anglo society, young adult Indians could decide whether they wanted to go on to college or set up in a trade or on a farm. Pratt hoped they would not want to return to living on their reservations, but should they decide so, they could bring civilization to their benighted kin.

Piegans who had attended Carlisle appear in Superintendent Campbell's 1921 survey: Irene Shoots, recently married to Peter Butterfly; Aloysius Pepion, age 25, living with a widowed sister; Lizzie Tatsey, 22, who "is housekeeper at the Old Agency day school and is making her home with the teacher and farmer, Mr. and Mrs. W. D. Helm"; Billy Hall, 23, "an intelligent young man" with a minimal farm; George Horn, 52, "one of the reliable men in the tribal herd activity; in fact, he was foreman during the last year before the herd was dispersed. George Horn has received his patent in fee but informs me that he still has his land and has not mortgaged it although he had pretty hard sledding during the hard winter and the droughts"; and Dick Grant, 44, with a three-room house, a well in a wellhouse, a log barn, and good mixed farm (Campbell 1921:2, 31, 34, 40, 84, 123). Carlisle closed in 1918 (and Pratt retired in 1903); there would be no more recent graduates after Campbell's administration.

Not on Campbell's survey list was the most widely known of Carlisle's Piegan graduates, Richard Sanderville (Fig. 18). Born, as Richard Sandoval, about 1866, he attended schools at Old Agency, St. Peter's Mission, and St. Ignatius until 1886, then was persuaded in 1889 by the Blackfeet Agent, J. B. Catlin, to enroll in Carlisle. Stan Juneau, an Amskapi Pikuni educator who has researched Piegan experiences at Carlisle, thinks it likely that it was at Carlisle that the family name was Anglicized from Sandoval to Sanderville. Richard graduated in 1892, was hired at Fort Shaw Indian School as boys' disciplinarian to oversee and drill the male students, then in 1894, came back to Browning to work in the Agency as clerk and interpreter. By 1940, after 37 years employment by the Bureau of Indian Affairs, Sanderville retired with a pension, continuing his ranching and service as a tribal councilman elected from Heart Butte. John C. Ewers, first curator of the Museum of the Plains Indian in Browning, wrote about his friend and colleague Dick Sanderville for a book titled *American Indian Intellectuals*.

The Sandovals were not the only family whose name was arbitrarily changed by schoolmasters. In 1897, the superintendent of the Crow Reservation boarding school wrote on the subject, quoting Commissioner of Indian Affairs Thomas J. Morgan's 1890 directive that agents should make an effort to find out the proper name of Indian employees and use it consistently as the surname for all members of the same family (that is, a man's wife and children). Morgan did admit that some Indian names may be "unusually long and difficult," and could be shortened (quoted in Terry 1897:302). Morgan cautioned that using English translations of Indian names, a practice prevalent for Piegan, was not advisable because the translations, by frontiersmen, were often "uncouth" and would embarrass the family once they became familiar with English. Legal names had become critical after the 1887 Allotment Act, in case children with surnames different from their parents' might be denied their inheritance. Morgan's directive to use Indian names notwithstanding, the Crow boarding school superintendent recommended that children such as Blanche Little-star should be renamed Blanche Brown, but to protect Miss Brown's inheritance, her parents should be renamed Brown, also!

Fɪɢ. 18. Chief Bull (Dick Sanderville). Credit: Blackfeet THPO.

Other Schools

Superintendent Campbell noted approvingly several 1921 Blackfeet residents who had been students at Fort Shaw when he was director there. Sam Randall, 49, a widowed full-blood still in ward status, "was formerly a school boy of mine [Campbell] and a tailor by trade. He is crippled having lost the entire use of one leg, walks with a crutch [but] . . . can make a hand in the hay field or elsewhere about the farm. . . . 22 horses, no cattle, 5 acres wheat, no oats, garden" (Campbell 1921: 45). Oliver Racine "and his wife were married at Fort Shaw while I was superintendent there. They had every prospect for a happy home but unfortunately it was broken up. . . . Oliver is a very good mechanic and at present is doing the blacksmithing and general repair work for the Indians of the Old Agency district. . . . He is also a good steam engineer" (Campbell 1921: 30). Victor Pepion, who would later paint the beautiful lobby murals in the Museum of the Plains Indian, was 20 in 1921, had been at Chemawa Indian School in Oregon but had run away and was working as a hired hand (Campbell 1921:92). Campbell seemed most pleased by a pair who had graduated from Fort Shaw under his supervision, Mathew Adams and his wife, the former Mary Williamson. Mary had bought out her brother's interest in the farm they inherited from their father, a white man; it was on the south bank of Birch Creek, so was not actually in the reservation. Matt, similarly of "mixed blood," was enrolled at Fort Belknap. He had "lost a brother in the war on which account he is receiving a pension of $57.00 a month. In addition to this he earns considerable money playing for dances in the vicinity . . . about $50.00 a month." Matt "plans on working through the harvest season and purchasing what wheat he needs for flour," rather than farming himself. Perhaps with tongue in cheek, Superintendent Campbell noted that "Mathew informed me that moonshine whiskey in that vicinity is now selling for $3.00 a quart and a few months ago was selling for $10.00, all of which goes to show that the cost of living is reducing" (Campbell 1921:89).

One of Superintendent Campbell's concerns, in his 1921 survey, was to determine what districts on the reservation ought to have day schools. As his team traversed the southern valleys, he noted families with school-age children and inquired whether they would like a local school. Among the Birch Creek allottees, he met several families who had moved to Valier to send their children to the public school there. Other families reported children away at the Genoa, Nebraska, Indian School. Nora Connolly Lukin's memoir details the difficulties families encountered:

Our school year was as long as it is today, about nine months.
Once in a while, Papa would have to keep us home for a week or
so to finish up the haying.

In my first grade of school, we went to Blackfoot Grade
School [in the village of Blackfoot, about seven miles from the
ranch. Blackfoot was the site of a train section-house where the
trains were repaired and washed. The Carbery family owned a
store there and handled the mail. A beanery, to house and feed
the train workers, was added in later years. Even later, it was
moved to East Glacier]. It was a good size building with lots of
south windows, which let in lots of sunshine. There were two big
rooms, one for all eight grades and the other for recreation. The
playground at Blackfoot had swings, teeter-totters, and probably
other things. . . . In cold weather we played in a large entrance
room; on each end were our cloakrooms, one for boys, one for
girls. The kids had a game in which they would race from one
cloakroom to the other. If you were caught, you became the coyote. Two young Chinese boys, whose parents worked at the Railroad Section House, attended our school mostly to learn English.
Their names were Kip Chung and Ying Yang. One day the oldest,
Kip Chung, was caught and he was to be the coyote. Instead, he
went home, got a knife, and pulled the knife on them. . . . When
the teachers found out, their schooling ended. . . .

We had only one teacher for all grades. One group had to study
or draw while the other group had oral work with the teacher . . .
all was a learning experience for us country kids who never traveled more than 20 miles from home. Just experiencing the modern
conveniences of electric lights, running water, and new foods that
we never had was a treat. . . . Our teacher had three small children of her own so she was constantly running to the teacherage
to check on them. . . . [p. 45] We did not learn a lot during the year.
The County Superintendent of Schools came to the school at the
end of the year to give us a test, and no one passed. Some students
spent summer vacations catching up. To get to school, we rode
about three miles horseback and left our horses at the Billy Kipp
ranch. We then went by car for the next four miles with a neighbor
who was hired by the school district to haul us to and from school.
But he was not always there to bring us home. Many times our
father had to hook up a team of horses and come get us after dark.
The wagon would be filled with hay so we could curl up in it for
warmth. After a year of this and the lack of good teaching, we
went to the Cut Bank Boarding School. . . .

In the fall of the year, Cut Bank Boarding School Superintendent, Charles Sellars, . . . would go out around the reservation and gather up kids to take them to the Boarding School. He did not wait for permission or even to let the children bid their parents goodbye. He just loaded them up. I guess we were lucky that this didn't happen to us. . . . The Cut Bank Boarding School buildings were nice but discipline was strict. . . . Doris Barlow and I were the only ones in the second grade at the normal age (possibly 7 or 8 years old) while the rest of the students were a lot older. One of our assignments was to embroider a dresser scarf. Doris and I worked on it nearly the whole school year. We would have to rip it out and do it over many times. . . .

The next year, a new school opened at the Joe Kipp home on Cut Bank Creek, about five miles north of the ranch. So we left the Boarding School and I began the third grade at the Cut Bank John School. It was the original home of Cut Bank John, as he was known. Our classrooms were at the top floor of their home. The Joe Kipp family lived on the ground floor. . . . At recess time, we would climb the rock formations near the School or just entertained ourselves. . . . We rode horseback to school but it wasn't an easy year as many blizzards came up. Our horses brought us home through many of these snowstorms. . . . In the 4th grade, it was back to the Cut Bank Boarding School for the remainder of grade school. It was the lesser of two evils. Discipline was severe as it was run like a military camp. We marched to meals, to school, and we spent many hours training. If we missed a step, it was back to more hours of drilling. . . .

When we arrived at the Boarding School, we were issued Hickory dresses made of a material which is like striped pillow ticking, big black blousy bloomers, long black stockings, and high top shoes we called "stogeys." . . . My memories of the Boarding School were not the discipline from the officials even though they were strict: it was more the older students who were the bullies. We were their slaves. Fighting was a must to survive so I did my share of fighting. I'm not proud of it but it was something you were forced to do "or else." I can say I didn't start a fight but it didn't take much to set me off. . . .

For me, a very major problem was "head lice." Somehow, those horrible critters really liked me. Maybe it was my "fine" hair. We would come home for the weekend and the first thing Mom would do was to check our heads. I always was the lousy one so I spent the weekend with Mom cleaning my hair. . . . Most

childhood illnesses I had while attending the Boarding School.
I do not remember having mumps but did have measles and
chicken pox. I was vaccinated for smallpox but it did not take.
The doctors think I may have had it but Mom did not think so. I
probably had a very mild case, if at all. There were about 10 of us
who had scarlet fever and we were completely quarantined with
one nurse to care for us in one wing of the dormitory. The only
other person allowed to enter was the doctor when he came to
examine us. I think we were "holed up" for about 10 days. I also
had a few sprained ankles and a broken arm once. My teacher,
Vivian Gifford gave my arm a yank to set it. When we got to the
doctor, he said she did a perfect job of setting it.

We had many school activities. We had an excellent track
team. Ursula (Walters) Higgins was one of our outstanding stars
and she participated in most events. George Kicking Woman was
another track star. . . . We also played softball, football and in later
years, some basketball after a gym was built. We had a Glee Club
and the choir sang at many functions. This was an extracurricular
activity. One was the mid-winter fair in Browning, which was a
reservation-wide fair. The men showed their garden crops and
leather and woodcraft accomplishments. The ladies displayed
their sewing, knitting, and crocheted items. They had baked
goods and canning. It really was a big event. We also held spelling bees in class. They taught penmanship, which I failed, as my
penmanship never improved. . . .

I remember, one time, going to Browning for a matinee. The
very smallest students went by wagon and the rest of us walked
[seven miles!]. This was the first movie I ever saw. . . .

The Boarding School gardens were just the greatest I've ever
seen; they were like the gardens of the Hutterites. [The school is
located in a sheltered valley adjacent to Cut Bank creek.] Albert
[Lukin?] said the reward for weeding was two hours of dancing
to an old time, windup phonograph. The garden was about four
acres by my estimate. The vegetables were stored in an under-
ground cellar that was dug out of the hillside.

Whatever the differences between home and the Cut Bank
Boarding School, I don't think we thought about it. I just accepted
it as something I had to endure. [Nora Lukin 2003:44–48]

Mrs. Lukin's experiences illustrate the severe difficulties of deliver-
ing schooling to ranching families. Considering how the Connolly children nearly perished in blizzards riding home from the district school,

FIVE

The Ranchers

The history of the Amskapi Pikuni covers a large number of families often called "mixed-bloods." It's been common to oppose "mixed-bloods" or "Progressives" to "full-bloods." Reality has been, from one point of view, much more complex than that, or from another point of view, simpler. Simpler, because by the 20th century, everyone on the reservation probably had at least one relative who was white; more complex, because some people who were only half Indian conservatively followed their Amskapi Pikuni mothers' ways, and everyone on the reservation had to deal with the Bureau of Indian Affairs, the agency, and the white business families such as the Sherburnes and Scrivers. Historian Paul Rosier notes that in 1885, only eighteen "mixed-bloods" were recorded living on the reservation, while a generation later, 1914, there were officially 1,452 "mixed-bloods" sharing it with 1,189 "full-bloods" (Rosier 2001:14).

Disdainfully called "squaw men," white men who married Piegan women—legally by U.S. law or according to Blackfoot custom—committed themselves to their wives and children. Many, many other white men used Indian women for a night's gratification, or at best as "country wives," to be left behind, with their children, when the white man returned to "civilization." Hudson's Bay Company policy discouraged "fraternization" with Indian people; the American Fur Company was more tolerant, notably when Alexander Culbertson persuaded the aristocrat Natoyist-siksina' ("Natawista") to become his wife and partner in negotiating with her nation. Some of the independent traders and freighters stayed with their wives for several years, only to abscond when times got tough, for example the father of Jack Wagner, well-known interpreter for the Northwest Mounted Police:

> My father was Captain Jack Collaly who ran a steamboat on the Missouri River, one of Armstrong's tow-boats. . . . Then Captain Jack freighted between Fort Benton and Calgary, and set up

a whiskey trading post on the Oldman River. Father was in the group [of traders and Heavy Shield's band] that was chased out [from Stand-off by the police]. We never heard from him again. . . . Mother remained at Fort Macleod with Mrs. Culbertson. It was here that my mother married Billie Wagner, whose name I took. [interview, 1968, by R. H. Willcomb]

Jack's mother, Pipe Woman, according to the 1907–08 Allotment census was married four times, each time to a white man, and bore two children to Billie Wagner and two to her succeeding husband, George Harrison.

The white men who remained with their Piegan wives usually ranched, even if their main income came from businesses. Once the reservation was allotted, in 1912, the Piegan wives and children had their shares, often enough for a good-sized spread (Fig. 19) if the family chose adjoining allotments. "Squaw men" were sometimes accused of marrying Indians in order to get land free. Whatever a man's motive, he was obliged to work the place, and likely cooperated with his wife's relatives, reciprocating labor and lending tools. For example, Superintendent Campbell notes in his June 1921 survey of reservation families that Joe Weatherwax, half-Piegan, and his full-Piegan young brother-in-law Pete Butterfly were living with their families in tents that summer while building homes adjacent to the land both were working. Butterfly put in wheat and Weatherwax, oats that he could exchange for some of that wheat. We understand how patronizing the reservation superintendent could be when he says that "[t]hose two boys [37-year-old Weatherwax and 23-year-old Pete Butterfly] plan on digging a well" (Campbell 1921:133–134. 154).

The Critical Problem of Obtaining Land

Cattle ranching does well on the Blackfeet Reservation, so long as the rancher can put up hay and give the animals some protection during severe winter weather. The drawback to ranching is that it needs a large amount of rangeland plus hay meadows. Allotted 320 acres each, with the choice of all grazing land or 280 acres of grazing and 40 of irrigable land (called "the forties"), Piegan soon faced disastrous fragmentation as each child grew up and married. Selecting contiguous allotments for two parents and their children in 1910 meant that by around 1925, the children had to decide whether to farm their own allotment or move to their spouse's, and to decide which of the younger families would assist the aging parents on their allotment. Another generation, and most

Fɪɢ. 19. Percy DeWolfe ranch, north section of Blackfeet Reservation.
Credit: Renee Miller Blaney.

of the original allotments had both too many heirs and a tangle due to marriages linking families. Unlike money or durable goods, an allotment could not be carried by an heir to a new place. The government and the missionaries apparently did not urge adoption of European customs of keeping farms intact through planning for dowries or apprenticeships in trades to compensate all but the one child destined to get the farm, nor did they favor cooperative farming until Campbell, in 1921, decided that small local cooperatives to purchase seed and share machinery might pull the Indian people out of the ruin inflicted by droughts and the terrible winter of 1919–1920.

There was a history of ranching on the reservation even as early as Campbell's planning. The first cattle officially carried on the reservation were 12 animals brought by 1875 superintendent John Wood to provide the agency's needs for beef and milk. Ten years later, Sam Burd moved about 500 cattle from the Missoula region to the Reservation. They did well over a relatively decent winter, persuading something like a dozen additional entrepreneurs to bring in grazing cattle, a total of more than 20,000 head. Then came the terrible winter of 1886–87, when

> 75 percent of the cattle on the Blackfeet reservation starved or froze to death. That winter will always be remembered by the stockmen, since the snow covered all the feeding grounds. All water holes were frozen solid and there was no shelter to protect the cattle, or any feed prepared. The agency cattle, under the

supervision of Eli L. Guardipee, survived throughout the winter. The reason for this was that Guardipee, knowing the country so well, was able to find feeding grounds. He also knew where to find natural shelter. Those big ranch owners came up into this country and stayed during the summer and then went back to their homes in the late fall, after the roundups. They left cowboys to care for their cattle. Cut Bank John [Kipp, ranching where Willow Creek joins Cut Bank Creek] had a place for the cowboys to board and room. . . . [A non-Indian rancher driving about five thousand cattle through the Reservation told Cut Bank John he could take thirty] calves had just been born and were too young to travel with the herd. After this big herd headed north, Cut Bank John and William Upham went after the calves and brought them back to their home. In the summer of 1886 Cut Bank John bought a milk cow from Sam C. Burd. Those calves and that one cow were the start of Cut Bank John's herd which in later years numbered almost 1,000 head. [Stewart 1940b:2–3]

Not surprisingly, the big cattlemen learned that grazing on the reservation was not as cheap and profitable as they had thought in 1886. Small operators—Jeff Devereaux (35 head), Henry Powell and Joseph Kipp (100 head each), and Joe Cobell (10 head)—claimed squatter's rights to grazing land in 1888; each of these men was married to a Piegan woman. Kipp was half-white, half-Mandan, the others white.

Great Northern Railway gave cattlemen an incentive to utilize the reservation again. In 1891, it inaugurated shipping from its depots along the Hi-Line; up until then, cattle had to be driven to Big Sandy to a railhead. The cattle industry was adapting to better-controlled management. Coincident with the extinction of the bison herds, cattlemen in central Montana let their stock graze with little supervision. An early Piegan stockman, Eli L. Guardipee, recalled,

May 20, 1882, the ranchers all met at the elbow of the Teton river. The purpose of the meeting was to have a roundup of all the cattle north of the Missouri river and west of the Marias river. Each rancher could then get his cattle and return them to their proper range. This was the first big roundup of that type. The roundup camp consisted of about 40 tents. There were between 200 and 300 men, which included ranchers, cowhands, cooks, nightherders and horse wranglers. Each day the cowhands made their circles and brought in all the cattle they had located. These circles averaged about a 15-mile radius from the camp. Many cattle were branded, each outfit doing its own branding. When all the cattle had been gathered together, each rancher took his cattle and his employees back to his rangeland. Guardipee estimates that this roundup amounted to over 100,000 head. [Stewart, Eli Guardipee Interview, 1940a:27–28]

The last big round-up was held in 1906; 1906–07 was another of the hard winters with serious loss of stock (Stewart 1940b:7).

Superintendent Campbell figured out, from his survey in May and June of 1921, that the generation settling the reservation in the 1870s and '80s would end their days living by agency rations. He described two old ladies managing by, of all things, gleaning wheat like Ruth in the Bible.[1] Mrs. Moves Out (Good Victory or Good Massacre) was 60, full Piegan.

Mrs. Moves Out is a rationer and of course will always be. She is the first in the Old Agency district to put in wheat. This woman provided her own seed wheat, the only one on the reservation. The farmer states that she gleaned this seed in the wheat fields on the bench and threshed it out by hand. They have also cooked wheat for a part of their subsistence during the winter and as shown kept sufficient for seed. Their wheat area is two acres and a half. We are very anxious about the success of this wheat field as it will be a lesson of thrift and industry to the other Indians when it is brought to their attention. . . . These old ladies are anxious to have chickens and state that there is always some one left at home and that they would be careful to take care of them. If they are successful in their wheat growing they will evidently have chicken food. If they are not and the old lady follows up her system of garnering they will have food anyway.

[Mrs. Moves Out and her fellow widow, Mrs. Two Stabs] both got lease money which helps them out during the year, also the [agency] field matron gives them special attention. In addition to their regular rations she takes her some meat and other supplies. They stated that they were getting along very well and had plenty to eat. They are living four miles from the sub-agency and are easily kept in touch with. [Mrs. Moves Out's divorced daughter lives with and assists the old ladies. A Piegan man from Heart Butte is camping on the allotment to farm for the women.] He is fairly industrious. He has no cattle, no horses and the farmer informs me he has sold the land [his fee patent] and disposed of the proceeds without anything to show for it. The man intends to marry Mrs. Moves Out's daughter. [Campbell 1921:204–208]

This household had no livestock except "a few head of horses running on the range," belonging to Mrs. Two Stabs. Campbell was asking every family to raise chickens, believing that the responsibility of caring for fowl would counteract people's inclination to leave their allotted places to camp with friends or relatives. Chickens, he seemed to think, would "civilize" them; he approvingly quoted Found A Gun, a 43-year-old full Piegan man, "If he had some [chickens] he would stay at home as he did not care to go around to dances and other gatherings" (Campbell 1921:158).

More typical than the Moves Out household was another visited by Campbell's survey team:

> Philip Aubrey, 29, was 1/4 Piegan, his father a White man married at the Agency by a priest in 1875 to the daughter of a White man employed by the American Fur Company before he took up ranching in the Sun River valley. Her mother's father was Piegan, mother's mother Kainai. This couple had nine children, of whom Philip was third youngest. Philip married Cora, daughter of Mary Jane Ripley White and Lorenzo White, "a Spaniard," making Cora, like Philip, 1/4 Piegan, and their three children 1/8 Piegan. Philip had his allotment in fee patent. The family had, in 1921, neither horses nor cattle. Philip had put ten acres in wheat, several acres in oats, and a garden. Their home was a small one-room "log cottage" near Cora's mother's house. Superintendent Campbell recorded that Philip "informed me that he had mortgaged his land and that it is now being foreclosed. He probably got as much on the land as the land could be sold for at this time; at least, that is his judgment. . . . He had one hundred sixty-five head of cattle when the bad winter struck and those that he pulled through were taken over by the mortgagors. He informs me that what chickens he had have been stolen. . . . It will be the plan of the district farmer to keep pretty closely in touch with these people and try to encourage them to put forth their best efforts . . . they plan on having sufficient vegetables with some chickens and eggs and milch cows to help out" (Campbell 1921:193).

Black Boy was, in 1921, a 64-year-old full Piegan widower, still legally a ward of the government, who

> lives part of the time with his sister Mrs. Four Horns, and when he is not living with his sister he visits from place to place. One of the lessees has offered him $350.00 per annum for the use of his allotment. The old gentleman refused to make the lease saying

that after the lease payment has been made for five years and the lessee has the signed receipts he will find then that his allotment is sold and he will have nothing left, the receipts acting as evidence of the purchase. He has a very good hay allotment . . . well watered the year around. If the old gentleman could be induced to lease his land, the $350.00, in addition to the rations he received, would make him a very good support. [Campbell 1921:164]

We may suppose that Black Boy knew of cases such as he foresaw if he leased his place. One of his neighbors, Chester Pepion, 38 years old, full Piegan, and like Black Boy legally a ward, told Campbell that he and his wife Mabel [Davis, "an Indian girl"—her father was white, mother full Piegan], had seven children.

They leased their own allotment a few years ago and are now living in a rented log house in the timber along Birch Creek on the allotment of his sister Mrs. Rutherford. He is having trouble with the lessees and we have been unable to collect his lease money for the past six months. It is a question whether the lessee or the bondsmen either are good for the amount. He desires to take his land back and move into his own home which he will do if he can again get possession of it. He also complains of losing a great deal of his property by theft and among other things he showed us an automobile standing near his home which had been robbed of all the accessories that could be very well carried away. This was done during his absence of a few days from his home. He has no cattle and says he lost them during the hard winter. [Campbell 1921:178]

Another discouraging case was that of Susie Pias Ziegler, a 25-year-old widow with two children, living with her 70-year-old father Frank Pias on her allotment on Birch Creek. Mrs. Ziegler's deceased mother was full Piegan. and a sister of Black Boy's wife. Frank Pias was Mexican, making Susie half Piegan. She owned her allotment in fee patent, and with her widowed father lived on it in

a very comfortable three room cottage. [Frank Pias, although] elderly, is still competent to manage for her and help her make a good living. . . . She is living on her own allotment [which] is mortgaged and it is probably only a question of time when it will be lost, as it will be difficult for them to pay the interest on the

mortgage and the taxes. . . . From a loan on her land she purchased a small bunch of cattle and has about ten head of cattle
now on hand. . . . [Frank] informed me that he lost forty head of
cattle during the hard winter and that stealing had been going
on continuously although he stayed carefully at home. About a
month ago they lost a four year old cow. . . . He] says he has lived
on this reservation for forty-five years, and informed me that after all these years of experience he preferred the north country to
that of Mexico, his former home. [Campbell 1921:173–174]

Contrast the poverty of these families with Joe and Martha Rutherford Kuka, both in their mid-forties. She was half Piegan, and Joe was
white; they had five sons and a daughter. Although they owned only a
few head of horses, they had 11 head of cattle, hogs, chickens, 130 acres
in wheat, 23 acres in oats, and a good garden. Mrs. Kuka had been married to another white man, Albert Hill, who died, leaving her a son from
this marriage. The Kukas' oldest son, 18, was in the Marines. They occupied a

very nice home consisting of four rooms . . . well kept and well
furnished. . . . Mr. Kuka is not doing a great deal in the livestock
business but is probably one of the best farmers on the reservation and has been farming successfully in this location for about
twenty years. He does not question but that the Indians on any
part of the reservation can make their living farming and garden-
ing if they would only devote their time and attention to it. We
happened in at this home unawares and Mrs. Kuka prepared a
very hasty meal for us which consisted of fresh pork and eggs,
potatoes, pickled beans, butter and cream and bread, all of which
were grown on the home ranch, the only other items on the bill of
fare not grown at home would be sugar, canned pears and coffee.
Mrs. Kuka is an excellent cook and is very much interested in a
public school and is otherwise progressive.
    They have eleven head of cattle which is really their dairy
herd. He has alfalfa. . . . This ranch has suffered from theft the
same as the others along this [Birch Creek] valley and he informed me that he had lost two sets of harness, a saddle, and a
great many chickens; that the heads of the chickens were usually
left as evidence of the absence of the body. They have raised a
good garden and of course have a root house. This is the third
place in this district that we found hogs. Mr. Kuka informed us
that he had bought neither lard nor bacon for twenty years and

had always raised his own. . . . He uses entirely horse power for his farming and advises against tractors. His land is susceptible to irrigation and is under one of the ditches and he informs me that he can always get water when he needs it. He advocated irrigating the native grasses and if one prefers, he says, by disking the native grass and sowing timothy a good stand of timothy can be secured without breaking. He has been successful in growing [squaw] corn for roasting ears and also for seed [Campbell 1921:194–195].

From these cases, we see that by 1921, ten years after Allotment, hope of making most Piegan families self-sustaining through raising cattle had been blighted by drought followed by an especially severe winter. Where loans had been secured by cattle, loss of most of a herd led to foreclosure on the allotment; non-Indians leasing allotments failed to make payments, leaving the Indian owner to pay taxes without income to do so, again leading to foreclosure; and some fee-patented allotments had been sold. Al Hirst, for example, a white man, married Margaret Champagne (also spelled Champine), nearly full Piegan, got a job with the Reclamation Service and in 1921 was buying allotments in fee patent while living in a rented house on land he leased along Badger Creek (Campbell 1921:103). Some of the people Campbell interviewed who had sold their land were using the proceeds "judiciously," as Campbell put it, while others had, as one young man admitted, "'blowed the whole works'" (Campbell 1921:123).

In 1982, Teddy Burns described in an interview the manipulation of fee patents. Burns, born in 1916, was a Babb resident whose German immigrant grandfather married a half-Piegan woman in 1879 at Fort Benton and settled on the reservation. According to Burns,

Joe Sherburne run the bank. . . . He bought land from the Indians for almost nothing. They had what they called forced patents . . . say if you was coming here, you wanted a place there, and this Indian had a piece of land over there. Well, your congressman, or whoever had a little pull and you tell him I want you to send him a patent. Then you'd write him a patent, send him a patent, he'd look it over like this, you know, pay no attention. Pretty soon here comes a bill on taxes. Soon as they get a patent, they start taxing. Sherburne would say, "Tell you what I'll do, I'll pay the tax off and I'll give you a thousand dollars cash, or five hundred or whatever. Or credit in my grocery store." Well, sure, oil rights and everything went with it too. . . . If you don't say I'm reserving the oil rights, it goes with it. The Indian never said that. [interview with Mary Murphy, April 8, 1982, 16]

Who should be declared "competent" and given their fee patent to their allotment, and who should be judged "incompetent" and kept in wardship seems to have taken into account people's earlier history. Mrs. Isabel [Brass Woman] Ripley, a full Piegan widowed from marriage to a white man, had ranched on the Teton River near Fort Benton with her husband. In 1921, she was living with a married daughter on the Reservation. Campbell noted,

[H]er daughter . . . states that she is always industrious and finds something to do. [Mrs. Ripley] does not speak English [but] was recently recommended for a patent in fee and has secured a loan on her allotment which is located near Fort Benton. . . . [S]he did not have any money [at time of survey visit] and her daughter said that her mother had helped her out during the hard times through the loans she made on her allotment. Although she is now a citizen, she is not competent to make her own ways and will evidently have to be continued as a rationer the rest of her life. [Campbell 1921:189]

The daughter was married to a white man, variously listed as "Mexican" or "Spaniard," and with him had been farming since 1892 on the north side of Birch Creek.

Cattle, or Sheep, or Horses?

Campbell had lived in central Montana long enough to realize that the Dawes Allotment Act of 1887 had not taken into account conditions on the northwestern High Plains of central Montana. He had been in the area during the drought and hard winter that had ruined both Indians and whites. The answer to making Piegan self-sufficient rather than dependent on government rations, he figured, would be to persuade every household to keep a milk cow, chickens, a vegetable garden with a root-house, raise enough wheat for the family's flour and oats for their work horses. Such a basic farm could fit within allotments' "forties," accessing irrigation ditches when rain failed. For cash, sheep might be the answer. Sheep don't require as much acreage or as high quality forage as cattle, and a sheep provides marketable wool for years in addition, eventually, to meat. That sheep can ruin range for cattle presumably wouldn't matter, after 1919–20's demolition of the cattle business. It's interesting that he seemed uninterested in horses other than teams kept as draft animals, although in visiting slightly more than 100 households in May and June 1921 he noted 732 horses plus, for 22 of the households, "a few horses" or "has horses running on the range"—altogether well over a thousand horses. Tellingly, he recorded for Mrs. Annie McKnight Fisher, an elderly widow, half Piegan, forty acres in wheat, thirty acres in oats, and a good garden,

> Most of her farming is done by hired men. She has twenty-five head of cattle; sold thirty head and lost about fifty head during the hard winter. She has forty horses on the range but no stallion. In her case as in almost all of the others, the best of her horses died and the ponies and hardier ones survived. [Campbell 1921:182]

In other words, the ponies Piegan had been breeding for two centuries survived. Imported "better" horses did not. If only the reservation superintendents could have hired a good creative 21st-century marketing expert to make a business out of the ponies!

Superintendent Campbell left for greener pastures after eight years, just before the Great Depression and the West's "Dirty Thirties" dustbowl. One result of Campbell's program had been to reinforce the difference between "traditional" Piegans, generally called "the full-bloods," and "mixed-blood" entrepreneurs. He could respect the full-bloods' lack of interest in amassing money, as long as they didn't simply expect government—taxpayers'—rations forever. Meanwhile, those white ranchers who had toughed out the 1919–20 disaster and the "mixed-blood" families who thought of themselves as having, as it were, dual citizenship, in the Piegan Nation and the United States, wanted to rebuild the cattle industry. Dustbowl desert farther south persuaded the Interior Department to relocate starving cattle from these regions to the Blackfeet Reservation, where proximity to the Rockies and timbered foothills lessened the impact of the drought. Nearly 6,000 beef cattle were shipped in 1934, only to be hit with another terrible winter killing one-third of the new stock. Still, there were now somewhat over 4,000 animals to restore the industry, and most were managed by the "mixed-bloods" occupying the northern and eastern districts of the reservation. There was questioning whether these "Progressives" had been improperly favored over the "full-bloods" who were subsistence farming in the southwestern districts, or merely received more because they had demonstrated greater commitment to ranching. Campbell had noted in 1921 of Owl Child, a son of Mountain Chief, that

> Owlchild [sic] was one of the very prominent and progressive full blood Indians of this reservation. He had accumulated about 300 head of cattle and the same number of horses. . . . [before he died in 1918]. The estate has now [1921] no cattle and but a very few head of horses . . . the culls of the bunch, the best having been sold out. [Mrs. Owl Child] lives around from place to place and usually travels with a tent. [Campbell 1921:165]

Owl Child had not been formally educated, so his ranching success did not stem from white schooling. He had been married "Indian custom" for years before accepting a legal ceremony by a priest, and his widow's "living around" suggests the couple had not rejected a Piegan way of life. It was the drought, winter, and poor market just after Owl Child's death that cut down the full-bloods' ranching, and Campbell's push for simple subsistence mixed farming that discouraged and impeded those who wanted to rebuild herds. Campbell's focusing of agency assistance on the southwestern districts, to the relative neglect, occasionally even opposition to, the northern and eastern ranching districts, left those districts primed to assert their interests once he left.

During the 1930s, in spite of the donated cattle, cattle ranching on the Reservation declined, as it did elsewhere in Glacier County, and Campbell's idea of sheep replacing cattle seemed at last to be prevailing. A 1940 compilation of livestock records showed that in 1919 there were approximately 77,000 head of cattle and approximately 77,000 horses on the range on the reservation. The next year, 1920, after the disastrous winter, only 30,000 cattle remained, now including all within Glacier County, not just the reservation. Glacier County's taxable livestock, that is to say, animals not owned by enrolled Indians on the reservation, amounted in 1921 to 13,716 cattle, 15,198 sheep, and 5,810 horses. By 1923, Glacier County counted 17,669 taxable cattle, 23,475 sheep, and 5,421 horses. Between 1924 and 1926 there occurred a sharp decline in taxable cattle in Glacier County, from 15,592 to 4,848, while taxable sheep increased from 29,230 to 44,089, and horses remained more or less the same, 4,864 in 1926. That year, 1926, the Blackfeet Livestock Company, a subsidiary of the Portland Loan Company—begun in 1914 as itself a subsidiary of Swift and Company—was dissolved after only three years in business. During those years, Portland Loan Company had a virtual monopoly on loans to cattlemen in Glacier County, and Blackfeet Livestock handled their marketing. The 1926 dissolution of Blackfeet Livestock cost the company a half-million dollars' loss, and the overall loss, 1914–26, for Portland Loan Company was estimated to have been five million dollars. The company's accountant attributed the business failure to a market in which cattle had been purchased at higher prices and ranchers were obliged to sell them at lower prices.

By 1930, the cattle industry in Glacier County had rebuilt to 10,280 taxable head. Sheep continued to attract investment, reaching 102,301 taxable head in 1930. Taxable horses remained about the same, 4,711. In 1940, a comparison was compiled of reservation stock and Glacier County taxable livestock over the decade of the 1930s. Prefacing this report, the reservation was described as "approximately 51 miles east and west by 54 miles north and south, and contains a grass area of 1,125,518.86 acres grazing, 50,000 acres of forest, 7,234 acres irrigated, 28,850 acres dry farm land and 238,439.58 acres alienated" from Piegan ownership (Stewart 1940b:1).

TABLE 5.1. Taxable Livestock, 1930s

1931: Extension agent Wallace Murdock's annual report:		
	Indian	*Lessee*	*Total*
Cattle	1,650	12,100	12,750
Sheep	13,000	120,000	133,000
Horses	3,400	2,280	5,280
Goats	25	0	25
Hogs	65	175	240
County assessment records compiled at Cut Bank:		
Cattle	8, 847		
Sheep	121,619		
Horses	4,367		

"Lessee" refers to ranchers leasing land from Indians. Their animals were taxable but for the most part not by Glacier County because the owners lived outside Glacier County and would be taxed elsewhere. It is clear from this table that (tax-exempt) Piegan, in 1931, had few cattle compared to outsiders who used their land or to other ranchers in Glacier County; that like other livestock owners they were investing more in sheep; and that unlike other stock owners, they kept more range horses. Extension agent Murdock's figures display, also, lessees' heavy exploitation of the reservation for sheep ranching.

In 1934, the 6,000 cattle brought to the reservation from worse drought regions appear in the extension agent's figures:

TABLE 5.2. Outline of the Livestock Industry in Glacier County

1934: Extension agent Earl Stinson's annual report		1934 County assessment records	
Cattle	10,308	Cattle	6,876
Sheep	7,260	Sheep	92,878
Horses	4,900	Horses	2,732
Hogs	116		

After the bad winter of 1934–35			
1935, Earl Stinson's annual report, Indian-owned		County assessment records	
Cattle	7,447	Cattle	7,977
Sheep	4,895	Sheep	90,994
Horses	2,691	Horses	2,434

And by 1939, still deep in the Depression			
1939, extension agent Rex D. Kildow's annual report		County assessment reports	
Indian-owned cattle	6,846	Cattle	3,425
Sheep	19,411	Sheep	48,733
Horses	2,500 (estimated)	Horses	1,512

(Year by Year Outline of the Livestock Industry in Glacier County, compiled by Research Worker Ernest H. Stewart, 1940:73–87)

Kildow reported, 1940, that

[t]he Galbreath family, who have been in the livestock industry since 1890, specialize in remount horses. Their entire ranching operations are devoted, at the present time, to the raising of remount horses on a commercial scale. Many are sold to the War department. This area is particularly adapted to horse raising, and undoubtedly more Indians will become interested as the demand increases for this type of horse. [Stewart 1940b:15]

The U.S. Cavalry soon replaced those horses with armored tanks.

Politics and Ranching

Piegan benefited from the Indian New Deal instituted by President Franklin Roosevelt's Commissioner of Indian Affairs, John Collier. An important part of Collier's campaign to revitalize Indian nations was a Revolving Credit Fund, lending at low interest rates to Indian people. Under the 1935 Blackfeet Corporate Charter, instituted through Collier's Indian Reorganization Act, the Blackfeet Tribal Business Council borrowed hundreds of thousands of dollars they could channel to entrepreneurs and needy persons. Blackfoot ethos of course demanded that the successful chiefs—now the members of the Tribal Council—be generous to the poor and elderly, regardless of whether they could ever repay with anything more than gratitude. The Bureau of Indian Affairs never did accept this ethos, and the difference between Blackfoot and Anglo ethos led to many charges of incompetent or unethical dealings. During World War II, with several hundred Piegan men and women in the armed forces, an equal number in urban defense industry jobs, and yet more working off-reservation as farm labor, family incomes improved, and loans from the Revolving Credit Fund enabled a number to build sheep flocks.

The end of the war, in 1945, brought hundreds back from military service and from terminated defense jobs. The federal government, wanting to terminate tribal reservations and treaty benefits, encouraged younger families to emigrate ("relocate") to big cities for industrial jobs. The majority who did so returned to the reservation, discouraged by low-wage employment and slum living in cities. With Piegan population steadily increasing and no abatement in selling parcels of land, reservation acreage was ever more inadequate for its most suitable economic enterprise, ranching. The Revolving Credit Fund, like acreage, could not be expanded to support the larger population's needs. One Piegan rancher recalled, in the 1960s,

> I started years ago to build a herd with repayment [loan] cattle. At that time they accepted repayment as a man was able to make it. I took ten years to pay back fifty head. Then they made changes and required that repayment be made within two years. One bad year made this impossible. 1947 was a bad year. The people needed hay to get their cattle through the winter. The government wouldn't finance feeding [purchase of hay]. Then, because the Indian wasn't able to feed, they came in and hauled away the cattle. I managed to borrow $700 from a friend in town and made it through the winter. [quoted in McFee 1972:58]

Throughout the 20th century, outsiders identified ranchers who persevered and made a living as "mixed-bloods," and people whose style of life more resembled early reservation times "full-bloods." This distinction never fit well with economic differences, and as generation after generation intermarried, the often large families of committed "squaw men" and the many children whose mothers were deserted or widowed by white men were integrated with families of full Piegan descent. Mingling in boarding schools, including the famous Carlisle Indian School in Pennsylvania, Fort Shaw, south of the reservation, and the mission schools, it was easy for young Indian people to fall in love with peers, disregarding "blood quantum." The critical differences have been access to capital and freedom from Bureau of Indian Affairs regulation, both factors favoring white men. Beyond these, there has been the drive to succeed in terms of American values. Carlisle Indian Industrial School seems to have instilled its vaunted work ethic in many pupils, some mixed-blood and others full-blood. Competent in English and trained to debate (one of the "cultural achievements" Captain Pratt showcased), Carlisle graduates were prominent on the Blackfeet Tribal Business Council during the first half of the 20th century (the school closed in 1918). An example is Brian Connolly, a contentious man, son of a white father and Piegan mother, whose daughter Nora Lukin has given us a good picture of this hard-driving rancher.

More recent is the picture painted by Woody Kipp of his family, founded by Cut Bank John Kipp who settled at the junction of Willow and Cut Bank Creeks. Cut Bank John (Night Gun was his Blackfoot name) was one of the children of Heavy Runner adopted by trader Joe Kipp after the 1870 Baker Massacre. Cut Bank John's son Joseph was full Piegan, but married a "mixed-blood." Their son "Big John" Kipp served in the Marines during World War II and the Korean War. Returning, he took out a loan from the tribe to purchase machinery to turn the family allotment of rangeland into a wheat farm. His younger brother Woody describes Big John and his wife "Bobby":

> Bobby would get up at 5:00 a.m.; by 6:00 we would have eaten breakfast and be heading for the plowing fields. When the tractor was readied by 7:30 a.m., there was nothing left to do but get into the seat and lower the shovels into Mother Earth and start plowing. . . . I summer fallowed or plowed with an International WD-9 wheel tractor and a TD-9 crawl tractor. . . . Our equipment was fairly small compared to some of the big non-Indian farmers who farmed close by. . . . Grinding monotony. Summer fallowing is dreary work—up one side of a wind strip and down the other, all day, up and back. . . . Rocks as big around and thick as a washtub were thickly deposited across parts of the farmland. . . . It's time-consuming to remove several thousands of acres of rocks. And they keep coming back . . . after a plowing or two they come out of the ground again. . . . We would plow till the sun went down. (I wish I had a videotape of one of our working days to show to white people who chant their mantra about lazy Indians.) We plowed till sundown, went home and ate, retired to bed by 10:00

p.m., and then woke up the next morning and did it again. . . . My ears would ring with the roar of steel on rock for hours. [Kipp 2004:23–25]

Woody Kipp escaped by joining the Marines. Big John hung in there, a successful Piegan farmer. After his death, none of his family continued the farm. Woody teaches in the tribal college, Blackfeet Community College (Kipp 2004:142, 145).

SIX

About Clark Wissler

Clark Wissler was born September 18, 1870, on an Indiana farm, and died August 25, 1947, in New York City. Between 1902 and 1905, he traveled to several northern Plains reservations to record cultural practices and collect representative materials for the American Museum of Natural History in New York, his employer. When he met the gifted half-Piegan David Duvall in Browning, Wissler concentrated his ethnographic research on the Montana Piegan, training Duvall to systematically interview elders and organize their memories of pre-reservation life. Duvall's tragic suicide, at age thirty-one, on July 10, 1911, cut short this fruitful collaboration. Wissler wrote up their material for a series of monographs published by the American Museum, the first listing Duvall as co-author, the succeeding with only Wissler as listed author. Twenty years later, Wissler decided to prepare a study of "The History of the Blackfoot Indians In Contact with White Culture." A partial manuscript, dated 1933, is among the papers left after his death. Why he did not complete this study, he did not indicate.

Wissler's 1933 manuscript is unusual for its time, not a political history but one focusing on, as he put it, "human ecology," relationships between people and their environment. Piegans' "standard of living," he noted, changed through the three centuries of European intrusions into their country. A people who more perfectly than any other represented nomadic bison hunters, the quintessential Plains Indians, Blackfoot led bison herds into corrals for slaughter for at least two millennia, then in the 18th century added care of horse herds to their way of life. Bison and the "Indian ponies" bred by Blackfoot were very well adapted to Blackfoot country, the northwestern Plains and Rockies foothills. Wissler believed that a history of the Piegan needed to understand the bison economy, the incursions of fur traders, and the nation's adjustments to the catastrophe of bison extinction. His student John C. Ewers wrote a history, after Wissler's death, titled *The Blackfeet: Raiders of the Northwestern Plains* (1958). Perhaps the title attracted Western lore aficionados; it certainly does not do justice to the Amskapi Pikuni. We think Wissler's manuscript, with narrative summaries and an outline drawn from annual reports of the Blackfeet Agency superintendents, deserved completion. His perspective on political economy and its ecological base clarifies the issues with which the Piegan had to deal.

Clark Wissler's Life

Clark Wissler's father's family, originally from southern Germany, and his mother's, from England, both emigrated to America in the early 18th century, and to the Midwest—Indiana—a century later when Midwestern First Nations were being dispossessed of their lands. Wissler grew up familiar with the struggles of farmers and lingering echoes of the frontier. His father worked for a time as a school superintendent and edited a county newspaper. Clark graduated from high school in 1887, taught for five years in rural Indiana schools, and then for a year served as principal of the high school he had attended. By 1893, he had saved enough to enter Indiana University, with some credits earned summers from Purdue University. Majoring in experimental psychology, Wissler obtained his BA in 1897 and a Master's degree two years later while supporting himself by teaching psychology and education at the Ohio State University. In 1899, he received an assistantship in psychology at Columbia University in New York, where he completed a PhD in that field in 1901. It happened that Wissler's major professor, James McKeen Cattell, had an office adjacent to that of Franz Boas, and encouraged Wissler to take courses in anthropology from him. For two years, Wissler continued to work in experimental psychological research with Cattell until there was an opportunity for a job at the American Museum, where Boas was Curator of Anthropology. A classmate at Columbia remarked that at that time, there were more jobs for young anthropologists than for young psychologists.

His boyhood tramping through farm fields collecting Indian artifacts, guided by a local enthusiast, infected Wissler with an abiding appreciation of First Nations cultures. He became experienced in scientific method during his studies in experimental psychology, and was, Boas wrote when recommending him for the American Museum position, "very adaptable and highly efficient" (quoted in Freed and Freed 1983:804). Initially, Wissler went to the Dakotas and Montana for ethnography with

Sioux, Gros Ventre, and Blackfoot, working winters in the American Museum. Boas resigned his Museum curatorship in 1905 to teach full time at Columbia, and Wissler was appointed Acting Curator and then permanently Curator of Anthropology, heading the Museum's Department of Anthropology until he retired in 1942. Although Wissler, like Boas, taught at Columbia in addition to his Museum duties, he gave up teaching in 1909. In 1924, he was appointed to a research position in a new Institute of Psychology at Yale University in New Haven, and when an anthropology department was established at Yale in 1931, Wissler was named professor of anthropology, holding that post until 1940. Usually, he took the train to New Haven on Saturday mornings, taught a class and met with graduate students, and returned to New York on Saturday night. Wissler's course was popular and well attended, and colleagues as well as students deeply appreciated his generous sharing of knowledge and experience, wise counsel, and interesting stories.

The one mystery in Clark Wissler's otherwise calm, proper, hardworking life was an illness that caused him to give up fieldwork. Several years later, this illness was still not diagnosed; a letter in the Wissler papers in Ball State University, recommends Wissler to see the Museum director's personal physician. Well-known anthropologist Margaret Mead said that the chronic illness cleared up in 1928, but that until then, Wissler appeared frail (quoted in Freed and Freed 1983:806). We wonder whether Wissler may have been sensitive to chemicals used as preservatives in the Museum; steel lockers holding collections lined the corridors around his office, leaking the smell of preservatives. We asked the Museum archivist whether, in 1928, conservators changed the chemicals they had been using up until then. He replied (personal communication, March 30, 2005) that he had no documentation on preservatives; retired curator Stanley Freed told us that mothballs were the basic preservative, and that he doubted they were the cause of the illness (personal communication, March 20, 2005).

Wissler's outstanding talent was for organizing. He could envision patterns that might be manifest as departments, committees, expeditions, surveys, mappings, classifications, ethnographic monographs, textbooks, handbooks—forms that would provide coherence and order. Unlike many who like to organize, Wissler did so as means to ends, not to enjoy power. His contemporaries characterized him as "somewhat casual, imprecise, and perhaps unintense in his attack on [a] problem; but he possessed an exploratory and pioneering mind" (Kroeber and Kluckhohn 1952:151). An anthropologist employed in the American Museum, later head of its anthropology department, said of Wissler,

He was perceptive but slow to action, judicious, and ready to seek a compromise. . . . He was realistic or practical. Because of this natural inclination, he rarely if ever revolted or spearheaded a drive, preferring to negotiate and to find a middle ground . . . he generally attained his objective. . . . During eighteen years as my chief, he never once laid the heavy hand of authority upon my activities. As a consequence his department was generally known throughout anthropological circles to be one of the happiest places in which to work. [Shapiro 1948:301–302, quoted in Freed and Freed 1983:808]

Margaret Mead added that he had "tremendous width and breadth of imagination and organization" (quoted in Freed and Freed 1983:808); she confessed that she never felt she really knew the man. He was married, father of a son and a daughter (she became a librarian at the American Museum); if he wrote letters to them or friends expressing more of his heart than he revealed to colleagues, they seem not to have been preserved. His principal student, John C. Ewers, acknowledged only that Clark Wissler's classes at Yale had been "stimulating," arousing an interest in Blackfoot that culminated in Ewers's two major books of the 1950s, on Blackfoot history and on Blackfoot horse culture (Ewers 1958:x).

A half-century after Wissler's death, anthropologists looking into the history of the discipline found Clark Wissler mentioned again and again. Genial in manner, he agreed, again and again and again, to chair committees, organize conferences, evaluate programs, and advise. One historian of archaeology credits Wissler with the most extensive planning for archaeology and deployment of field projects, beginning at his first assuming his curatorship in 1905 (Lyon 1996:9). His elected offices included:

1915, vice president, American Association for the Advancement of Science

1919, president, American Anthropological Association

1920–21, chairman, Division of Anthropology and Psychology, National Research Council[1]

1921–24, chair, Committee on State Archaeological Surveys (a committee of the National Research Council, organized by Wissler in 1920 when he was chair of the NRC)

1930–31, president, New York Academy of Sciences

1937, vice president, American Association for Adult Education

1938–43, president, American Association of Museums

1940–43, vice president, Advisory Board, National Park Service

He served as advisor to the Bishop Museum in Honolulu and the Carnegie Institution in Washington, D.C. (sponsor of major archaeological projects, especially in Latin America). His professional memberships included, in addition to those above in which he held office, the National Academy of Sciences, American Philosophical Society, Royal Anthropological Institute of Great Britain and Ireland, Phi Beta Kappa, Sigma Xi, and Educational Research Association. Indiana University and Yale University awarded him honorary degrees.

Wissler's many publications show his ability to organize data to illuminate significant aspects of a subject. He was invited to contribute chapters on "Anthropology" to a pair of volumes in the 1920s, *Recent Developments in the Social Sciences* (1927) and *Research in the Social Sciences* (1929). All the contributors to these volumes were eminent professors, for example, philosopher John Dewey, historians Arthur Schlesinger and Charles Beard, legal scholar Roscoe Pound, sociologist Robert Park, political scientist Charles E. Merriam, and geographer Carl Sauer. Wissler argued, in his chapters, for the critical importance of distribution maps of culture traits, from which culture areas could be recognized. Environmental factors in area culture patterns could be sought, and also historical relationships. Mentioning the value of stratigraphy for archaeology—a relatively new technique for archaeologists in America—Wissler proposed the "age-area" model in which widely distributed culture traits are "overlaid" by more limited traits: a cultural trait (behavior or artifact) would be invented in a culture area center and diffuse outward, sequences of inventions producing a "stratigraphy" indicating which are older, which more recent. This age-area concept was also used in Europe where it was called *kulturkreislehre* (culture-circle theory). Subsequently, scholars have found that there are too many exceptions to the model to justify applying it as a principle; Wissler used it judiciously, as in his discussion of feather mosaics including Plains war bonnets (Wissler 1926:52–61), and his interesting analysis of moccasin types (1926:19–27). His espousal of age-area models reflects his talent for organization and analyses cutting through to basic structures.

A member of his Museum staff who knew him well remarked that it was his style "to write first what he had to say and then afterwards to check with the authorities" (Nelson 1948:247). This is exactly what we see in his 1933 manuscript on Blackfoot history, writing out what he had to say after studying and absorbing a range of source materials, noting where he intended to go back and copy exact quotes or details. These notes are explicit, enabling us to fill in with confidence and preserve what he meant to say. Actively concerned with bringing knowledge to a broad public, Wissler's popular books include:

1912: *North American Indians of the Plains,* an American Museum
handbook for visitors
1917: *The American Indian: An Introduction to the Anthropology of
the New World*
1923: *Man and Culture,* an introductory anthropology textbook
1926: *The Relation of Nature to Man in Aboriginal America*
1929: *An Introduction to Social Anthropology*
1938: *Indian Cavalcade* (reprinted 1971, in paperback, as *Red Man
Reservations*)
1940: *The Indians of the United States*

Most of these went through several editions. His five monographs on
Blackfoot (primarily Amskapi Pikuni [Southern Piegan]), the first listing
David Duvall as co-author and the following with Wissler alone as author, are models of salvage ethnography, preserving in systematic records
the way of life recalled by Blackfoot who knew firsthand the buffalo days.
Indian Cavalcade is Wissler's ethnography of reservation life, descriptions
not considered worth publishing early in the 20th century that had to
await a new generation in the discipline before they could be appreciated.
Wissler carried on Franz Boas's project to record salvage ethnography
from all the Plains First Nations, published as Anthropological Papers of
the American Museum of Natural History. His 1914 paper, "Influence of
the Horse in the Development of Plains Culture," published in *American
Anthropologist,* was a landmark in making readers aware that Plains nations had dynamic histories.

Wissler's colleague at Yale University said that "the number and
range of the ethnographic publications of [the American Museum] demonstrate that Wissler must share with Boas the credit for establishing
field research as the hall-mark of American anthropologists" (Murdock
1948:295). He assisted Arctic explorer Vilhjalmur Stefánsson not only in
obtaining funds and planning expeditions, but in writing them up. He obtained funds to send Robert Lowie and Alfred Kroeber to Hopi and Zuni,
respectively, to obtain data from Southwestern nations relevant to questions raised by British anthropologist W. H. R. Rivers in his monograph
Kinship and Social Organization. Lowie had also questioned whether Plains
"age-societies" were really similar to age-based grade levels in Western
schools, whereupon Wissler created a cooperative survey of several Plains
nations, producing in-depth comparative data clarifying all-comrades
societies (Lowie 1949:527). He took up another American Museum staff
member's suggestion, in 1914, that tree rings in building beams might enable archaeologists to date prehistoric Pueblos, writing to astronomer A.
E. Douglass, pioneer in dendrochronology, and arranging for American

Museum archaeologists to give specimens to Douglass (Nelson 1948:246; Nash 2000:62). In 1925, he traveled to Australia, New Zealand, and Hawaii to assist in developing anthropological field researches in the Pacific. Margaret Mead's famous studies were encouraged by Wissler, and his approval of ethnographic studies of human sexuality eventually led to the National Research Council supporting Alfred Kinsey's monumental research on American sexual behavior (Gathorne-Hardy 1998:93).

Human Ecology

Clark Wissler's failure to complete his 1933 manuscript on Blackfoot history can certainly be excused, given his multiple commitments to museums, university teaching, public education, and protection and research into heritage resources. That he undertook preparing a manuscript indicates how important he believed the human ecology perspective could be for history. "Ethno history" he promoted from his first years in the American Museum, writing this term on page xiii in a foreword (pages xiii–xv) to the Museum's Anthropological Paper number 3 (1908), on "The Indians of Greater New York and the Lower Hudson"—possibly the first use of the term *ethnohistory* in print (Robert Grumet, citing his teacher Robert Schuyler, personal communication, February 2005). In his 1923 *Man and Culture* and particularly his 1926 *The Relation of Nature to Man in Aboriginal America,* Wissler thought deeply about the topic of the 1926 book. His standpoint, presented in the 1917 *The American Indian,* was that the principal sustainable subsistence resource for humans in an area powerfully affected the construction of societies' culture in that area. The idea of "culture areas" was not original with Wissler: it had been argued in the mid-19th century by German geographers Ratzel and Bastien, both influential on Franz Boas's thinking, and embodied in museum methods by Otis Mason in his 1880s exhibits for the Smithsonian Institution's Museum of Natural History (for the German geographers and Boas see Lowie 1937; for Mason and Smithsonian, Hinsley 1981).

The American Indian opens with "The Food Areas of the New World," because, Wissler states, "[i]t is obvious that the fundamental necessity for man's existence is a sufficient quantity of some kind of edible organic substance" (Wissler 1922:1). Later, "while the environment does not produce the culture, it furnishes the medium in which it grows, and . . . once rooted in a geographical area, culture tends to hold fast" (Wissler 1922:373). This conclusion came out of detailed examinations of the American Museum's extensive collections of artifacts. Wissler presented his analyses in 1915, in a long paper, "Material Cultures of the North American Indian," prepared for an international conference cancelled by the start of World War I. Including a map (used in hall labels in the American Museum) dividing North America into nine culture areas, the paper revealed three underlying culture areas, north, west, and east, and linked the Southeast through the Caribbean with eastern South America. He found arbitrary motor habits, such as mounting horses from the right or sewing coiled baskets clockwise or counterclockwise, suggest the persistence of learned cultural behavior, supporting his finding that much of the similarity characterizing a culture area is not a direct function of environmental factors but a cultural complex (for example, horse management was learned as a complex, or we might say a package). Why material culture is likely to be learned, and persist, as "packages," and conversely, why ceremonial acts and accompanying beliefs seem to vary more between nations in a culture area, Wissler posed as scientific questions.

Finally, Wissler argued that

> culture . . . is, after all, the only distinctly human phenomenon . . . [and anthropology] conceives of it as historical phenomena. . . . But anthropology is something more than the study of culture; it is essentially a coordinating and synthetizing science. It seeks to bring to bear upon the problem of man the full joint force of geology, zoology, and history . . . a task which offers the greatest possible scientific opportunity of the age. [Wissler 1922:388]

This perspective, giving primacy to historical events and movements while undergirding them with ecological factors, is beautifully realized in the 1933 manuscript on Blackfoot.

The original, 1917, edition of *The American Indian* was a breakthrough in mapping America's First Nations as encountered during European invasions. The expanded 1922 edition, the edition most used by anthropologists, was truly scientific in that it postulated a testable hypothesis—that ecological factors significantly affected human societies—adduced a large amount of data, and demonstrated that these data validated the hypothesis. As he stated, Wissler saw that he needed to synthesize material from the natural sciences with human histories to explain cultures. Nels Nelson's comment, that Wissler would "write first what he had to say and then afterwards to check with the authorities," indicates how Wissler differed from many of his (and our) colleagues who plod along piling on one observation after another in expectation that when the last field note is down, readers will somehow intuit some valuable conclusions. Years of study, by observations, reading, and discussions, led to Wissler formulating explanatory hypotheses: these he wrote out as descriptive text, then filled in necessary additional data and references to demonstrate to readers that his interpretations were valid. Franz Boas was notorious for accumulating huge amounts of detailed descriptions, a good part through the work of collaborators in First Nations communities, yet never satisfied he had enough to permit substantial interpretation. Perhaps because Wissler grew up in Midwestern farm communities less intellectual than Boas's urban background, and Wissler's father and he were both rural teachers, Wissler was comfortable writing to wide audiences.

Wissler's accomplishment in realizing the six great "food areas" of North America paralleled that of his contemporary Edward Sapir in recognizing six great language stocks, a classification not available to Wissler until after publication of the 1922 *The American Indian*. (Sapir first published his synthesis in 1921, then more fully in 1929.) "Six" is a coincidence in number; the linguistic stocks only very roughly reflect ecological food areas, because speaker communities moved historically, for example the Navajo and Apache into the maize-growing Southwest from their earlier home with fellow Athabascan-language speakers in the Caribou Area of northwest Canada. Both Wissler and Sapir were bold in proposing their macro-groups, Wissler reducing Otis Mason's 12 "ethnic environments" to six staple-subsistence ecological areas, and Sapir reducing John Wesley Powell's 58 language groups, published in 1891, to the six superstocks. Both reductions were powerful not because they simplified classifications, but because they highlighted critical features of assemblages of data.

Ecology was a fairly new science early in the 20th century. The word itself (spelled oecology) was coined by the German marine biologist Ernst Haeckel in 1873 , and the concept utilized around the turn of the twentieth in several American studies of plant geography. Originally looking to explain "the balance of nature" or equilibrium, by 1905 Frederick Clements had published a textbook, *Research Methods in Ecology,* and argued for "dynamic ecology" reflecting observed changes in plant communities through time. Clements really only modified the equilibrium model, in that he looked for regular successions as in regeneration of woodlands after clearing (McIntosh 1982:11–16). Classics in ecology, including the work of the mathematician Lotka and zoologists Shelford and Allee, were yet to come when Wissler's second edition of *The American Indian* was published, and only Lotka's major work was available in 1933; novelist H. G. Wells had spoken of "the ecology of the human species" in a 1931 book, but meaning that economics is the equivalent of ecology for humans (Oxford English Dictionary: "ecology"). Sociologists at the University of Chicago in the 1920s picked up the term *human ecology* to describe the structure of cities, emphasizing competition for space and societal resources; their usage practically excluded the natural environment (see Young 1983:20–48), while geographer Harlan Barrows urged his colleagues to see geography as uniquely human ecology (reprinted in Young 1983:49–62). Alfred Kroeber, in his *Cultural and Natural Areas of Native North America,* used "ecology" to refer to the natural environment (see index to his volume), explaining how societies adjust their cultures to their environments (e.g., 1939:22–23). Wissler in 1933 had a stronger understanding of humans in ecological relationship with their country, not so dualistic as Kroeber's more traditional view of here culture, there environment.

What Wissler understood was the concept today discussed by evolutionary biologists as "niche construction." Organisms affect their environment as they remove what they consume, deposit waste and secretions, and destroy, or perpetuate or nurture, other organisms and inorganic matter. Organisms may move from one habitat to a different one, this of course being true of humans, and the ecological effect is especially significant if the movement tends to be seasonal and repeated (Odling-Smee, Laland, and Feldman 2003:44–45). Blackfoot did not simply adapt to their northwestern Plains/Rockies front range environments, they affected the landscape and many populations of animals and plants as they hunted, burned bison pasture, cultivated and harvested camas, prairie turnip, berries, and medicinal plants, collected and burned firewood and buffalo chips, left bison bones and carcass remnants in pounds, and during historic times, pastured and watered horse herds. Development of a cattle ranching economy more drastically affected the environment with its irrigation dams and channels, fences, grazing by an invasive species and introducing foreign grasses. Thus, the concept "niche construction" well conveys the active role Blackfoot played in their land, even before introduction of horses and slaughtering for the fur trade.

Other Analytic Approaches

Early in the 20th century, Franz Boas challenged the then-dominant assumption in anthropology that human societies evolved from small simple hunting-gathering bands into pastoral or agricultural tribes and eventually civilized states, *and that many existing societies represented fossilized primitive types.* Anglo middle and upper classes, or bourgeois European culture generally, were most evolved. "Inferior races" had failed to evolve further because they were physically and mentally weaker. Philosopher Herbert Spencer's phrase "survival of the fittest" explained why the European "race" conquered "inferior races" and predicted these would die out, "vanish," as the "fittest" overwhelmed the earth. Boas used anthropometry (measurements of the human body) to demonstrate that American Indians and children of Indian-Euro-American marriages were not physically inferior to Euro-Americans, and he and his students recorded and published ethnographies and linguistic studies exhibiting richness and complexity in First Nations' cultures. Clark Wissler, though WASP by descent, recognized the validity of Boas's work, perhaps because his own research in experimental psychology at Columbia revealed poor science in intelligence testing. The Smithsonian's William Holmes's labeling Wissler "a two-faced Jew of the most cunning variety" exhibits how closely mainstream cultural evolutionism, accepted by Major Powell and his deputy Holmes, was tied to WASP power. In the light of Holmes's fanatic anti-Semitism, Wissler's staunch commitments to empirical science and respect for human dignity are remarkable: where Boas's challenges to WASP bias might seem self-serving, coming from an immigrant Jew, Wissler was speaking against the class he could claim as birthright. To assert, in the first, 1917, edition of *The American Indian,* that indigenous America forms "one of the two grand world divisions" (Wissler 1917:1) was a bold rejection of the common myth that American First Nations were savages in wilderness.

Another approach might have been that of Karl Marx, whose emphasis on the social relations of production took into account societies' environmental settings. A Marxist approach would characterize relations between humans and their nonhuman surroundings as a dialectic, each party responding and reacting to the other, on and on, a dynamic relationship. Wissler's emphasis on "food areas" is an economic approach delineating how production of a region's most reliable and profitable staple food supported certain social structures and called forth symbolic expression in cosmology, myth, ritual, and art. For Blackfoot, fluid bands were the societal form best suited to dependence on herds that for most of the year moved and grazed in similar small, widely separated bands; indeed, Blackfoot clearly saw strong parallels between their human societies and those of bison. It may be that because Marx focused on urban industrial capitalist societies, seeking to understand how they evolved, Wissler didn't notice the overlap with a dynamic human ecology. More likely, Wissler found the ecology concept, drawn from natural history research, sufficient to understand how Blackfoot culture developed, persisted, and changed.

Political anthropologist Joan Vincent called attention to 1920s and 1930s scholars ignored by the mainstream of anthropology (Vincent 1990:174–177, 180–188), when fashion celebrated culture-and-personality hypotheses copied from Sigmund Freud, or "acculturation" charting indigenes' courses toward assimilation into dominant Western behavior and beliefs. Outside these fashions, political economist William Christie MacLeod published an iconoclastic *The American Indian Frontier* in 1928, showing how similar had been the Roman and English-Scottish frontiers to the American frontier. MacLeod went against contemporary usage when he recognized American First Nations as sovereign nations, rejecting the label "tribe" (MacLeod 1928:21). C. Daryll Forde was an English geographer on a fellowship to University of California, Berkeley, who conducted an ethnography of the Yuma of southeastern California, published in 1931, that aligned him with the marginalized Anna Gayton, ethnographer for Yokuts and Western Mono, and Julian Steward, recording Great Basin Shoshone and Paiute, in a perspective framed by University of California historical geographer Carl Sauer. Citing Wissler's definition of anthropology as "trying to show what all the forms and forces of nature have done to man, but even with more emphasis what man has done to nature," Sauer remarked it was a good description of geography, too (Young 1983:385; Sauer referred to a paper Wissler published, 1924, in the journal *Ecology* [5:311–318]). Like Wissler, Sauer was keenly aware of historical events and contingencies, mapped onto landscapes. Daryll Forde's *Habitat, Economy and Society,* published in 1934 and republished after World War II, quickly became a standard text for a heavily anthropological ecology. Julian Steward achieved fame with his 1938 Bureau of American Ethnology monograph, *Basin-Plateau Aboriginal Sociopolitical Groups,* apparently describing an extremely simple culture dominated by its desert habitat.

Steward was so fascinated by survival in the western desert that he failed to take notice of Mormon expulsion of First Nations from their stream and lake valley homelands, not to mention their decimation by disease, settlers' attacks, and enforced poverty. He clung to his notion that desert Shoshone, and Inuit, represented primeval patrilineal bands, notwithstanding neither group of peoples lived in such communities. Steward's drive to theoretical models culminated in his 1955 *Theory of Culture Change,* presenting the concept of "multilinear evolution" to replace racist unilinear evolution. Although comparatively liberating, stimulating, and in line with evolutionary biology, Steward's mid-century work remained wed to abstract modal types he postulated to independently evolve in suitable environments (Steward 1955:184–185). Bloodless theoretical models appealed to the postwar generation sick of real carnage. Wissler's mature, strongly historical, dynamic human ecology was eclipsed in the 1960s and 1970s by equilibrium models and closed systems listing only a few factors, differentiating an ecological focus from the interdisciplinary field of ethnohistory emerging, in the 1970s, from research carried out for the Indian Claims Commission.

Wissler and Blackfoot

Wissler's experience with Blackfoot was limited but intense, heightened by the mediation of the gifted, tragic Dave Duvall. Through Duvall, Wissler not only obtained a very detailed picture of Piegan life in the mid-19th century, but opportunity to sit with people such as "Wolf Chief" and "Mother-of-All," dignified, humorous, kind, and intelligent (Wissler 1971:275–289). The pathos of Duvall's anomie, feeling neither Indian nor white, affected Wissler, illuminating for him the human cost of forced assimilation, just as the comfortable old couple led him to respect a Piegan way of life. His last two books, *Indian Cavalcade* and *Indians of the United States,* express outrage against United States treatment of First Nations; reaching retirement age, he no longer needed to be circumspect. His manuscript history of the Blackfoot, thoroughly researched and outlined, left no doubt over the calamitous effects of white contact.

The illness that debilitated him from 1909 to 1928 discouraged Wissler from fieldwork, and by the time his health improved, he was nearing 60, busy with administrative work in the American Museum, national committee engagements, and helping build an anthropology department at Yale. Difficulty in obtaining fieldwork funds for ethnography during the 1930s Depression may have further dampened thoughts of returning to the field. He does not seem to have corresponded with Piegan after Duvall's 1911 death and his nephew James Eagle Child's inability to fill his role of fieldworker. By the time Duvall shot himself, hundreds of pages of his manuscript notes awaited Wissler's editing for publication in the American Museum Anthropological Papers. On top of this enterprise, Wissler was directing other anthropologists' fieldwork and comparative studies with Northern Plains nations. His American Museum Anthropological Papers on Blackfoot comprise volume 2, with Duvall as co-author, 1908; volume 5 number 1; volume 7 numbers 1 and 2; volume 11 number 4; volume 11 number 12; to volume 16 number 3, 1918, with volumes 11 and 16 including colleagues' contributions on other Plains nations.

In part because of Wissler's talent for clear organization, the American Museum series on Blackfoot stands as one of the most thorough and accessible records of any 19th-century American First Nation way of life. Their great value comes from Duvall's commitment to his culture, his determination to document fully and translate accurately; a man who felt himself too Indian to be white, too white to be Indian, he found his niche in interviewing the men, and a few women, a generation older than he, the last generation to grow up before the reservation. Most were residents of Duvall's mother's community, Heart Butte, or lived along the rivers in the southwest sector of the reservation. Although Duvall did not usually identify his informants individually, we can list them from the accounts for payment he mailed to Wissler: Talieu Ashley; Bad Old Man; Bear Skin; Big-brave (Frank Mountain Chief); Black-bear; Boy Chief; Bull Child; Chief Crow; Comes-at-Night; Curley-bear; Eagle Child (his uncle); Elkhorn; Flat Tail; Heavy Breast; Heavy Gun; Heavy Runner; Last Star; Lazy Boy; Mad-plume; Sam Many Guns; Mistaken Buffalo Rock; New-breast; Henry No Bear; Mrs. (Gertrude) No Chief (Piegan name: Fetched Back); Owl Top Feathers; Red-plume; Steep Short Face; Mrs. Strangling Wolf (wife of Duvall's uncle); Jappy Takes-Gun-On-Top (Duvall's step-father); The Boy; Three Bears; Shorty White Grass; White Man; White Quiver; Mrs. (Strikes First) Wolf Plume (Fig. 20); and most significant, Tom "Kiyo"—Kyaiyo, English name Tom Sanderville—owner of Head Carrier's beaver bundle and principal ritual leader for the Heart Butte community. Of these, all but Ashley, Bear Skin, Elkhorn, and Mrs. Strangling Wolf are listed on the 1907–08 Blackfeet Allotment Census (DeMarce 1980); Bear Skin and Elkhorn may be listed under other names.

Walter McClintock, George Bird Grinnell, James Willard Schultz, John Ewers, and other white authors writing significant Piegan ethnographies revisited the reservation for years. None of them found a David Duvall. McClintock and Schultz romanticized their experiences, Grinnell limited his Blackfoot research, and Ewers, Wissler's student from Yale, came too late to listen to a range of men and women who had been adults before the bison disappeared. Dutch linguist C. C. Uhlenbeck meticulously took down texts in Blackfoot during the summers of 1910 and 1911, giving us memoirs and tales as they were told, but his purpose was language, not culture. Those of the Columbia University students carrying out Ruth Benedict's ethnographic project in 1938 and 1939 who published their research focused on the political economy of the Canadian Blackfoot reserves (Goldfrank 1966; Hanks and Hanks 1950; Lewis 1942 was a library dissertation). Calgary historian Hugh A. Dempsey, married into a prominent Blood (Kainai) family, has produced notable collections of Blackfoot historical accounts and biographies, primarily of his wife's people. Black-foot scholars are now publishing independent of white collaborators, struggling to convey in English what they feel to be authentic Nitsitapi ("Real People") experience and thinking (see, e.g., Bastien 2004).

Surveying the literature on and by Blackfoot, we see nothing that quite matches Wissler's 1933 manuscript. His monographs written from

FIG. 20. Wolf Plume. Credit: Blackfeet THPO.

his and Duvall's fieldwork have no historical dimension; their purpose was to preserve knowledge of a way of life no longer possible, and the style was scientifically objective, not from arrogance but to persuade readers this was serious matter. Twenty years later, Wissler had status in the academic world. He could explore material, confident that his experience and work in the scientific mode would give it respect. The outrage he had felt witnessing so much injustice on South Dakota and Montana reservations, his sorrow over Duvall's pain, and the fascination raised by correlations between staple foods and cultural patterns could be pursued as he deemed best. He recognized human ecology to be an informative framework for tracing out the indigenous life and, as he titled it, the effects of white contact upon the First Nation with which he was most familiar, Piegan. Then he put the sketched-out manuscript aside to record his observations on reservations thirty years earlier, and to prepare his last Museum handbook, *Indians of the United States*. Handsomely published by Doubleday, its lively language succinctly describes the nations, grouped under linguistic stocks, and histories characterized as hard-fought frontiers. Its aim is clear: to make Americans realize that the First Nations are integral components in American history. We can understand that Wissler believed this more important than chronicling the ecology of one nation. Still, that study was well conceived, and enough written that the manuscript can be completed. This we offer in the preceding pages.

Addendum:
Definitions of Blackfeet
Reservations Lands, 1855, 1851, 1875

The extent of Blackfoot lands in the United States was defined (in 1855 "Treaty with the Blackfeet Nation," or "Lame Bull's Treaty," on the Judith) as follows:

> Bounded on the south by a line drawn eastward from the Hell Gate or Medicine Rock passes to the nearest source of the Musselshell River, down that river to its mouth, and down the Missouri to the mouth of Milk River; on the east by a line due north from the mouth of Milk River to the forty-ninth parallel (the Canadian border); on the north by this parallel; and on the west by the Rocky Mountains. [Ewers 1958:217]

> Fort Laramie Treaty, 1851:

> Commencing at the mouth of the Muscle-shell river, thence up the Missouri river to its source—thence along the main range of the Rocky Mountains, in a Southern direction to the head waters of the northern source of the Yellow Stone river—thence down the Yellow Stone to the mouth of Twenty five Yard Creek—thence across to the head waters of the Muscle-shell river—and thence down the Muscle-shell river to the place of beginning. [Ewers 1958:207]

Extent of their lands in the United States was defined in 1875 as follows:

Commencing at a point on the Muscle-Shell River, where the same is intersected by the 47th parallel of north latitude; thence east with said parallel to the south bank of the Yellowstone River; thence down and with the south bank of said river to the south boundary of the military reservation at Fort Buford; thence west along the south boundary of said military reservation to its western boundary; thence north along said western boundary to the south bank of the Missouri River; thence up and with the south bank of said river to the mouth of the Muscle-shell River; thence up the middle of the main channel of said Muscle-Shell river to the place of beginning, be, and the same hereby is withdrawn from sale and set apart as an addition to the present reservation for the Gros Ventres, Piegan, Blood, Blackfeet, and Crow Indians. [Executive Order, U. S. Grant, in Report of the Commissioner of Indian Affairs for 1877:243]

Notes

Chapter 1. Wissler's 1933 Manuscript

1. Horses were released in the southern plains by DeSoto and Coronado about 1541; hence, there is nothing impossible in horses having reached the Blackfoot country early in the 1600s. The highly integrated culture of the Canadian Plains tribes in 1754 suggests at least a century of development.

2. Editor's note: We now do have evidence. See Ewers 1958:197, Dempsey 1994:38.

3. Thompson records a narrative of a Cree Indian living among the Piegan relating to events that he believed to have happened before 1750. A fight between Snakes and Piegans, assisted by a few Cree and Stone Indians is described. A few guns were in use among the Cree and Stoneys and the Snakes had horses. Whether the narrator confined his statements to events in his own lifetime is not certain, nor is it clear that Thompson is not writing from memory many years afterward [Editor's note: This in fact was the case]. It is significant, however, that this is consistent with later statements as to the source of horses and the presence of the Snake tribes in the Canadian Plains (Thompson 1916:329–344).

4. White and mixed-blood "peddlars" made their early appearance, first as "engagés" of the fur companies, later as more or less independent operators. Some of these lived with the Indians and raised families. How extensive this penetration was we have no way of estimating, but the number in any one camp probably rarely exceeded one man. Nevertheless, such an individual could have exerted considerable culture influence.

5. Mooney (H.B.) considers 500 miles the average annual range for the horse tribes.

6. It is usually overlooked that the beaver were greatly reduced in the wooded country at an early date. David Thompson records how thick they were when the trade first entered the Bay and the Lakes. It was the presence of this dense beaver fauna that stimulated the fur trade. The new methods introduced by the trade and the importation of white and mixed-blood hunters soon reduced the beaver east of Lake Winnipeg and stimulated movements into the Plains and into the northwest. The beaver were not wholly exterminated, but they were so depleted in certain areas as to cause collapse and disorganization among the tribes concerned. In 1797 Thompson remarks that the Indians are now in poverty (Thompson 1916:206).

7. (Wissler's own footnote here contradicts the statement.) No beaver. "The trade with the Slaves is of very little consequence to us. They kill scarcely any good furs a beaver of their own hunt is seldom found among them; their principal trade is wolves, of which of late years we take, while our H. B. neighbors continue to pay well for them. At present our neighbors trade with about two-thirds of the Blackfeet, and I would willingly give up the whole of them. Last year, it is true, we got some beaver from them; but this was the spoils of war, they having fallen upon a party of Americans on the Missourie, stripped them of everything, and brought off a quantity of skins" (Henry 1897:541).

8. Catlin estimate[ed] Indians living on buffalo at 300,000. Estimate[ed] 1,500,000 wolves. Indians now [1830s] killing 200,000 excess [i.e., above number needed for food and other Indian uses] for skins to trade for whiskey (Catlin 1844:262–263j). Mackenzie: Wolf they "never eat, but produce a tallow from their fat," trade this and skins (Mackenzie 1902: c11).

9. Gallatin (1836:151): It is worthy of remark that the population of those hunting nations does not appear to have ever reached the maximum of which it was susceptible.
Proof in the number of game animals.
Famine due to crude methods.
Wars.
(p. 262): Estimates the Indians living on buffalo at 300,000.

10. Hinsdale reckons that according to modern diet tables, 3,000 calories per day were necessary for each Indian, to secure which he must have eaten either 6.7 lbs. of fish, 1.6 lbs. of lean meat, 1.9 lbs. of maple sugar, 1.8 lbs. of corn meal, etc. This is in general agreement with Henry's tables (1897:8). Hinsdale has discussed the sustaining resources of aboriginal Michigan [1932] without venturing to commit himself to specific figures, but seems to accept Thompson's ratio,

which would suggest about 1,700 ferns (?) [Ed.: therms?]. However, since some maize was raised in part of the state, this number might safely be doubled and 3,500 ferns (?) might be maintained. He reports [p. 15] that in 1877 over 10,000 deer were killed for market, presumably more than were produced in the year, but this would barely have fed 1,000 Indians through the year.

Thompson makes no comment upon the density of Plains population but rates the Cree between the Pass [the Pas] and Hudson Bay as "ninety families, each of seven souls, giving to each family an area of 248 square miles of hunting ground; or 3 square miles to each soul, a very thin population" (p. 109). The country south of Lake Superior he estimated at 130 families and 206 square miles per family: the annual hunt for each family averaged about sixty to seventy skins (267).

11. Editor's note: Shaw (1995:150), citing McHugh's (1972) assumption of 26 bison per square mile for carrying capacity, states the estimate was "simplistic" and at best, only "a theoretical maximum."

12. Editor's note: Denig was figuring "Each cow has a calf yearly and the fourth year these also have calves" (Denig 1930:462), i.e., Wissler includes the original cow's progeny, following Denig in assuming half the cow's calves are bulls, leaving two females to have respectively five and four calves themselves in the eight-year period. Figures in brackets are supplied by this Editor. Wissler left question marks, no figures.

13. Editor's note: Fye et al., 2003, summarized extensive tree-ring data to show a pluvial (high rainfall) period between 1825 and 1840, producing "lush grassland teeming with bison" (Fye et al. 2003:905). Before this pluvial, there had been a severe drought in the 1790s (according to Alwynne Beaudoin [personal communication, October 24, 2005], worse than the 1930s Dust Bowl drought). Again, between 1841 and 1848 there was a widespread drought, and further droughts between 1855–1865 and 1870–1883, the latter somewhat less severe. Thus, during the 58 years of expansion of the Northern Plains fur trade, there were an initial fifteen years of pluvial, twelve years of "normal" rainfall, and thirty years of drought. Clearly the last 44 years of wild bison herds were predominantly years of drought that must have severely stressed herds expanded to a maximum during the preceding fifteen years of unusually lush grazing.

14. June berry, saskatoon [sarvis berry], red haw, wild plum, sand cherry, chokecherry, high-bush cranberry—[at] Pembina, coral berry, wolf berry. A brief note in Science, May 27, 1932, shows the hack berry Celtis occidentalis L.-Urticaceae, used by many Plains Indians is rich in calcium salts.

15. Editor's Note: Blackfoot did make cooking pots prehistorically, and as Wissler postulated, gave up the craft in the early 19th century (Duke 1991:125).
16. Judging from his photographs, Wissler observed tanning deer or possibly elk hide (Wissler 1910:Plates 1, 2–5). Bison were no longer available to Piegan in the early 1900s. Deer skins are much smaller, lighter, and less heavily haired than bison, so time needed for tanning is considerably less. John Moore calculated tanning a bison hide to require 70 hours, about 15 hours more than tanning a cow hide as recorded by Mooney in a 1903 manuscript (Moore 1996:129).
17. Editor's Note: "Insignificant" perhaps compared to the total number of Indian women, but nevertheless involving thousands of women, many from prominent families, e.g., Natoyist-siksina', wife of Alexander Culbertson, chief trader for the American Fur Company's Upper Missouri Outfit.
18. Editor's Note: Canada did not exist as an independent government until 1867, when it was constituted by the British North American Act. Initially, only the four principal eastern provinces were included. Manitoba entered in 1870, while Alberta and Saskatchewan remained part of the Northwest Territories, formerly Rupert's Land, until that was sold to Canada in 1870.
19. Editor's Note: Figures differ on the number killed in Baker's attack. The Blackfeet agent, William Pease, reported ninety women and fifty children killed, in addition to several dozen men (Ewers 1958:250–251).
20. Editor's Note: Except for his notion that a 12-year-old virgin was sacrificed annually.
21. Editor's Note: Estimates by the Indian Rights Association and a Piegan count put the number between 400 and 555, approximately one-quarter of the population (Ewers 1958:294).
22. Editor's note: The assumption that all Indians must become farmers derived from contemporary philosophy teaching that human societies evolved from wandering savages through a stage of village agriculture to civilization. Indians' evolution could be accelerated by white tutelage.
23. Editor's note: Blackfoot did raise their own tobacco, and women understood how to maintain sustained yields of their vegetable staples, prairie turnips and camas bulbs.
24. Editor's Note: I.e., wagons were to replace travois, men to replace women in hauling.
25. Editor's Note: Wissler does not give citations to Henry's text. The instances are scattered, e.g., pages 73, 105 for stabbings, 1800, page 156

for burning, page 161 for men tearing a baby apart, page 162 for bit-ing, page 164 for beating, 1801, page 168 for shooting, etc.

26. Editor's Note: Wissler makes no attempt at such a count. There are instances, for example a bully who was finally beaten up by a strong man to end his exploitation of young men, page 135.

27. Editor's Note: This is not correct,; both are, like Blackfoot, Algonkian languages but distinct.

28. Clark Wissler was told that, having never seen them before, "some of the Indian women took the green coffee beans, put them into a kettle and boiled and boiled; each time they tasted the mess it was worse than before. So, at last, they abandoned the coffee in disgust" (Wissler 1971:46).

29. John Slidell and James Mason were Confederate politicians en route to England to persuade Britain to support the Confederacy, when the British ship was stopped, November 1861, by an American and the two seized. British troops in Canada were alerted for possible war. The United States released the two men, and Britain decided for a policy of neutrality.

30. This is disingenuous. A little over a year after his arrival as Blackfeet agent, Wright was accused by a Fort Benton saloon keeper of selling him eighteen yards of government-issue ration cloth, selling "two or more cases" of ration goods to merchant T. C. Power as security for a loan of $75 Wright owed the saloon, and in 1867, selling four bales of annuity payment blankets to merchant I. G. Baker, who in turn sold the blankets to the Indians (Dobak 2003:41).

31. The absurd length to which Anglo ideology could legitimate policy regarding First Nations is seen in Canadian Indian Commissioner Hayter Reed's 1889 decree that Indian farmers had not evolved to use modern machinery but must be limited to small plots worked with medieval peasants' hand tools (Carter 1999:168–69). Reed's de-cree was actually intended to prevent Indian farmers from competing with white agricultural enterprises (Carter 1990:188).

32. Courts of Indian Offenses were created in 1882 to abolish "barba-rous and demoralizing practices . . . Indian dances, plural marriages, practices of medicine men, theft, destruction of [others'] property, payment for cohabiting with Indian women, drunkenness, and intro-ducing intoxicating liquors" (Morgan 1890:lxxxiii).

33. Latin for "father of a family." "Family" would include wife, children, servants, and slaves.

34. Britain's famous prime minister Winston Churchill was invited to join the NCAI in 1963 (Cowger 1999:144). Churchill's mother, the Ameri-can Jenny Jerome, was one-eighth Indian.

35. In 1947, "Bureau" rather than "Office" became the official name of Indian Affairs.

Chapter 2. The Amskapi Pikunis from the 1950s to 2010

1. Robert Scriver, a white man born on the reservation and making it his home, collected holy medicine bundles from economically distressed Piegan and those who converted to Christian denominations that would not countenance them. Late in his life, Scriver sold his collection to the Provincial Museum of Alberta, which agreed to respect them. The Montana Piegan preferred to repatriate their ancestral holy bundles to Amskapi Pikuni custody.

Chapter 3. Bungling

1. Campbell was "at Large" supervising livestock on a number of reservations. Animals at large were only part of his responsibilities.

Chapter 5. The Ranchers

1. See the Book of Ruth in the Old Testament. Ruth and her mother-in-law Naomi were both widowed, and to support them Ruth went into the field following the wheat harvesters. Whatever seed fell to the ground as the stalks were cut and carried away, was collected by a household's young women; the owner of the field permitted Ruth to join his young women gleaning, and then married her, praising her devotion to her mother-in-law.

Chapter 6. About Clark Wissler

1. His appointment was opposed by Smithsonian archaeologist William Henry Holmes, whose 1921 letter to Smithsonian director Charles Walcott shows the blatant anti-Semitism permitted then: "[A] new chairman of the [National Research] Council must be selected and it is most important that he should not be of the Hebrew kind." Holmes then warned Walcott that Clark Wissler "is . . . a two-faced Jew of the most cunning variety and an understudy of Boas" (Secretary's Correspondence, Box 62, Folder 1–2, National Anthropological Archives). Cunning indeed, to hide in the person of a seventh-generation English-German Protestant American! (I thank Valerie Pinsky for bringing this letter to my attention).   •

References

NOTE: RCIA = (Annual) Report of the Commissioner of Indian Affairs

Abbott, Frederick H.
    1915 The Administration of Indian Affairs in Canada. Report of an Investigation Made in 1914 under the Direction of the Board of Indian Commissioners. Washington, DC: Board of Indian Commissioners.

Adams, David Wallace
    1995 Education for Extinction: American Indians and the Boarding School Experience, 1875–1928. Lawrence: University Press of Kansas.

Adams, Hank
    1995 Presentations, Conference on Indian Self-Rule, Institute of the American West, Sun Valley, ID, 1983. *In* Indian Self-Rule, Kenneth R. Philp ed. Pp. 239–242. Logan: Utah State University Press. Reprint of 1986 edition.

Allen, Reuben A.
    1884 RCIA for 1884:106–108.
    1885 RCIA for 1885:117–119.

Armitage, J.
    1872 RCIA for 1871:No. 46.

Atkins, John D. C.
    1885 RCIA for 1885:3–72.
    1886 RCIA for 1886:3–55.
    1887 RCIA for 1887:3–83.

Aubrey, Charles
    1919 First Strike of Record in State. Newspaper article, 1 page, from Blackfeet Tribal Historic Preservation Office.

Baldwin, Mark D.
    1886 RCIA for 1886:170–172.

1887 RCIA for 1887:130–132.

1888 RCIA for 1888:150–153.

Banner, Lois W.

    2003 Intertwined Lives: Margaret Mead, Ruth Benedict, and Their Circle. New York: Knopf.

Bartlett, W. A.

    2001 The Pablo-Allard Herd; Origin. *In* "I Will Be Meat for My Salish:" The Montana Writers Project and the Buffalo of the Flathead Indian Reservation, Robert Bigart, ed. Pp. 69–101. Pablo, MT: Salish Kootenai College Press; see additional accounts pp. 103–113 by other Salish.

Bastien, Betty

    2004 Blackfoot Ways of Knowing: The Worldview of the Siksikaitsitapi. Jürgen W. Kremer, ed. Calgary: University of Calgary Press.

Belyea, Barbara, ed. and commentary

    2000 A Year Inland: The Journal of Hudson's Bay Company Winterer Anthony Henday, 1754–55. Waterloo, ON: Wilfrid Laurier University Press.

Berger, Joel, and Carol Cunningham

    1994 Bison: Mating and Conservation in Small Populations. New York: Columbia University Press.

Blakiston, Thomas

    1859 Report. *In* Further Papers Relative to the Exploration of British North America, by Captain John Palliser. London: George Edward Eyre and William Spottiswoode. Facsimile reprint by Greenwood Press, New York, 1969.

Bryson, Reid

    2004 Climate Change and Bison Range Conditions on the 19th Century Great Plains. Oklahoma Archeology 52(4):23–25.

Burnham, Philip

    2000 Indian Country, God's Country: Native Americans and the National Parks. Washington, DC: Island Press.

Campbell, Fred C.

    1921 Field Survey and Individual Indian Report of the Old Agency District, Blackfeet Indian Reservation, Montana. Unpublished document in Blackfeet Planning and Development Office, Browning, MT.

Carter, Sarah

    1990 Lost Harvests: Prairie Indian Reserve Farmers and Government Policy. Montreal: McGill-Queen's University Press.

    1999 Aboriginal People and Colonizers of Western Canada to 1900. Toronto: University of Toronto Press.

2003 Transnational Perspectives on the History of Great Plains Women: Gender, Race, Nations, and the Forty-ninth Parallel. American Review of Canadian Studies Winter 2003:565–596.

Catlin, John B.
1889 RCIA for 1889:222–223.
1890 RCIA for 1890:114–115.

Chapman, Augustus
1868 RCIA for 1867:No. 77.

Clow, Richmond
2003 Presentation on Piegan water rights, Nizipuhwahsin Conference, August 15, 2003, Browning, MT.

Clum, H. R.
1872 RCIA for 1871:1–21.

Coleman, Michael C.
1993 American Indian Children at School, 1850–1930. Jackson: University Press of Mississippi.

Cowger, Thomas W.
1999 The National Congress of American Indians: The Founding Years. Lincoln: University of Nebraska Press.

Cumming, Alfred
1858 RCIA for 1857:No, 54.

Dare, J. Z.
1906 RCIA for 1905:236–237.

DeJong, David H.
1993 Promises of the Past: A History of Indian Education in the United States. Golden, CO: North American Press.

Deloria, Philip S.
1995 The Era of Indian Self-Determination: An Overview. *In* Indian Self-Rule, Kenneth R. Philp, ed. Pp. 191–207. Logan: Utah State University Press. Reprint of 1986 edition.

DeMarce, Roxanne, ed.
1980 Blackfeet Heritage, 1907–1908. Browning, MT: Blackfeet Heritage Program.

Dempsey, Hugh A.
1972 Crowfoot, Chief of the Blackfeet. Norman: University of Oklahoma Press.
1978 Charcoal's World. Lincoln: University of Nebraska Press.
1980 Red Crow, Warrior Chief. Lincoln: University of Nebraska Press.
1994 The Amazing Death of Calf Shirt and Other Blackfoot Stories. Lincoln: University of Nebraska Press.
2002 Firewater: The Impact of the Whiskey Trade on the Blackfoot Nation. Calgary: University of Calgary Press.

2003 The Vengeful Wife and Other Blackfoot Stories. Norman: University of Oklahoma Press.

Denig, Edwin Thompson
1930 Indian Tribes of the Upper Missouri. J. N. B. Hewitt, ed. Bureau of American Ethnology, 46th Annual Report. Pp. 377–628. Washington, DC: Government Printing Office.

Dobak, William
2003 "The Primary Object Is Money": Robe Traders and Federal Contractors in Territorial Montana. *In* The Fur and Robe Trade in Blackfoot Country, 1831 to 1880. National Fur Trade Symposium Proceedings, 2003. Pp. 40–47. Fort Benton, MT: River and Plains Society.

Dole, William P.
1861 RCIA for 1861:9–30.
1865 RCIA for 1864:No. 85 3/4.

Drinnon, Richard
1987 Keeper of Concentration Camps: Dillon S. Myer and American Racism. Berkeley: University of California Press.

Duke, Philip
1991 Points in Time: Structure and Event in a Late Northern Plains Hunting Society. Niwot, CO: University Press of Colorado.

Edwards, J. E.
1902 RCIA for 1901:258–259.

Eggermont-Molenaar, Mary, ed.
2005 Montana 1911: A Professor and His Wife Among the Blackfeet. Calgary: University of Calgary Press; and Lincoln: University of Nebraska Press.

Ensign, William T.
1874 RCIA:No. 40.

Ewers, John C.
1945 Blackfeet Crafts. Washington, DC: United States Department of the Interior, Bureau of Indian Affairs.
1955 The Horse in Blackfoot Indian Culture. Bureau of American Ethnology, Smithsonian Institution, Bulletin 159. Washington, D.C.: Government Printing Office.
1958 The Blackfeet: Raiders on the Northwestern Plains. Norman: University of Oklahoma Press.
1974 Ethnological Report on the Blackfeet and Gros Ventre Tribes of Indians. New York: Garland. (Original report presented to Indian Claims Commission, docket No. 279-A).
1978 Richard Sanderville, Blackfoot, 1873–1951. *In* American Indian

Intellectuals, ed. Margot Liberty. St. Paul MN: West Publishing. Reprinted 2001 by University of Oklahoma Press, Norman. Pp. 132–143 in Oklahoma edition.

1984 An Appreciation of Karl Bodmer's Pictures of Indians. *In* Views of a Vanishing Frontier. Pp. 51–93. Lincoln: University of Nebraska Press. (Exhibit catalog).

Fawcett, Melissa Jayne
2000 Medicine Trail: The Life and Lessons of Gladys Tantaquidgeon. Tucson: University of Arizona Press.

Foley, Michael F.
1974 An Historical Analysis of the Administration of the Blackfeet Indian Reservation by the United States, 1855–1950. Indian Claims Commission Docket 2790:1–31.

Forde, C. Daryll
1934 Habitat, Economy, and Society. London: Methuen.

Freed, Stanley, and Ruth Freed
1983 Clark Wissler and the Development of Anthropology in the United States. American Anthropologist 85(4):800–825.

Fuller, Thomas P.
1898 RCIA for 1898:182–186.

Fye, Falko K., David W. Stahle, and Edward R. Cook
2003 Paleoclimatic Analogs to Twentieth-Century Moisture Regimes Across the United States. Bulletin of the American Meteorological Society 84(7):901–909.

Gallatin, Albert
1836 Synopsis of the Indian Tribes within the United States East of the Rocky Mountains, and in the British and Russian Possessions in North America. Cambridge, MA: Archaeologia Americana, Transactions and Collections of the American Antiquarian Society, Vol. 2. Reprinted 1973 by AMS Press, New York.

Gathorne-Hardy, Jonathan
1998 Kinsey: Sex Is the Measure of All Things. Bloomington: Indiana University Press.

Goldfrank, Esther
1966 Changing Configurations in the Social Organization of a Blackfoot Tribe During the Reserve Period: The Bloods of Alberta, Canada. American Ethnological Society Monograph no. 8. Seattle: University of Washington Press.

Hanks, Lucien M., Jr., and Jane Richardson Hanks
1950 Tribe Under Trust: A Study of the Blackfoot Reserve of Alberta. Toronto: University of Toronto Press.

Harrod, Howard L.
1971 Mission Among the Blackfeet. Norman: University of Oklahoma Press.

Hatch, E. A. C.
1857 RCIA for 1856:74–77.

Henday (Hendry), Anthony –*see* Barbara Belyea 2000.

Henry, Alexander
1897 The Manuscript Journals of Alexander Henry, Fur Trader of the Northwest Company. Elliott Coues, ed. Minneapolis: Ross and Haines. Reprinted 1965.

Hinsley, Curtis M. Jr.
1981 Savages and Scientists: The Smithsonian Institution and the Development of American Anthropology 1846–1910. Washington, DC: Smithsonian Institution Press.

Indian Claims Commission
1967 Docket No. 279-A, *The Blackfeet and Gros Ventre Tribes of Indians, Petitioners, v. The United States of America, defendant.* Published 1974 by Garland, New York.

Iverson, Peter
1994 When Indians Became Cowboys: Native Peoples and Cattle Ranching in the American West. Norman: University of Oklahoma Press.

Jenkins, N. E.
1898 RCIA for 1898:187–188.

Jenness, Diamond
1955[1934] The Indians of Canada. National Museum of Canada Bulletin No. 65, Anthropological Series no. 15. Ottawa: National Museum of Canada.

Jones, William A.
1898 RCIA FOR 1898:1–107.
1902 RCIA for 1901:1–171.

Kehoe, Alice Beck
1995 Introduction. *In* Mythology of the Blackfoot, by C. Wissler and D. C. Duvall. Pp. v–xxxiii. Bison Book reprint by University of Nebraska Press, Lincoln.
1996 Transcribing Insima, a Blackfoot "Old Lady." *In* Reading Beyond Words: Native History in Context, Jennifer S. H. Brown and Elizabeth Vibert, eds. Pp . 381–402. Orchard Park, NY: Broadview Press.
1956-present Unpublished fieldnotes, Blackfeet Reservation.

Keller, Robert H., and Michael F. Turek
1998 American Indians and National Parks. Tucson: University of

Arizona Press.

Kennerly, Henry A.
1982[1912–1913] The 1855 Blackfeet Treaty Council: A Memoir by Henry A. Kennerly. David A. Walter, ed. Montana Episodes. Montana: The Magazine of Western History 32(1):44–51.

Kipp, Darrell Robes
2003 Strangers in Strange Lands: Visitors Amongst the Blackfoot People (1620–2003). *In* The Fur and Robe Trade in Blackfoot Country, 1831 to 1880. National Fur Trade Symposium Proceedings, 2003. Pp. 99–105. Fort Benton, MT: River and Plains Society.

Kipp, Woody
2004 Viet Cong at Wounded Knee: The Trail of a Blackfeet Activist. Lincoln: University of Nebraska Press.

Kroeber, Alfred L., and Clyde Kluckhohn
1952 Culture: A Critical Review of Concepts and Definitions. Papers of the Peabody Museum of American Archaeology and Ethnology, vol. 47, no. 1, Harvard University.

Larpenteur, Charles
1933 Forty Years a Fur Trader. Milo Milton Quaife, ed. Chicago: Lakeside Press, R. R. Donnelley and Sons.

Leupp, Francis E.
1906 RCIA for 1905:3–155.

Lewis, David Rich
1994 Neither Wolf Nor Dog: American Indians, Environment, and Agrarian Change. New York: Oxford University Press.

Lewis, Oscar
1941 Manly-Hearted Women Among the North Piegan. American Anthropologist 43(2):173–187.
1942 The Effects of White Contact Upon Blackfoot Culture. Monograph 6, American Ethnological Society. Seattle: University of Washington Press.

Lindsey, Donal F.
1995 Indians at Hampton Institute, 1877–1923. Urbana: University of Illinois Press.

Lowie, Robert
1937 The History of Ethnological Theory. New York: Holt, Rinehart and Winston.
1949 Supplementary Facts About Clark Wissler. American Anthropologist 51(3):527–528.

Lukin, Nora C.
2003 My Early Years. 2nd edition. Privately published; in archives of Blackfeet Tribal Historical Preservation Office.

Lux, Maureen K.
    2001 Medicine That Walks: Disease, Medicine, and Canadian Plains
        Native People, 1880–1940. Toronto: University of Toronto Press.
Lyon, Edwin A.
    1996 A New Deal for Southeastern Archaeology. Tuscaloosa: Univer-
        sity of Alabama Press.
Mackenzie, Alexander
    1970 The Journals and Letters of Sir Alexander Mackenzie. W. Kaye
        Lamb, ed. Published for the Hakluyt Society. Cambridge: Cam-
        bridge University Press.
MacLeod, William Christie
    1928 The American Indian Frontier. New York: Knopf.
Manypenny. George W.
    1855 RCIA for 1854:1–23.
    1856 RCIA for 1855:1–21.
Matson, W. F.
    1898 RCIA for 1898:186–187.
    1901 RCIA for 1901:257–258.
Maximilian, Prince of Wied
    1906 Travels in the Interior of North America. In Early Western Trav-
        els, 1748–1846. Reuben Gold Thwaites, ed., vols. 22–24. Cleve-
        land: Arthur H. Clark.
May, R. F.
    1874 RCIA for 1874: 259–260.
McFee, Malcolm
    1968 The 150% Man, a Product of Blackfeet Acculturation. American
        Anthropologist 70:1096–1103.
    1972 Modern Blackfeet: Montanans on a Reservation. New York:
        Holt, Rinehart and Winston.
McHugh, Tom
    1972 The Time of the Buffalo. New York: Knopf.
McIntosh, Robert P.
    1982 The Background and Some Current Problems of Theoretical
        Ecology. In Conceptual Issues in Ecology, Esa Saarinen, ed. Pp.1–
        61. Dordrecht: D. Reidel.
Miller, J. R.
    2003 Troubled Legacy: A History of Native Residential Schools. Sas-
        katchewan Law Review 66(2):357–382.
Mix, Charles E.
    1858 Report of the Commissioner of Indian Affairs for 1858. Pp. 1–16.
        Washington, D.C.: William A. Harris.

Monteath, James H.
     1901 RCIA for 1901:256–257.
Mooney, James
     1928 The Aboriginal Population of America North of Mexico. John R.
          Swanton, ed. Smithsonian Miscellaneous Collections, vol. 80, no.
          7. Pp. 1–39. Washington DC: Government Printing Office.
Moore, John H.
     1996 Cheyenne Work in the History of U.S. Capitalism. *In* Native
          Americans and Wage Labor, Alice Littlefield and Martha C.
          Knack, eds. Pp. 122–143. Norman: University of Oklahoma Press.
Morgan, Thomas J.
     1889 RCIA for 1889:3–91.
Morison, Samuel Eliot, and Henry Steele Commager
     1942 The Growth of the American Republic, 3rd edition. New York:
          Oxford University Press.
Murdock, George Peter
     1948 Clark Wissler, 1870–1947. American Anthropologist
          50(2):292–304.
Nash, Stephen E.
     2000 Seven Decades of Archaeological Tree-Ring Dating. *In* It's About
          Time: A History of Archaeological Dating in North America, Ste-
          phen E. Nash, ed. Pp. 60–82. Salt Lake City: University of Utah
          Press.
Nelson, Nels C.
     1948 Clark Wissler, 1870-1947. American Antiquity 13(3):244–247.
Oberly, John H.
     1885 RCIA for 1885: Report of the Indian School Superintendent,
          LXXV–CCXXV.
     1888 RCIA for 1888:5–89.
Odling-Smee, F. John, Kevin N. Laland, and Marcus W. Feldman
     2003 Niche Construction: The Neglected Process in Evolution. Princ-
          eton: Monographs in Population Biology 37, Princeton University
          Press.
Old Person, Earl
     1995 Presentations, Conference on Indian Self-Rule, Institute of the
          American West, Sun Valley, ID, 1983. *In* Indian Self-Rule, Kenneth
          R. Philp, ed. Pp. 107–108, 252–254. Logan: Utah State University
          Press. Reprint of 1986 edition.
Palliser, (Captain) John
     1859 Papers Relative to the Exploration by Captain Palliser of that Por-
          tion of British North America which Lies Between the Northern

Branch of the River Saskatchewan and the Frontier of the United States; and Between the Red River and Rocky Mountains. London: George Edward Eyre and William Spottiswoode. Reprinted 1969 by Greenwood Press.

Pease, F. D.
1870 RCIA for 1869:No. 80.

Philp, Kenneth R.
1999 Termination Revisited: American Indians on the Trail to Self-Determination, 1933–1953. Lincoln: University of Nebraska Press.

Pratt, Richard Henry
1964 Battlefield and Classroom: Four Decades with the American Indian, 1867–1904. Robert M. Utley, ed. New Haven: Yale University Press.

Price, Hiram
1881 RCIA for 1881:3–70.
1882 RCIA for 1881:3–72.
1883 RCIA for 1883:3–71.
1884 RCIA for 1884:3–55.

Prucha, Francis Paul
1986 abridged edition The Great Father: The United States Government and the American Indians. Lincoln: University of Nebraska Press. (Original unabridged edition 1984, same press.)

RCIA = Report of the Commissioner of Indian Affairs, issued yearly. Washington D.C.: A. O. P. Nicholson for 1855, 1856, 1857; William A. Harris for 1858a, 1858b; George W. Bowman for 1859, 1860; Government Printing Office beginning with 1861.

Reed, Henry W.
1863 RCIA for 1862:No. 36.
1864 RCIA for 1863:No. 72.

Robinson, A. M.
1858 RCIA for 1858:No. 22.

Roe, Frank Gilbert
1951 The North American Buffalo: A Critical Study of the Species in Its Wild State. Toronto: University of Toronto Press.

Rogel, Amy Lyn
1990 "Mastering the Secret of White Man's Power:" Indian Students at College, 1872 to 1884. Beloit, WI: (Beloit College) Archives Publication Number One.

Rosier, Paul C.
2001 Rebirth of the Blackfeet Nation, 1912–1954. Lincoln: University of Nebraska Press.

Samek, Hana
  1987 The Blackfoot Confederacy 1880–1920: A Comparative Study of Canadian and U.S. Indian Policy. Albuquerque: University of New Mexico Press.
Schaeffer, Claude E.
  Manuscripts in Glenbow Museum Archives, Calgary, filed under M-1100.
Shaw, James H.
  1995 How Many Bison Originally Populated Western Rangelands? Rangelands 17(5):148–150.
Shepardson, Mary
  1983 Development of Navajo Tribal Government. *In* Handbook of North American Indians, vol. 10. Pp. 624–635. Washington, DC: Smithsonian Institution Press.
Sheridan, Philip
  1870 Telegram, January 31, 1870, published under 41st Congress, 2nd Session, House of Representatives Executive Document No. 269.
Shewell, Hugh
  2004 "Enough to Keep them Alive:" Indian Welfare in Canada, 1873–1965. Toronto: University of Toronto Press.
Simmons, A. J.
  1872 RCIA for 1871:No. 47.
Smith, Edward P.
  1874a RCIA for 1873:3–25.
  1874b RCIA for 1874:3–83.
Smyth, David
  2001 The Niitsitapi Trade: Euroamericans and the Blackfoot-Speaking Peoples, to the Mid-1830s. PhD dissertation, Carleton University, Ottawa.
Sommers [Dietrich], Sue
  1939 Ms., interviews on Blackfeet Reservation, summer 1939. On file in Marquette University Archives, Milwaukee, WI.
Sorenson, Mark W., and Guy Senese
  2001 Clarence Karier's Influence on Two Careers in Native American Policy Studies. *In* Inexcusable Omissions, Karen Graves, Timothy Glander, and Christine Shea, eds. Pp. 101–117.New York: Peter Lang.
Stevens, Isaac I.
  1855 RCIA for 1854:No. 86.
Steward, Julian H.
  1938 Basin-Plateau Aboriginal Sociopolitical Groups. Smithsonian

Institution, Bureau of American Ethnology Bulletin 120. Washington, DC: Government Printing Office.

1955 Theory of Culture Change. Urbana: University of Illinois Press.

Stewart, Ernest H.

1940a Interviews, Eli L. Guardipee and Richard Sanderville (March 16, 1940). Document in Blackfeet Planning and Development Office, Browning, MT (from Merrill G. Burlingame Special Collections, Montana State University Libraries, Bozeman, MT).

1940b Year By Year Outline of the Livestock Industry in Glacier County. Document in Blackfeet Planning and Development Office, Browning, MT (from Merrill G. Burlingame Special Collections, Montana State University Libraries, Bozeman, MT).

Stuart, Granville

1925 Forty Years on the Frontier. Paul C. Phillips, ed. Cleveland: Arthur H. Clark.

Sundstrom, Linea

1997 Smallpox Used Them Up: References to Epidemic Disease in Northern Plains Winter Counts, 1714–1920. Ethnohistory 44(2):305–343.

Taylor, M. Scott

2007 Buffalo Hunt: International Trade and the Virtual Extinction of the North American Bison. Working Paper 12969, National Bureau of Economic Research. http://www.nber.org/papers/w/12969.

Tax, Sol

1995 Comments. In Indian Self-Rule, Kenneth R. Philp, ed. Pp. 132–133. Logan: Utah State University Press. Reprint of 1986 edition.

Terry, Frank

1897 Naming the Indians. American Monthly Review of Reviews (March 15):301–307.

Thompson, David

1916 David Thompson's Narrative of his Explorations in Western America, 1784–1812. J. B. Tyrrell, ed. Toronto: Champlain Society, Publication 12. Reprinted 1965, Greenwood Press, New York.

Tough, Frank

1996 "As their Natural Resources Fail": Native Peoples and the Economic History of Northern Manitoba, 1870–1930. Vancouver: University of British Columbia Press.

Treaty Seven Tribal Council, Walter Hildebrandt, Dorothy First Rider, and Sarah Carter

1996 The True Spirit and Original Intent of Treaty 7. Montreal: McGill-Queen's University Press.

Trobriand, Philip de
    1870 Letter, February 18, 1870, published under 41st Congress, 2nd Session, House of Representatives Executive Document No. 269.
Upson, Gad. E.
    1865 RCIA for 1864:No. 137.
Vail, James H.
    1865 RCIA for 1864:No. 138.
Valentine, Robert G.
    1912a RCIA for 1911:1–51.
    1912b RCIA for 1912:5–72.
Vaughan, Alfred J., Jr.
    1855 RCIA for 1854:No. 28.
    1858a RCIA for 1857:No. 55.
    1858b RCIA for 1858:No. 23.
    1860 RCIA for 1859:No. 30.
Viall, Jasper A.
    1872 RCIA for 1871:No. 42.
Vincent, Joan
    1990 Anthropology and Politics. Tucson: University of Arizona Press.
Walker, Francis A.
    1872 RCIA for 1872:3–105.
Weibel-Orlando, Joan
    1999 Indian Country, L.A. Revised edition. Urbana: University of Illinois Press.
Wessel, Thomas R.
    1979 Agriculture on the Reservations: The Case of the Blackfeet, 1885–1935. Journal of the West 18(4):17–24.
    1986 Agent of Acculturation: Farming on the Northern Plains Reservations. Agricultural History 60(2):233–245.
Wilkins, David E., and K. Tsianina Lomawaima
    2001 Uneven Ground: American Indian Sovereignty and Federal Law. Norman: University of Oklahoma Press.
Wilmoth, Stanley Clay
    1987 The Development of Blackfeet Politics and Multiethnic Categories, 1934–84. PhD dissertation, University of California-Riverside.
Wischmann, Lesley
    2004 Frontier Diplomats: Alexander Culbertson and Natoyist-siksina' Among the Blackfeet. Norman: University of Oklahoma Press. (Originally published 2000, Spokane, WA, by Arthur H. Clark.)
Wissler, Clark
    1910 Material Culture of the Blackfoot Indians, Anthropological

Papers, vol. 5, Pt. 1, pp. 1–175 + 5 plates. New York: American Museum of Natural History.

1911 The Social Life of the Blackfoot Indians, Anthropological Papers, vol. 7, Pt. 1, pp. 1–64. New York: American Museum of Natural History.

1912 Ceremonial Bundles of the Blackfoot Indians, Anthropological Papers, vol. 7, Pt. 2, pp. 65–289. New York: American Museum of Natural History.

1915 Material Cultures of the North American Indian. *In* Anthropology in North America. Pp. 76–134. New York: Stechert. (No editor given for this volume of papers prepared for a 1914 International Congress of Americanists that was not held due to the outbreak of World War I.)

1922 The American Indian: an Introduction to the Anthropology of the New World. Second edition (first edition 1917, Douglas C. McMurtrie). New York: Oxford University Press.

1926 Relation of Nature to Man in Aboriginal America. New York: Oxford University Press. (This book comprises a series of lectures Wissler delivered at the Wagner Free Institute of Science in Philadelphia.)

1927 Recent Developments in Anthropology. *In* Recent Developments in the Social Sciences, Edward Cary Hayes, ed. Pp. 50–96. Philadelphia: Lippincott.

1929 Anthropology. *In* Research in the Social Sciences, Wilson Gee, ed. Pp. 83-111. New York: Macmillan.

1938 Depression and Revolt—The Story of the Last Indian Uprising and its Youth Movement. Natural History 41(2):108–112.

1940 Indians of the United States: Four Centuries of Their History and Culture. New York: Doubleday, Doran.

1971[1938] Red Man Reservations. New York: Collier. (Originally published 1938 as Indian Cavalcade or Life on the Old-Time Indian Reservations, by Sheridan House.)

Wissler, Clark and D. C. Duvall
1908 Mythology of the Blackfoot Indians, Anthropological Papers vol. II, Pt. 1, pp. 1–163. New York: American Museum of Natural History.

Wood, John S.
1875 RCIA for 1875:299–301.

Wright, David E., III, Michael W. Hirlinger, and Robert E. England
1998 The Politics of Second Generation Discrimination in American Indian Education: Incidence, Explanation, and Mitigating Strategies. Westport, CT: Bergin and Garvey.

Wright, George B.
   1868a RCIA for 1867:No. 76.
   1868b RCIA for 1868:No. 48.
Yellowhorn, Eldon
   2003 Regarding the American Paleolithic. Canadian Journal of Archaeology 27:62–73.
Young, Gerald L.
   1983 Origins of Human Ecology. Benchmark Papers in Ecology 12. Stroudsburg, PA: Hutchinson Ross.
Young, John
   1877 RCIA for 1877:131–132.
   1878 RCIA for 1878:82–84.
   1879 RCIA for 1879:89–91.
   1880 RCIA for 1880:105–107.
   1881 RCIA for 1881:111–113.
   1882 RCIA for 1882:98–100.
   1883 RCIA for 1883:96–98.

Index

Treaties, Canada, 33–35, 98; United
States, 34–37, 82, 83, 85, 118; Stevens'
at Fort Benton, 1853, 67

Uhlenbeck, C. C. and Wilhemina, 139,
142–152, 242
United States government, 1856 policy
to settle Northern Plains, 70–71,
74; 1872 policy, 89–90; New Deal,
159–161, 193, 224–225; Termination,
167–168, 170

War, 39, 62, 63, 69, 83–84; World War II,
165–166

Whiskey, 39–40, 56–57, 88–89; liquor
sales on Reservation, 178; violence
and drinking, 58, 60, 93
Williamson, Mae Coburn (prominent
twentieth-century Blackfeet leader),
163
Wissler, Clark, xi–xii, 2, 229–244
passim
Women, captives, 20; labor, 27–28, 63,
112; wives of traders, 30
Wood, John (exemplary Indian Agent),
41–42